The Brain-Friendly
Workplace

The Brain-Friendly Workplace

Why Talented People Quit and How to Get Them to Stay

Friederike Fabritius
Foreword by Scott Barry Kaufman

ROWMAN & LITTLEFIELD
Lanham • Boulder • New York • London

Art courtesy of Carolin Nischwitz

Published by Rowman & Littlefield
An imprint of The Rowman & Littlefield Publishing Group, Inc.
4501 Forbes Boulevard, Suite 200, Lanham, Maryland 20706
www.rowman.com

86-90 Paul Street, London EC2A 4NE

Distributed by NATIONAL BOOK NETWORK

British Library Cataloguing in Publication Information Available

Library of Congress Cataloging-in-Publication Data

ISBN: 978-1-5381-5953-8 (cloth)
ISBN: 978-1-5381-5954-3 (electronic)

♾™ The paper used in this publication meets the minimum requirements of American National Standard for Information Sciences—Permanence of Paper for Printed Library Materials, ANSI/NISO Z39.48-1992.

To my husband, Jochen, and our children,
Benita, Wolf, Heinrich, Sylvester, and Nike.
You mean the world to me.

Contents

Foreword

When Friederike Fabritius asked if I would write the foreword to this book, I immediately said yes! I met Friederike when she was a guest on my show, *The Psychology Podcast*. Ever since then, I've really admired Friederike not just for her work, but also as a person. She is deeply committed to using neuroscience to help people reach their full potential. This resonates with my overarching belief in neurodiversity. I believe that this book is contributing to a broader discussion about how people's brain wirings can be very different from each other and can influence the way we see the world.

I know how this works personally. As a kid growing up in special ed, people didn't know how to classify me because nothing in my school system's rulebook covered understanding a neurosignature for creativity and imagination. So, I think this book is contributing to a broader conversation that deeply resonates with me personally. We need some sort of framework that is understanding and inclusive of different ways of processing information and different ways of seeing the world.

This book also takes a fresh perspective on what it takes for people to flourish in the workplace. It points to a higher north-star goal than a lot of companies tend to focus on. What you find in most companies is that they focus on the company's goal actualization first, and the worker's actualization comes second. What Friederike is saying is that when you focus on neurodiversity, you respect the deeper drives and motivations of people, and the company will naturally achieve better results as an outgrowth.

One thing to keep in mind is that neurosignatures shouldn't be thought of as static. All of our neurosignatures change throughout the day. It's worth thinking thoughtfully through this as a manager as well, about time of day and when you give people a certain task. When I get right out of the bed in the morning, my testosterone neurosignature is very high. But by evening, it's almost nonexistent. I don't want to conquer my goals at eight at night; I want to watch Netflix and chill. Neurosignatures are fluid, and they should serve as guidelines, as a helpful framework in understanding people, rather than as categories and boxes to classify people.

This book highlights the basic fact that we need more thought diversity, but also highlights that people's motivations differ very much from each other. Being able to orchestrate that in a workplace—like an orchestra conductor—is essential. A good conductor is not someone who tells all the instruments how to play but is really good at helping the instruments come together in a harmonious way to have a beautiful sound. That is a very fresh approach.

This book is very timely, as there is so much uncertainty in the world. Stress levels are incredibly high. People are starving for meaning and for a way to understand their unique place in the world and in the workplace. They want to matter. Their need to matter is such a fundamental human need. I think that this book can really play a pivotal role in people feeling like they matter in the workplace by allowing them to bring their unique neurosignature to the table.

But it's not just the brain: the brain and the body are all so deeply interconnected in the environment. Your neurosignature serves as a shorthand—a quick way for people to understand themselves on a deeper level—but it's really part of a bigger system. The neurosignatures interact with the environment, and we know that the need for autonomy is really important in the workplace.

This book can help people increase their sense of mattering as well as a sense of autonomy, a sense that they are making decisions based on their unique being, as opposed to the pressure to perform or to do things just for the sake of external rewards. So, there's also a real intrinsic motivation and fostering of our autonomy that understanding your neurosignature can help provide.

People don't really give themselves the time in life for self-discovery. We don't focus on it because we're constantly trying to meet the demands of others, creating a career and juggling a family. We face so many external demands that we don't think that we even could make time for self-discovery. But the journey of self-actualization—which is my main focus—is being able to recognize that first of all, you're worth it: you're worth understanding, you're worth cultivating a real sense of how you can best contribute to the world. Being able to say "no" to things that are not right for you is also a very important part of the self-actualization process.

The Brain-Friendly Workplace gives people permission to start seeing themselves in a way that maybe they haven't been able to before. Maybe they have felt it intuitively but haven't been able to put their finger on it. Maybe this book can also inspire them to say "no" to things that haven't been working for them with the self-compassion to realize that it wasn't a good fit. It doesn't mean that they were deeply broken.

Scott Barry Kaufman, PhD
Psychologist, author, host of *The Psychology Podcast*
January 2022

Introduction

We have a once-in-a-century opportunity, right now, to create a better future for work. The old corporate paradigm of extreme hours, little sleep, endless meetings, and nonstop travel is dead. No one wants to go back to that. It's bad for performance and for everyone's mental and physical health. The future of business is hybrid and requires a flexible new paradigm that helps everyone reach peak performance: the brain-friendly workplace.

I'm a neuroscientist and keynote speaker who teaches Fortune 500 executives easy, brain-friendly ways to reach peak performance and experience greater joy and well-being.

Everybody's talking about reinventing work—but no one is sure how to do it. In *The Brain-Friendly Workplace*, I offer a science-backed, field-tested blueprint that my clients already love. Now, they plan to use it to reverse the coming mass exodus of expensively trained and educated professionals and win the talent war.

In July 2021, the *Wall Street Journal* confirmed, "More American professionals are quitting their jobs than at any time during the last two decades . . . as people gravitate to jobs more suited to their skills, interests and personal lives."[1] The 2021 Women in the Workplace study from McKinsey and LeanIn .org reports that two million women could exit corporate America.[2]

My clients need both these problems solved—fast. As Riaz Shah, a global talent leader for EY (formerly Ernst & Young), who leads learning for more than 340,000 people, told me, "Once things open back up fully, those who have been unhappy will make their move to where they really want to be."

1

The brain-friendly workplace retains talent because it encourages you to work in line with what *your* brain needs to function optimally. It values employees with different kinds of brains for the diverse ideas they bring to their teams. It even values fun! As I tell my clients, "If you're not having fun at work, you're not performing at your best."

In *The Brain-Friendly Workplace*, you'll discover your own "neurosignature," a unique mix of four key brain chemicals that strongly affects your personality and how you process stress and information. You'll learn to hit your "optimal stress point" and manipulate "fun, fear, and focus" so you can easily reach peak performance. Ideas will flow. You'll feel energized, inspired, and alive.

You'll also gain a valuable framework for understanding colleagues with different neurosignatures. This works at home, too. Things that used to annoy my husband and me about each other we now happily chalk up to our different, yet complementary, neurosignatures.

My clients report improved performance, talent retention, and gender diversity for themselves and their employees. Why? Because when you learn how to use fun, fear, and focus to easily enter the flow state, you can get more done in less time. When you get enough sleep, exercise, healthy food, and personal time, you feel happier. When employees feel respected and their needs for child care, remote work options, and flexible schedules are met, they stay. This is especially true for women, which is why the brain-friendly workplace naturally improves gender diversity.

Instead of trying to change the people, my clients are changing the workplace. They're cutting time-wasting meetings and unnecessary travel to the bone, supporting employee biorhythms with flexible schedules, and encouraging "strategic rest" to keep everyone operating at peak performance. Brain-friendly practices provide my clients with a concrete competitive advantage, as they siphon off pools of talent that less-aware companies lose to attrition.

Formerly jet-setting executives are speaking out about how the enforced break from global travel, extreme stress, and protracted workweeks has improved their productivity—and their lives. *New York Times* reporter Ginia Bellafante interviewed her neighbor, a jet-setting investment banker with a young family. Before the shutdown, she notes, "he might call into our monthly condo meetings from Dallas, but he had been in Tokyo the day before and was on his way to Brussels the next."

Bellafante expected the banker to be itching to resume his swanky globe-trotting lifestyle. Surprisingly, he told her, "I have not missed one second of domestic or international travel. What has replaced it? Exercise. Being with my kids. Greater productivity. No one in my world is saying, 'Wow, I can't wait to get back to doing everything the way we did it before.'"[3]

Frankly, an exodus from corporate life had already begun before the global crisis. Highly educated women in particular were ditching corporate life at an alarming rate. According to *Workforce Management*, American companies were spending roughly $8 billion per year on gender diversity training. This included teaching female executives to "lean in" and sending male executives to "unconscious bias training." Yet, these costly efforts were tanking.

In 2019, *Forbes* reported in "Why Women Quit" that female participation in the labor force dropped from 51.4 percent in 1990 to 47 percent in 2020. Only 4.8 percent of Fortune 500 companies have female CEOs. This pathetic percentage of female leaders has been flat since 2010. To cite one example, just 18 percent of Microsoft's top executives are women.

My clients are desperate to get more women into upper management, because workplaces staffed with female executives are more profitable. As CNBC reported in "Companies with Female Executives Make More Money—Here's Why," there is "substantial evidence that gender diversity at the management level enhances a company's performance."[4]

Brain-friendly practices naturally decrease female attrition while raising overall employee satisfaction, productivity, and diversity. What's good for women, it turns out, is good for companies. Create a brain-friendly workplace, and you won't have to organize a single "gender diversity day" ever again. The brain-friendly workplace nurtures and attracts all neurosignatures and empowers them to perform at their best.

In each chapter, I interview a prominent thought leader about this new vision for the future of work. I talk with Thrive Global CEO Arianna Huffington, Boston Consulting Group Managing Director and Partner, Chief Recruiting/Talent Officer Amber Grewal, cognitive scientist/author/podcaster Dr. Scott Barry Kaufman, *Brain Rules* author John Medina, longtime Ben & Jerry's board member Jeff Furman, EY Women Fast Forward Global Leader Julie Linn Teigland, *The Five-Hour Workday* author and Tower CEO Stephan Aarstol, VaynerMedia Chief Heart Officer Claude Silver, and more.

They confirm that a huge cultural shift is taking place. The shutdown helped executives like our investment banker realize that they like getting enough sleep and being there for their children. I want to encourage them to compete about that, instead of about how many hours they work. Soon, they'll be comparing sleep trackers and bragging about how much quality sleep they get.

My clients share their stories, too. In chapter 4, Dr. Janin Schwartau, global head of learning and transformation for thyssenkrupp, describes the fluid new workspace and flexible schedules she designed for her seventy-person team after experiencing my brain-friendly program. Dr. Schwartau established a personal meditation practice after our workshop as well. She also mentions my favorite participant—a cranky sixty-year-old who declared, "If God had wanted me to move fast, he would have given me wheels." He became an avid jogger after learning that exercise staves off dementia better than any drug.

Each chapter of *The Brain-Friendly Workplace* also delivers brain-health tips, fun stories, and weird neuroscience nuggets. You'll learn about the Siberian hamsters whose testicles shrank when the hamsters were dosed with melatonin and why Angelina Jolie may have a high-testosterone brain. You'll discover how a role-playing game transformed a new chemo drug from a dog into a top performer and why I can't stand yoga (hint: it's my neurosignature).

The fight against discrimination on the basis of gender, race, or sexual orientation is extremely important, and I am behind it 100 percent. In *The Brain-Friendly Workplace*, I also advocate for a new, next-level inclusion based on our invaluable thought diversity as human beings. Diversity isn't only about race, gender, or sexual orientation.

It's also about how you think—and how you choose to work.

1

The Neurogap

Women are not the problem; they are the answer.

—Julie Linn Teigland

I arrived at the massive top-floor conference room of a five-star hotel ready for a full day of company-sanctioned "lean-in" training. The forty-something instructor wore a tailored navy pantsuit and sensible pumps. Her hair was cut in a crisp bob, laced with expensive blond highlights. She began by explaining to our group of accomplished female executives that men play by different rules and that we must learn to use male power plays if we want to rise to the top.

I was working grueling hours—including lots of international travel—for a top-tier management consulting powerhouse. Women comprised less than 25 percent of the firm's roster and only 5 percent of the partner group. Management was eager to improve these numbers by helping the firm's female executives to get ahead. Sending me and my colleagues to learn how to lean in was a gender-diversity initiative.

As a neuroscientist obsessed with human behavior, I was very excited about attending this training. Could leaning in really help women achieve more power and rise up into the male-dominated upper echelons of the corporate universe?

DON'T SMILE

Our instructor worked the room briskly, shaking hands with each of us. If our grips were "weak," we had to shake her hand until our handshakes met with her approval. My polite squeeze was deemed insufficient. It took several increasingly hardy efforts on my part before she was satisfied. By the time she moved on, I felt like a lumberjack.

After the instructor made her rounds, she had us all work the room, giving each other hearty handshakes and instant feedback. Shouts of "Stronger!" and "That felt like touching a dead fish!" filled the air, accompanied by peals of laughter, met with disapproving glares from our tutor.

Next, we were informed that to be taken seriously, we must always give orders and never ask questions. We were divided into pairs. One woman played the boss; the other played a team member. I had to demand "I need that report in tomorrow!" five times before I succeeded in lowering my girlish voice to sound sufficiently authoritative for our instructor.

There were lots of giggles during this exercise, too. It felt so awkward. To most of us, it felt more natural to ask our team member, "Would you be so kind as to turn in this report by tomorrow? I'd really appreciate it," followed by a smile.

But smiling? Big mistake.

"Don't smile!" our instructor barked. "The men around you will see this as a sign of weakness and low status. You can smile after work." More muffled giggles as she stared us down. She motioned us to sit around an enormous conference table.

"When you're seated at a table like this in a meeting," she began, "I want you to only address the 'top dog' in the room. Ignore everyone else. When the top dog is listening, you have everyone else's attention."

I raised my hand. She nodded brusquely.

Pitching my voice as low as I could and being careful not to ask a question, I said, "When I meet with my clients, I usually seek to create an inclusive, friendly atmosphere by acknowledging everyone in the room."

"That's weak!" our instructor declared. "Talk to the boss, and everyone else will listen. Shoulders back. Spread out in your chairs. Take up as much space as possible. Don't let anybody invade your space. You are the queen, and nobody touches the queen."

Next, we watched the infamous clip of U.S. President George W. Bush slipping behind German chancellor Angela Merkel as she sat at an even more impressive conference table than ours. Our instructor watched with horror as Bush warmly squeezed Merkel's shoulders.

"This was a male power play in action!" our teacher shouted. "Don't you *ever* let anyone do this to you!" We worked the room again, clapping each other on the backs as powerfully as we could, trying to create the ambiance of a male locker room. More giggling ensued.

As our training wound down, our new mentor imparted one final tip: "never order the smallest company car. Women tend to choose the smallest, most practical eco-friendly car. But status symbols matter a great deal to men, as they must now to you. The big car, the fancy watch, the expensive jewelry, the designer purse—these are all status symbols. They will earn you respect from your male colleagues. Go big. Or go home."

FAILING TO "FIX" THE WOMEN

Companies spend big bucks trying to get more women into upper management because numerous studies show that workplaces run by female executives are more productive, enjoyable, and profitable. In 2018, for example, CNBC

reported that "there's substantial evidence that gender diversity at the management level enhances a company's performance."[1]

Did sending female execs to empowerment training work for my firm? Did it retain us and increase the number of women being promoted? Nope.

More gender-diversity initiatives followed: female leadership training, mentoring networks, women's lunches—you name it. Nonetheless, every woman from my peer group, including me, left this company, taking with us our expensive training, along with our skills, talents, and insights. Not a single woman I knew is still working there. Frankly, we were frustrated by the exhausting travel, insane hours, extreme stress, and dearth of child care. Hefty bonuses and other perks weren't worth the cost of our health and sanity. Let me be clear: it's not that we couldn't cut it. We didn't *want* to cut it.

Last I checked, still only four women were on the thirty-member shareholders' council. The percentage of female senior leaders was stalled at 11 percent. Meanwhile, many men who were hired when I was have made partner.

The global pandemic worsened this situation. According to the Women in the Workplace 2021 study, coauthored by McKinsey and LeanIn.org, one in four women plans to leave the workplace or downshift their careers. Up to two million women could exit corporate America.[2]

A primary driver that women cite for leaving is the burden of unpaid care—shopping, cooking, cleaning, taking care of children and parents—that is disproportionately carried by women. Pre-pandemic, women took on nearly twice as much unpaid care as men. The crisis only increased this disparity, the Women in the Workplace 2021 report notes.[3]

TRYING TO "FIX" THE MEN

Companies also try to narrow the gender gap by putting their executives through "unconscious bias training." Unconscious bias training is supposed to arm employees with tools to recognize their biases and neutralize them. Almost all the big tech firms offer it, including Facebook, Salesforce, and VMware, with more joining every day. At Google, for example, 75 percent of 114,000 employees have taken unconscious bias workshops.

Evidence is strong that both male and female executives can be biased against women. These biases negatively affect hiring, payment, and promotion of female executives. It's both logical and ethical that companies take action against these biases. You don't need a neuroscientist, though, to tell you that nobody can be guilt-tripped into changing a prejudice.

In 2018, *Newsweek* published "How Diversity Training Infuriates Men and Fails Women,"[4] a fascinating dissection of unconscious bias training. Harvard organizational-sociology professor Frank Dobbin had combed through thousands of data points and concluded that unconscious bias training just made things worse, wrote reporter Joanne Lipman. "The training infuriated the men it was intended to educate," Lipman explained. "Their primary take-away was that they would have to 'walk on eggshells' around women and minorities."

According to *Workforce Management*, American companies spend roughly $8 billion per year on diversity training. Yet, Dobbin's study of 829 companies over thirty-one years showed that diversity training had "no positive effects in the average workplace."[5] An editorial in *The Economist* joked that the twelve most terrifying words in the English language are "I'm from human resources, and I'm here to organize a diversity workshop."[6]

⌦

Mental Break—In *Long Walk to Freedom*, Nelson Mandela recounts experiencing "a strange sensation" when he boarded an Ethiopian Airways flight and noticed that the pilot was black. Having never seen a black pilot before, Mandela felt overwhelmed by rising panic. The leader of South Africa's anti-apartheid movement found himself wondering, "How could a black man fly an airplane?"

Mandela wrote, "I had fallen into the apartheid mind-set, thinking Africans were inferior and that flying was a white man's job. I sat back in my seat and chided myself for such thoughts." Mandela vividly describes how even the most "woke" person can succumb to unconscious bias. His story also points to a solution—simply being exposed to greater diversity helps us overcome our biases.

⌦

IT'S ABOUT OUR BRAINS

Four powerful chemicals shape your personality: the neurotransmitters dopamine and serotonin, and the hormones estrogen and testosterone. Together, they form four distinct systems that stimulate specific areas of your brain. These are your dopamine, serotonin, estrogen, and testosterone brain systems.

⌦

Neurotransmitters are molecules the brain uses to transmit messages between nerve cells called neurons and from neurons to muscles.

⟐

You might have lots of activity in your serotonin system. I might have more neurons firing in my estrogen brain system. If I say your neurosignature is "high in dopamine," what I mean is that you score high on personality traits associated with the dopamine brain system. That's a mouthful! It's easier to simply say your brain is "high in dopamine," so that's what we'll do.

Let's take a deeper dive into the four brain systems. See if you recognize yourself.

Dopamine

People high in dopamine are curious, energetic, and future-oriented. Inventors and entrepreneurs tend to have this neurosignature. They get bored easily and are always looking for the next new exciting project.

Thrill-seeking British billionaire and Virgin Group founder Richard Branson fits the high-dopamine neurosignature. "As soon as something stops being fun, I think it's time to move on," Branson has famously said.[7] Never letting his dyslexia slow him down, Branson followed his own advice throughout his career—from starting a magazine at sixteen, to creating Virgin Records, founding Virgin Atlantic Airways, and zooming into space in 2021 on his Virgin Galactic space plane.

Serotonin

People high in serotonin are reliable, detail-oriented, cautious, and loyal. They thrive on routine and structure and enjoy consistency and stability.

Legendary investor Warren Buffett expressly avoids the dopamine rush provided by e-mail and Twitter. Instead, Buffett says, "I just sit in my office and read all day." His Berkshire Hathaway partner, Charlie Munger, notes, "Neither Warren nor I is smart enough to make decisions with no time to think. We make actual decisions rapidly, but that's because we've spent so much time preparing ourselves by quietly sitting and reading and thinking."[8]

Testosterone

People high in testosterone are tough-minded, direct, and enjoy wielding power. They tend to be analytical and use systems thinking, which involves moving logically from one step to the next to solve a problem, based on a system's "rules." They enjoy tinkering with "systems" such as car engines or computers.

Apple founder Steve Jobs was a driven high-testosterone leader. His great strength was harnessing the intellect of gifted people, such as his friend Steve Wozniak, and keeping them focused. But Jobs was also famously demanding and could be a bully. Jobs's mantra was "focus and simplicity," and his obsessive focus on design at Apple had a purpose. "Design is a funny word," Jobs said. "Some people think design means how it looks. But, of course, if you dig deeper, it's really how it works."[9]

Estrogen

People high in estrogen are empathetic and good at building personal connections and community. Estrogen increases secretion of the "cuddle hormone" oxytocin, which enhances feelings of bonding and trust. This neurosignature excels at nonlinear "lateral thinking," which involves examining a problem from multiple angles until insights emerge. Lateral thinkers are also good at envisioning long-term implications of a decision.

Apple cofounder Steve Wozniak exhibits the traits of a high-estrogen lateral thinker. Wozniak noted in a 2020 interview with CNBC that, unlike Steve Jobs, he was "never hungry for fame, power, or money." [10] Imaginative and creative, Wozniak recalled that as a teenager, "I had a TV set and a typewriter, and that made me think a computer should be laid out like a typewriter with a video screen."[11] Perhaps Jobs and Wozniak were successful partners because they had such different, yet complementary, neurosignatures.

༒

Lateral thinking involves solving a problem by examining multiple possibilities at once. Lateral thinkers prioritize intuition and insight and make connections that other types of thinkers may miss.

༒

THE HIDDEN NEUROGAP

Scientist and best-selling author Helen Fisher has spent decades researching how these four brain systems drive personality. The Fisher Temperament Inventory (FTI) has been taken by more than sixteen million people in forty-plus countries.[12] Helen's personality inventory, based on neuroscience and validated with functional MRI testing, is also used by Match.com. She's one of my mentors, and I've learned a great deal from her.

In 2015, Fisher cofounded NeuroColor, a consultancy that helps businesses and governments use neuroscience-backed tools to help their executives reach peak performance. I was thrilled when NeuroColor CEO and cofounder Dave Labno agreed to consolidate some anonymized data sets for me that might shed light on the role gender plays in our brains. What he found was fascinating.

According to this data, "tough-mindedness," a personality marker for an active testosterone system, is strongly indicated in 53 percent of men and 39 percent of women in the general population. But when top executives at Fortune 500 corporations are tested, tough-mindedness rises to around 73 percent in male executives and 65 percent in female executives.

⌒⟨⟩⌒

Tough-mindedness is characterized by a no-nonsense, unsentimental point of view and a tendency to be strong-willed, persistent, and not easily swayed.

⌒⟨⟩⌒

Results were similar for another high-testosterone brain trait: systems thinking. In the general population, NeuroColor found it strongly indicated in 40 percent of men and 23 percent of women. Among top executives, however, systems thinking was predominant in 61 percent of male executives and 57 percent of female executives. In addition, in the data sets NeuroColor shared exclusively with me, testing also uncovered a five percentage-point decline in empathy in male *and* female top-level executives when compared to the general population.

⌒⟨⟩⌒

Systems thinking is a way of thinking and reasoning that tends to progress in a linear, analytical fashion. In order to pinpoint and correct a problem, it looks at how the parts of a system, such as a car engine, interact.

⌒⟨⟩⌒

NeuroColor CEO Dave Labno and I discussed the fascinating results uncovered in these previously unpublished data sets. "Executives at the top tend to score higher on traits associated with the testosterone and dopamine systems than the average person—and that is true for both men and women," Labno noted.

This means that our executive suites are dominated by people with high-testosterone/dopamine neurosignatures—regardless of their gender. This hidden neurogap—I call it a "stress gap"—may be even wider than the gender gap that diversity efforts seek to address.

MAD MEN . . . AND WOMEN

Don't get me wrong. High-testosterone/dopamine leaders have loads of positive qualities. They are tough-minded, direct, and logical. They thrive on insane work hours, skull-cracking pressure, and blood in the water. They are charismatic, impatient risk-takers. I love working with them because they're exciting and fun. They never waste my time, and they get straight to the point.

But some testosterone-dominant executives can come off as rude, insulting, and short on impulse control. They can create extremely stressful workplaces and fail to understand why other neurosignatures aren't spurred by all the "excitement" to perform at their best. A high-testosterone executive genuinely

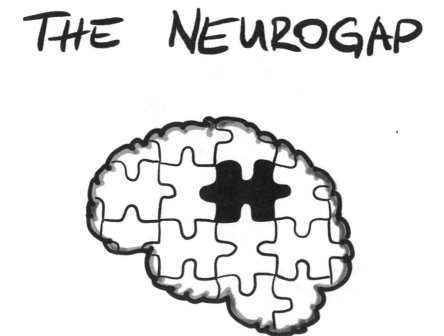

doesn't get it when people with different neurosignatures say they're exhausted. She just thinks they're lazy. In actuality, their productivity is being negatively affected by the work environment she's created.

Taken to an extreme, a leader souped up on dopamine and testosterone may reward employees who exhibit the "dark triad" of narcissism, Machiavellianism, and psychopathy—and punish those who react negatively to extreme stress. Think Don Draper in *Mad Men*. This creates a toxic work environment that turns off employees with other neurosignatures. They'll suffer in silence, or they'll quit. This vicious cycle will lead to a profound lack of neurosignature diversity at that company.

Imagine Steve Jobs without Steve Wozniak. Would Apple ever have gotten out of the garage?

⁓∾

Brain Food—Sometimes we feel cranky at work because we're dehydrated. When you feel sluggish at work, drink some water. Hydration can boost brain performance by as much as 14 percent, according to a *Frontiers in Neuroscience* study.[13] Even mild levels of dehydration can have a negative impact on mood and cognitive performance.

⁓∾

THE "BAD" FEMALE BOSS

Some female executives who have successfully scaled the corporate ladder to the top have earned a surprising rap as abusive bosses. Once hailed as "SheEOs" who would usher feminism into the modern office, disgraced female bullies such as former Yahoo CEO Marissa Mayer have been outed as prettier packaging of the same old exploitative corporate culture. As pop culture blog *Jezebel* noted bluntly, "The Problem with Shitty Women Bosses Isn't That They're Women. It's That They're Assholes."[14]

Female executives with high-testosterone/dopamine neurosignatures often have a strong drive to succeed. Others may be promoted because they feel more familiar to the men at the top. Some are exciting, inspiring, hard-driving bosses. Others may come off as rude and insulting, create extreme stress for their employees, and exhibit low empathy and poor impulse control.

Let's also acknowledge, however, that according to NeuroColor's data, roughly one-third of women have high-testosterone brains, yet women don't come anywhere close to making up one-third of corporate leaders. Women clearly still face tremendous bias in executive suites. In 2020, just one in five direct reports to a corporate CEO was a woman, and only one in thirty was a woman of color, according to Women in the Workplace. As of June 2021, only 8 percent of Fortune 500 CEOs were female.[15]

A meta review of sixty-three studies that the American Psychological Association collected and analyzed shows that when women act assertively and dominant, their behavior is viewed more negatively than when men exhibit the very same behavior. Women who assert their ideas, make direct requests, and advocate for themselves are liked less, the study concluded.[16] As Wharton organizational psychologist Adam Grant noted in his tweet about this study, "When will we stop punishing dominant women for violating outdated gender stereotypes?"[17]

The boss who sent me for "lean-in" training was female. Under her leadership, fourteen- to sixteen-hour workdays were the norm, and extreme stress was worshipped as proof of productivity. If you weren't sleep-deprived, you were underperforming. My average workday ran from 7 a.m. to 10 p.m. and sometimes lasted until midnight or later. I would often have to catch an early flight the next morning and run that entire day on two to three hours of sleep, without lunch or dinner breaks. I was exhausted and worried about my health, because I wasn't sleeping enough, working out, or eating right.

When I approached my boss to ask for an hour exercise break once a week, she testily informed me that my request was "unprofessional." I pressed her. She finally relented but told me I would have to sneak out so no one else would notice.

Was my boss simply conforming to the expectations of her superiors? Or was she driven by her own brain in her failure to recognize that by denying her employees basic needs such as sleep, healthy food, and exercise, she was destroying their productivity and job satisfaction? Regardless, highly educated, talented female employees were leaving this company instead of rising to the top. And they were taking the resources the company had poured into their training and development with them.

❦

Mind Bender—A whopping 86 percent of millennial women in a 2017 REAL study said they had ditched cushy corporate jobs. Thirty-three percent had felt restricted and unhappy. Forty-three percent said they weren't following their passion. Ten percent said they weren't progressing fast enough and couldn't influence the company in a meaningful way.[18]

❦

WHY THERE IS A NEUROGAP AT THE TOP

My lean-in training was designed to teach me to act like a powerful man. Now we can see that it was designed to teach me to behave like someone with a high-testosterone neurosignature. But what if you're a woman with a high-estrogen neurosignature? You may be able to fake high-testosterone traits such as tough-mindedness and linear thinking, but it won't be genuine, because you excel instead at empathy and lateral thinking.

Imagine if we sent male executives to "lean-out" training to teach them to shake hands more gently, smile encouragingly, and take ladylike steps. Flipping the script illuminates how insulting "empowerment" training is to smart, talented women—and why it fails to prevent them from ditching corporate life in droves.

Today, we understand how demoralizing it is to require a gay person to pretend to be straight. To have to pretend to be someone you're not in order to advance at your job sucks up cognitive resources. It can cause anxiety and depression.

I'd like to add that lots of men have high-estrogen neurosignatures and may also feel unable to perform at their best in certain corporate environments. NeuroColor data shared with me shows that roughly 28 percent of men in the general population and around 72 percent of women exhibit traits associated with the high-estrogen brain. The data reinforces that gender should never be used to stereotype anyone's personality or thinking styles. Your gender *affects* your neurosignature, but it does not *determine* your neurosignature.

This applies to both cisgender and transgender people, by the way. Please know that whenever I say "women," I am including transwomen; and when I say "men," that includes transmen. Nonbinary and gender-fluid individuals also have unique neurosignatures, just as the rest of us do.

Your race has little to no influence on your neurosignature. That's why, as a neuroscientist, I don't feel qualified to directly address racial diversity at work. I have noticed, however, that when companies apply my brain-friendly recommendations for the workplace, they naturally attract greater gender and racial diversity.

THE POWER OF "THOUGHT DIVERSITY"

You could solve your gender-diversity problem by promoting women with high-testosterone brains to the executive suite. They may perform just like the guys. But you haven't actually diversified how your team thinks and solves problems.

Helen Fisher suggests that different neurosignatures evolved in hunter-gatherer societies for a reason. "Imagine a group of hungry humans walking together in Africa, hundreds of thousands of years ago," she told me. "Suddenly, they come across some mushrooms. The impulsive high-dopamine people would jump right into eating the mushrooms and possibly be poisoned. You need cautious high-serotonin folks to say, 'Hold on; it's not in our tradition to eat these mushrooms,' and high-testosterone types to say, 'Let's do an experiment and feed a couple of these mushrooms to the dog' while the high-estrogen people suggest, 'Let's sit down and pool our knowledge about these mushrooms.'"

Humans evolved to think differently so we could put our heads together and come up with smart solutions to problems. Thought diversity makes for a more effective team. "Unfortunately," Helen explains, "when organizations think about diversity, they look at race, gender, or cultural background—but not diversity of mind. So, you may have women represented, and that's great—but if they all share the same temperament, the group isn't as diverse as you think."

A CHANCE TO REIMAGINE WORK

In 2020, millions of people began to work from home. Corporate offices were profoundly disrupted with a far greater impact than any ambitious human resource executive could ever dream of having. This is an unprecedented opportunity to kick-start a workplace revolution that has been needed for decades. A brain-friendly workplace that supports all neurosignatures provides an exciting new paradigm for this revolution.

In March 2021, an internal Goldman Sachs report leaked to the press provided a shocking peek into the company. First-year analysts reported working on average ninety hours per week and sleeping just five hours per night. One hundred percent reported that their personal relationships had deteriorated and that they faced unrealistic deadlines. Forty-two percent said they had experienced unjustified blame. Seventeen percent reported frequent shouting and swearing.[19]

Here are two quotes from the leaked document:[20]

I didn't come into this job expecting a nine a.m. to five p.m. workday, but I also didn't expect consistent nine a.m. to five a.m. days, either.

Being unemployed is less frightening to me than what my body might succumb to if I keep up this lifestyle.

You may be thinking, *what did they expect, working for an investment bank?* True, yet I would argue that the real loser here is the company. It is likely to become a workplace that only attracts people with a dopamine/testosterone neurosignature. As a result, the company steadily loses the talent and insights that a variety of neurosignatures can provide.

⌘

Brain Boost—Julie Linn Teigland, a managing partner at EY (formerly Ernst & Young), travels the globe on an extremely demanding schedule. I see her at many events, and she always seems energized and upbeat. She never looks tired. I asked for her secret. "Before I have to speak to an audience," Teigland told me, "I love to get out and walk around the block for a couple minutes. And don't laugh, but I have one of those little under-the-desk pedaling machines. It really helps me keep my energy up."

⌘

THE TIMES THEY ARE A-CHANGIN'

Corporations mistakenly place the highest value on executives who can jet around the globe on no sleep and gallons of coffee. Companies think these are their "high performers." It's time to build awareness that all neurosignatures are equally valuable.

Women and men with high-estrogen or high-serotonin neurosignatures are strong in empathy and associative lateral thinking. They crave connection and build harmonious relationships. This can make them excellent, insightful, team-building leaders. But companies lose them when they are shamed for wanting reasonable hours, parental leave, child care, and a healthy work/life balance.

Women are expected to return to work a few short weeks after delivering a baby, for example, and never show signs of fatigue or longing to be with their infants. Men are expected to spend very little time with their families if they want to make it to the executive suite. None of this is normal.

⌘

Mind Bender—How did Americans use time saved from commuting during the 2020 shutdown? A Becker Friedman Institute paper reveals that Americans were commuting sixty million fewer hours per day and devoting two-thirds of that time to home improvement, chores, family time, and leisure.[21]

⌘

GIVE WOMEN WHAT THEY WANT—
AND GET MORE DIVERSITY

In 2007, Google extended paid maternity leave from three to nearly five months. Attrition rates for female Google employees who had babies plunged by 50 percent. If only gender diversity training had such a track record.

Google's move set off a maternity arms race, with a growing number of tech firms offering gender-neutral paid parental leave to men and women, including Twitter (20 weeks), Etsy (26 weeks), Facebook (4 months), and Change .org (18 weeks). Netflix and Virgin Management increased paid parental leave to a year. The practice is spreading beyond the tech industry to other sectors as well.

My clients have discovered that brain-friendly practices such as extended parental leave naturally decrease female attrition while raising overall employee satisfaction and productivity. What's good for women, it turns out, is also good for companies, because it restores neurosignature diversity.

In the next chapters, we'll explore how to create a brain-friendly workplace that encourages all neurosignatures to develop into their happiest and most productive selves. This will naturally decrease female attrition while raising employee satisfaction and productivity.

For starters, let's do away with the worship of extreme stress and insanely long work hours in favor of practices that genuinely enhance productivity. Even your most revved-up, high-testosterone/dopamine execs will perform better—and face fewer lawsuits from throwing tantrums—after a good night's sleep and a healthy snack.

CHANGE THE WORKPLACE, NOT THE PEOPLE

Setting up a brain-friendly workplace that is naturally attractive to all neurosignatures has wide-ranging benefits. It's far easier to reform the workplace than it is to change people. Let people play to their strengths instead of wasting energy trying to change their personalities.

The Network for Executive Women reports 31 percent attrition for female executives.[22] It only gets worse as they climb the corporate ladder. By the time women reach the top, they leave their jobs *three times* more often than their male colleagues. Corporations that don't understand neurosignatures and fail to listen to what women want are losing massive pools of talent.

Perhaps we should view female brain drain as a leading indicator—the canary in the coal mine. Something isn't right, and we'd better fix it before it's too late.

A company will thrive when it hires and respects employees with different neurosignatures. They will bring wonderfully complementary strengths into the workplace. By raising awareness of neurosignature diversity's importance to a company's productivity and profitability, bias should diminish as well. Companies that encourage and support *all* neurosignatures become more productive, more profitable—and naturally, more diverse. In the next chapter, we'll dive into *your* neurosignature.

THE BRAIN-FRIENDLY INTERVIEW

Julie Linn Teigland, managing partner, EY Europe, Middle East, India, and Africa

Teigland is a widely beloved senior executive at global accounting power-house EY. She is managing partner of EY Europe, Middle East, India, and Africa (EMEIA), overseeing more than 121,000 people across ninety-seven countries. She is also global leader for EY Women Fast Forward and serves on boards in Europe and the United States. Born in the United States, Teigland has lived in Germany for thirty years and is married with four children.

Teigland is an inspiring executive who is a genius at motivating her team and exuding positive energy, despite her demanding career. I was eager to learn some of her secrets.

Friederike: Was there a pivotal challenging moment in your career that motivated you to want to create a "better working world" at Ernst & Young?

Julie: Initially in my career, with four young children, I was focused on surviving. Trying to be a good wife, a good mother, and good at your job is a lot. It took some time to reach enough stability in my career that I could think about how to create a better work environment. To be honest, it wasn't until my kids were around nine or ten that I could truly begin to balance things better in my own life. That's when I started to say, "OK, I've made it. How can I give back?"

Friederike: What is EY doing today to better support working mothers?

Julie: In June 2019, we announced EY's collaboration with SheWorks!, a cloud-based technology platform that provides women access to remote and flexible job opportunities. Leveraging the power of digital to attract more women to the global workforce is a key objective. I still remember the days when if you wanted to leave the office, you waited for the partner to go to the restroom so you could sneak past his office to get to the exit. There are so many more mothers in our workforce today than there were when I started out. That's fantastic to see. It's a far more diverse workplace today.

Friederike: Millennial women in particular are demanding a workplace that is more sensitive to their needs as working mothers.

Julie: Yes, and we have not fully solved this problem. At EY, we offer a lot of flexibility, but we also demand a lot. Our focus now is to make sure our people can design their careers within our unique approach to work at EY. Our value proposition is that it's "yours to build." It does take strong women to be able to do that, though, and handle it all. I want to be honest about that.

Friederike: Do you have any hacks you use to cope with everything?

Julie: My secret hack is that I love long flights. They're my mini vacations. I feel like I can completely shut off, watch a chick flick, and thoroughly enjoy myself. I've also become a Peloton fan. I love to hop on and do twenty minutes in the morning to get my energy up, and then I'm ready to go.

Friederike: Exercise is so important to brain health and our moods. What do you do during a meeting when you sense that the energy is flagging?

Julie: In the Frankfurt office, we have a coffee bar. My entire leadership team knows that if I'm feeling a bit bored or frustrated in a session, I'll announce, "I'm going to go get coffee. Who wants a coffee?" People thought I was crazy, because I was always buying like twenty coffees. And I'm not a big coffee drinker.

But that allows me to leave the room, get in a little walk, and do something for others, which makes me feel good. When I return, it's usually with a positive change in my perspective that helps change the dynamic in the room.

If you don't like what you're hearing or seeing, you have to change perspective, and you have to get other people to change perspective, too. That can be as simple as getting them to look up, or drink a coffee. Anything to break them out of the rut. Actually, I shouldn't be sharing this because now everyone will know my coffee trick.

Friederike: People truly seem to appreciate you and your welcoming leadership style. What makes your leadership style work?

Julie: That is so nice of you to say. Two things drive my leadership style, I think. First, I know I'm incredibly privileged, and I seek to always remember to be grateful and to feel honored to have this position.

If you walk into work every day as if you're the king—or queen—people may look up to you and respect you. But they're not as appreciative of you if they don't sense that you are grateful to have your position. I do not come from a wealthy family, and I do not feel that I was given all this because I am the best. I truly feel grateful, and I think gratitude is a big portion of what drives happiness and satisfaction with oneself. And then you can share those good feelings with other people.

Second, I endeavor to be straightforward. I try to be open, honest, and transparent. I do also try to be gentle with people, but I think people appreciate it when you get straight to the point. It shows you respect them.

I also try to be honest about my shortcomings and mistakes. You're not a true leader unless you can demonstrate vulnerability in some way, shape, or form. You have to be able to show people that you're human and that you see them as human. Then, empathy can flow both ways, creating much more positive interactions.

Friederike: It is so challenging to be a corporate leader and also have a healthy, happy family life. What key advice would you give a man or woman seeking to have both?

Julie: If I had it to do all over again, I would set better boundaries at work. Early in my career, I didn't know how to set boundaries. I took on too much, and then I blamed the company—I was at Arthur Andersen at the time. In actuality, it wasn't the firm forcing me to work eighty hours a week. I had to learn to set my boundaries around how many hours I was willing to work and the fact that I also had young children who needed me home.

Friederike: Do you think people fail to set those boundaries out of fear, mostly?

Julie: It wasn't fear that was driving me but, rather, an inaccurate perception that every minute, every second mattered. But looking back on my entire career span, do you think it would have mattered if I decided to work a bit less when my kids were really young? No, it wouldn't have mattered. The employer has an obligation, in my view, to respect your boundaries if they value you as a talent. That's where I think EY has gotten smarter. I encourage my employees to make honest choices and to leverage the flexibility we can offer when they need it.

Friederike: Is there a shift in culture driving this change at EY?

Julie: Yes, especially post-pandemic, we see a shift away from presenteeism toward an outcome-based paradigm where it doesn't matter how much or how little time you spend as long as you get the job done. How well you do the job is much more important than the hours that you spend at work. If we can get comfortable with flexibility and diversity, we will achieve even better outcomes.

It's the difference between trying to control the processes versus trusting employees and letting them figure out how to get it done and giving them guardrails and guidance. It's a different type of leadership. At EY, we use an apprenticeship model. "You learn by watching those in front of you," whether you're following a partner or a senior manager. I don't think we have this approach all figured out yet, but I definitely like the direction we are headed.

2

Your Neurosignature

The Good, the Bad, and the Ugly

In diversity there is beauty and there is strength.

—Maya Angelou

A multinational pharmaceutical company was struggling to launch a thrilling new product—a pill as effective as chemotherapy against cancer, yet with far fewer side effects. This pill did not cause hair loss, vomiting, severe anemia, and other horrific chemo reactions. It saved patients from spending hours tethered to an IV pumping poison into their veins. Patients should have been choosing this new drug over chemo in droves. But in prelaunch marketing tests, cancer patients consistently chose chemo over the new pill. Nobody wanted this breakthrough drug.

THE MIRACLE DRUG NOBODY WANTED

I was the only female member of an elite four-person consulting team hired to travel to the pharmaceutical company's headquarters and investigate this problem. So, what innovative approach did my male colleagues suggest to solve this confounding mystery?

"We'll just ask them," one fellow announced proudly. "Let's hand out surveys to patients and doctors with questions like, 'Why did you choose chemo instead of the pill?'"

The other men enthusiastically agreed with this brilliant plan. As Spock might say, it was highly logical. As someone with a high-estrogen neurosignature, I thought this plan lacked nuance, to say the least.

"People don't know why they do things," I blurted. "You can't simply ask a cancer patient why she chose chemo. There's a good chance she doesn't know."

I had previously been a researcher at the famed Max Planck Institute for Brain Research. There, I learned that people *think* they know why they make decisions, but most decision making actually takes place in brain areas associated with the subconscious mind. Simply asking patients why they were choosing chemo, therefore, was unlikely to elicit the real reasons behind this seemingly irrational decision.

In family therapy, psychologists have patients role-play to uncover truths hiding in their subconscious minds. As family members play each other in scenes, the therapist gains insight into their unconscious fears and motivations. I suggested that we try playacting to draw the truth out of cancer patients, too.

My male peers thought my plan was ridiculously fluffy. "Why are you making this so complicated?" one groaned. Luckily, my high-estrogen neurosignature also makes me good at coalition building and persuasion. My colleagues eventually, reluctantly, agreed to give my approach a try.

PLAYACTING

The pharmaceutical company's marketing manager brought in cancer patients and their doctors. We had them act out doctor-patient consultations regarding the choice between chemo and the new pill while the marketing team watched from behind a one-way mirror. Then we'd ask patient and doctor to switch roles. Sometimes I had patients play chemo itself.

My colleagues really groaned at that one—but they did a great job tracking the data and keeping our efforts focused and on track. Their drive, energy, and interest in the statistics we were compiling dovetailed well with my focus on the behavior of the people in our study. Our different neurosignatures were quite complementary and were making us a very effective team.

Here's what we uncovered: Patients didn't trust the pill *because* it didn't have horrible side effects. Suffering through chemo made them feel as though it was working.

"We discovered that people wanted to feel the pain so they would believe the drug was working," the marketing manager told me. "They don't trust the pill—precisely because it has fewer side effects."

Few patients would have admitted on a survey that they wanted to vomit and watch their hair fall out. But, subconsciously, patients viewed chemo's terrible side effects as a reassuring indication that they were taking the strongest possible medicine to fight their cancer. Getting violently ill from chemo was the price they expected to pay for regaining their health. The thought of not having to pay that price made patients very uneasy.

Armed with this knowledge, the pharmaceutical company decided to make the pill bigger and emphasize in its brochure how unpleasant the (few) side effects were and how uncomfortable the pill was to swallow. The company's sales team was instructed to tell doctors to emphasize these factors to their patients.

"We had a fantastic launch," the marketing manager reported.

The miracle drug nobody wanted became the top product in the market. The marketing team even won an internal company award for its handling of the launch.

"This experience was so full of emotion," the marketing manager told me later. "I remember one patient breaking down as he shared how heartbroken he was that he couldn't attend his daughter's wedding. It became clear what an emotional disease cancer is."

She added that the company loved my role-playing approach and copied it for future launches. She also confided that she had found me easy to talk to but the men on my team "unapproachable."

HAPPY TO BE FIRED

Our team's insights helped our client develop a winning new marketing strategy and successfully launch its product. Together, my colleagues and I had brought a complementary range of neurosignature diversity to this project, and we knocked it out of the park.

When we returned from our business trip, I was fired. My team members had complained to our boss that my approach was "unstructured." They took credit for our success, as well.

Tears welled up in my eyes as I sat in our boss's huge corner office, complete with floor-to-ceiling windows and a stunning view. With his expensive suit, gleaming watch, and slicked-back hair, he was the picture of the accomplished high-testosterone/dopamine leader. He came out from behind his polished wood desk and perched on a corner of it.

"You just don't know how to communicate," he said. And that was that.

Ironically, after leaving this company, communication became my business. Today, I'm a busy keynote speaker to Fortune 500 companies, as well as an author. I couldn't be happier to have been fired, because it put me on a career path that plays to my neurosignature's strengths. But that company lost some valuable thought diversity, not to mention the money it had poured into my training.

I have since coached lots of female executives with high-estrogen neurosignatures. Many have received similar feedback from high-testosterone bosses that they "just don't know how to communicate." When I meet these women, they are empathetic, warm, and excellent communicators.

High-testosterone leaders of both genders tend to prefer linear, concise communication. They can become impatient with lateral thinkers and their wandering, free-association brainstorming. Sometimes, though, a high-estrogen brain is just what's needed to solve a thorny business problem.

As a lateral thinker, my process is nonlinear, which is great for coming up with creative ideas. Unfortunately, in corporate environments that are dominated by high-testosterone leaders, lateral thinking is undervalued. It can even be viewed as a liability in workplaces that prioritize "more logical" step-by-step thinking.

I am not saying that linear thinking is bad and lateral thinking is good. Both styles are great and highly complementary. I love working with linear thinkers and enjoy the structure they impose on our work. I'm saying that teams have the best shot at success when both thinking styles are understood, accepted, and valued. This is the power of thought diversity at work.

My message is clear. Nurture all neurosignatures and play to their strengths, and your team will succeed beyond your wildest expectations.

While working from home, many people have discovered that they are more productive when they have the freedom to go for a brisk walk outdoors when they feel stuck, or dive into a project at whatever time of day (or night) they feel the most focused. In a sense, people have already started creating their own brain-friendly workplaces. It will be tough to stuff them back into the old paradigm.

In the coming chapters, we'll explore ways to create a new brain-friendly paradigm for business that is more productive and enjoyable for all types of brains. But first, let's dive deeper into the four neurosignatures so you understand the tremendous value that each brings to the table. Along the way, you may discover yourself.

TOSS THE MYERS-BRIGGS

It's not like companies haven't tried to understand their employees' personalities in order to correctly place them and provide them with appropriate training. Unfortunately, business leaders have leaned heavily on debunked personality tests.

Personality tests found their way into business with the creation of the Myers-Briggs Type Indicator in 1962, which has been widely used in recruiting, team building, and leadership development. Unfortunately, the Myers-Briggs and other personality tests lack scientific basis and are highly susceptible to confirmation bias. As behavioral economist and Duke University professor Dan Ariely told me at the Digital Life Design conference in 2016, "instead of taking the Myers-Briggs, read your horoscope. It's just as valid and takes less time."

Confirmation bias is the tendency to search for, interpret, favor, and recall information that confirms or supports your beliefs or values.

In 2015, researchers confirmed strongly inconsistent results in roughly 50 percent of test takers who filled out the Myers-Briggs twice within a five-week period.[1] Even so, the company that provides the Myers-Briggs still earns around $20 million annually from corporate and government contracts. Companies still use it to separate employees into "types" and assign them to different training programs and responsibilities.

Mental Break—In 1948, psychologist Bertram Forer administered a personality test to his students. But when Forer received their completed tests, he threw them out. Instead, unbeknownst to the students, he returned an identical personality profile to every student in the class. Next, he asked the students to rate their profiles' accuracy on a scale of zero to five. Five meant "excellent"; four, "good."

The students gave their phony profiles a cumulative average of 4.26 for accuracy. Then, Forer told them he had clipped their "personality profile" out of a newspaper horoscope column. Like most horoscopes, it was ambiguous but vaguely complimentary. Every student had concluded that it was an accurate assessment of his or her personality.

THE LOVE STUDY

The Fisher Temperament Inventory created by Helen Fisher in 2005 is the first personality test validated by functional brain MRIs. Today, the Neuro-Color Personality Assessment based on Fisher's research is recognized as a science-based breakthrough in assessment.

Fisher's research began with a question posed to her by the leadership team at Match.com: "Why do we fall in love with one person rather than another?" Fisher decided to conduct a large-scale study to explore connections between brain activity and mate choice. The goal was to help Match.com do a better job of matching people romantically.

"When Match.com asked me, 'Why does someone fall in love with one person rather than another?' I tried to find a neurological answer," Fisher told *Harvard Business Review* in 2017.[2] "I found that four biological systems—dopamine, serotonin, testosterone, and estrogen/oxytocin—are each linked to a particular suite of personality traits. I found this not only in humans but also doves, lizards, and monkeys."

Fisher created a questionnaire to measure the degree to which a person expresses these personality traits. Then, it was put on Match.com and Chemistry.com. Next, Fisher explained, "I did two fMRI studies—one with young couples, the other with older couples. The subjects answered my questionnaire and then went into the scanner."[3]

The functional MRIs confirmed that Fisher's new personality test was accurate. "People who scored high on my scale measuring traits linked with the dopamine system showed lots of activity in their brains' dopamine pathways," Fisher noted.[4] The same was true for the other three brain systems. Results were consistent when repeated, proving that the test was not only valid, but also reliable. Fisher's results were published in the peer-reviewed *PLoS One* journal in 2013.[5]

So far, Fisher's personality test is the only one validated by neuroscience. The four brain systems it measures have been proven by further research to be universal—found across all cultures, even in animals.

⸰⸎⸰

Brain Food—Chocolate is the food of love . . . and the brain. Just make sure you get the dark stuff! Dark chocolate is linked to better cognitive performance and a "neuroprotective" effect on the brain, according to a 2013 study published in the *British Journal of Clinical Pharmacology.* "Chocolate induces positive effects on mood, and the flavonoids preserve cognitive abilities during ageing in rats, lower the risk for developing Alzheimer's disease and decrease the risk of stroke in humans," the study reports.[6]

Just don't eat dark chocolate too close to bedtime—the caffeine in it could keep you awake.

⤛

ON A SPECTRUM

The four neurosignatures I'm about to describe are based on my interpretations of Fisher's research. Before we dive deeper into understanding neurosignatures, I want to explain that they vary widely on a spectrum. You may have a very active dopamine brain system, for example, yet only express some of the personality traits associated with a high-dopamine brain. In addition, nature and nurture are equally important factors. Our fetal brains are shaped by estrogen and testosterone in the womb, for example. And our brain system development is affected by positive and negative experiences as we grow up.

Your current environment also has a huge impact on how your personality is expressed. At an extremely stressful workplace, for example, a person with lots of activity in her testosterone brain system might become angry and aggressive. A high-estrogen person, in contrast, may react by getting very indecisive, emotional, and overwhelmed. People with brains high in dopamine might become extremely impatient or even hyperactive. High-serotonin neurosignatures may react by becoming rigid, stubborn, and beset with worry.

In a brain-friendly workplace, high-testosterone people will lead with decisiveness and energy. High-estrogen people will nurture team relationships and use lateral thinking to brainstorm surprising solutions to challenging problems. High-serotonin folks will stay on top of critical details such as regulations and compliance. High-dopamine people will bring creativity to problem solving and keep everyone feeling optimistic and goal-oriented.

In addition, we each have all four brain systems, so our personalities express various combinations. As Helen Fisher explains, "We all are made up of an array of traits. I'm high estrogen, and in a group those traits come out: I listen carefully, I try to get along. When I'm alone at my desk, I'm all dopamine: I'm creative, focused on my work. Because I'm lower on testosterone, I'm not tough-minded or good at math. But I am logical—certainly in business, if not always in love. In evaluating yourself and others, you have to think about all four systems. When you understand where someone lands on each scale, you begin to see the full personality."[7]

DIVING INTO DOPAMINE

People with the high-dopamine neurosignature seek out sensation and novelty. They are energetic, curious, creative, and impulsive. They also tend to be optimistic and generous. On the flip side, they can be reckless and vulnerable to addictions. Statistically, they tend to have shorter marriages than other neurosignatures and get divorced more often.

Spanx shapewear founder Sara Blakely is a wonderful example of a creative, energetic high-dopamine leader. She came up with the idea for Spanx because she hated wearing panty hose for her sales job in humid Florida—but loved the slimming effect of control-top hose. Blakely took a pair of scissors and cut off the hose. Voilà, the first Spanx shapewear prototype was born.

In 1998, Blakely founded Spanx at age twenty-seven with just $5,000 in personal savings. Her bubbly personality enabled her to handle multiple rejections of her product. She persevered until she landed her first investor and then her first sales orders. By 2012, Blakely had made *Time*'s coveted Top 100 list. She was also crowned the youngest female billionaire by *Forbes* that year.

In 2006, Blakely launched the Sara Blakely Foundation to support education and entrepreneurship for women. She was mentored by her fellow high-dopamine entrepreneur, Virgin's Richard Branson, who encouraged her philanthropic bent. In 2020, for example, Blakely pledged $5 million to support female-run small businesses during the pandemic.

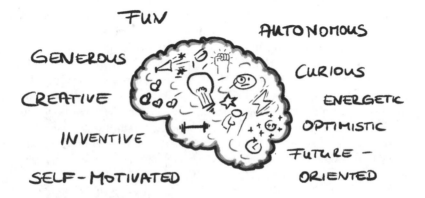

❧

Mind Bender—Parkinson's patients who have been prescribed L-dopa—the precursor to the neurotransmitter dopamine—have sometimes gambled away the family fortune or become sex addicts because it raised their brain dopamine levels too much.

❧

DOPAMINE AT WORK

High-dopamine neurosignatures love to explore and try new things. They handle change and travel well. They can roll with the punches when their company goes through restructuring—and they will probably enjoy it. They bring humor and fun to the workplace and can be very charismatic and inspiring.

❧

Brain Boost—I once had a high-dopamine colleague who kept me and the rest of our team in stitches. He was always cracking jokes, telling funny anecdotes, and finding humor in even the bleakest moments. He boosted my performance by raising my dopamine levels to new heights, keeping me feeling energized and positive. This happened because laughing releases dopamine, and dopamine is a natural brain booster. It creates euphoria and increases motivation. If you have someone like this on your team, he's a keeper, even if he's not one of your best performers. He will raise the mood and performance of the entire team. A fun workplace is a brain-friendly workplace.

❧

If you want to keep high-dopamine people happy, give them creative freedom and autonomy. Combine this with new projects, frequent promotions, and job rotations. Keep their work lives interesting, fresh, and rewarding. Don't stifle them with too much routine, or they will lose their minds.

Keep in mind that high-dopamine people can stress out your other neurosignatures because they have lots of energy, are whirlwinds of change, and can be unstructured and impatient. When someone is high in both dopamine and testosterone, in particular, it would be helpful for them to be aware of their tendency to be domineering and the possibility that they can become aggressive when stressed.

SAILING WITH SEROTONIN

People with a high-serotonin neurosignature tend to be loyal and conscientious. Duty, respectability, traditions, and morals are important to them. They respect authority, follow the rules, and adhere to social norms and customs. They love traditions, such as family holidays and anniversaries. Status and what other people think matters to them. They want to belong and enjoy rising to high-status leadership positions.

Interestingly, a study of vervet monkeys found that the alpha males have twice the serotonin levels circulating in their blood as their subordinates. High-serotonin leaders—whether they are monkeys or corporate executives—bring a calm, balanced quality to their leadership.

High-serotonin people can be cautious, though not fearful unless really stressed. Because serotonin triggers release of estrogen and oxytocin, the "cuddle hormone," they're great at building relationships, trust, and community.

Serotonin tends to suppress testosterone, which can spike in response to fear, anger, and aggression. This helps high-serotonin folks remain calm and stable in a crisis. They can be less aggressive under pressure than other neurosignatures. All of these factors further enhance their value at work.

People with high-serotonin neurosignatures generally prefer orderly and organized environments. Some have a special genetic variant in the serotonin system that enhances their ability to understand and process numerical infor-

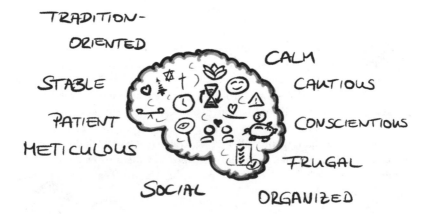

SEROTONIN NEUROSIGNATURE

TRADITION-
ORIENTED
                                            CALM
STABLE   CAUTIOUS
PATIENT   CONSCIENTIOUS
METICULOUS
                                        FRUGAL
            SOCIAL   ORGANIZED

mation. For instance, this could explain how someone such as Warren Buffett gains insights from financial statements when seeking undervalued companies to invest in.

In the extreme, high serotonin is correlated with anxiety and worry. When stressed, people with this neurosignature can become paralyzed by anxiety about what other people think of them, for example.

~≋~

Mental Break—Certain psychedelic drugs have chemical structures that resemble serotonin. These include MDMA, LSD, DMT, and psilocybin. Scientists believe that activation of a serotonin receptor is key to their hallucinatory effects and the feelings of joy they can engender. Of course, too much serotonin activity in the brain can also produce anxiety—and freak-outs.

~≋~

Kate Middleton provides an example of how a high-serotonin person might handle the glare of being constantly in the public eye. The Duchess of Cambridge is always perfectly put together, fashionable yet conservative. She remained calm in the face of snide tabloid remarks about her "middle-class" and "commoner" background. As a result, the highly critical British tabloids started embracing her as the country's future queen consort. The *Sun* reported, for example, that "Kate Middleton looked every inch the graceful and stoic royal at Prince Philip's funeral."[8]

Prince Harry and his wife, American actress Meghan Markle, tried and failed to push the British monarchy into modernity. Middleton, in contrast, appears content to conform to royal traditions. She has focused on building her family with Prince William and her philanthropic work with pregnant women and new mothers.

As pop-culture blog *Jezebel* put it, "Over the last decade, the commoner from Berkshire successfully fashioned herself into a perfect, smiling, briskly competent but never flashy vision of modern, polished, up-market motherhood—posting her own photographs of the kids on Instagram, and chatting kindly through her charity efforts with new mothers struggling to adjust."[9]

~≋~

Brain Boost—At Christmas and Thanksgiving holidays, we boost feelings of cheer with foods such as turkey and chocolate. Both are rich in the amino acid L-tryptophan, which helps our bodies produce serotonin.

~≋~

Serotonin at Work

People high in serotonin make great managers, because other employees sense that they are trustworthy and stable. High-serotonin executives can remain calm under pressure. They are good at building team relationships and mediating conflicts.

People with high-serotonin brains are meticulous—more likely to read the fine print on every deal and make sure all details have been triple-checked. This is the level of meticulousness you would want in a corporate lawyer, for example, where one small mistake could wind up costing millions.

Some corporate scandals and financial crises might have been avoided if more high-serotonin executives were in charge. They function as an excellent counterbalance to "big picture" high-dopamine or high-testosterone leaders. Again, one neurosignature is not "better" than another; rather, a brain-friendly workplace will be more productive and more likely to avoid disasters because it values all neurosignatures.

A high-serotonin employee will function best in a position that provides a steady daily routine with few surprises. He will value security, benefits, and opportunities to rise to positions of greater responsibility.

These days, many corporations led by high-testosterone/dopamine CEOs place high value on "continuous improvement" and constant change "for the better"—because that's what the CEOs prefer in their own careers. But frequent job rotations and change for the sake of change will drive a high-serotonin employee nuts—or out. An executive with a high-serotonin neurosignature will prefer to develop deep team relationships and stay with that team long-term.

~≋~

Mental Break—Who loves doing their taxes? Raise your hands. I can tell you one person who loves doing taxes—my accountant. He seems to genuinely get a kick out of working on tax returns. So, I asked him, "Ludger, do you *really* love doing taxes?"

"Yes!" he exclaimed. "Doing someone's tax return is like playing chess. I make one move, and I think three steps ahead about its ripple effects. Or I pretend I'm working on a big puzzle, and I think of the beautiful picture I will have once all the pieces are in the right place."

Ladies and gentlemen, this is how a high-serotonin person has fun. People with this neurosignature genuinely love patterns and order.

~⊗~

THRIVING WITH TESTOSTERONE

People with high-testosterone neurosignatures enjoy competition and are wonderfully independent. They are outspoken, straightforward, and focused. They get stuff done! Many folks high in testosterone are brave and altruistic as well. You'll find them dashing into a burning building to save a stranger.

People with high-testosterone neurosignatures tend to be decisive and rarely second-guess themselves. Research published in the *Proceedings of the National Academy of Sciences* (*PNAS*) showed that wielding power increases testosterone levels in women. Of course, the relationship between behavior, genetics, gender, and the environment is highly complex. Hormones are just one piece of an intricate puzzle.[10] Another *PNAS* study found that people high in testosterone are more likely to pursue high-risk careers.[11] They are linear thinkers who enjoy figuring out how machines and other systems work. Neuroscience research has uncovered that the right hemisphere of the brain, which provides spatial skills, is shaped by testosterone.

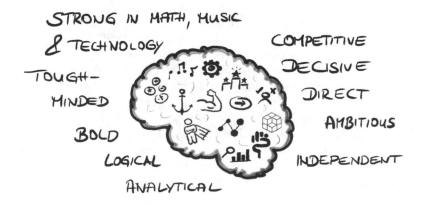

TESTOSTERONE NEUROSIGNATURE

STRONG IN MATH, MUSIC
& TECHNOLOGY

COMPETITIVE

TOUGH-
MINDED

DECISIVE

DIRECT

AMBITIOUS

BOLD

LOGICAL

INDEPENDENT

ANALYTICAL

Sometimes, people with this neurosignature lose their cool. They are vulnerable to being flooded by their emotions—particularly by rage—and can resort to bullying and power trips to assert their dominance. Interestingly, researchers have found that women become more self-confident, assertive, and bold after menopause, when estrogen levels start to decline, "unmasking" the testosterone activity in their brains.

The actress Angelina Jolie may seem like a surprising example of the high-testosterone neurosignature. But Jolie matches with many of its traits. Jolie pilots her own plane, for example, flying solo in and out of her movie locations. Although she could afford her own private jet and crew, Jolie enjoys zipping around in her small Cirrus SR22-G2 and tinkering with it herself.

Jolie is also known for doing her own dangerous stunt work. She even scarred her famous face during a fight scene for the film *Salt*. In one sequence, Jolie leaped off a bridge, landed on top of a speeding container truck, and then jumped from one moving truck to another before bike-jacking a motorcyclist and escaping between lanes full of stopped traffic. At a Comic Con convention in San Diego, Jolie and her director confirmed that she performed those stunts herself.[12]

When Jolie discovered that she carries the BRCA gene associated with the breast cancer that killed her mother at fifty-six, she moved decisively forward with a preventive double mastectomy. Jolie is also strongly altruistic. She has adopted children from multiple countries and travels the world as special envoy to the UN Refugee Agency.

Testosterone at Work

High-testosterone executives are analytical and direct. They respect logic, reasoning, and systemic investigation. Surprisingly, they also enjoy "dominance matching," which means that they like it when subordinates stand up to them. Just make sure you have something smart to say before you try it. High-testosterone neurosignatures enjoy debate, but only if it's intelligent.

High-testosterone employees value achievement and want to respect and enjoy their colleagues. One high-testosterone CEO I know announced that he wanted "all internal office politics" gone when he took over. He modeled and encouraged honesty and directness and came down hard on any backstabbing or manipulative behavior.

High-testosterone neurosignatures can sometimes be "mind blind" to what others are feeling. This can make them come across as aloof or impersonal. They prefer a workplace that provides them with lots of autonomy and minimal supervision. They want to get things done quickly, without having to constantly check in with a superior. They strongly prefer to be self-directed and trusted to get the job done.

High-testosterone employees can neglect their health, especially when strongly focused on a project. They can be so driven that they don't sleep enough or mindlessly grab junk food. Encourage your high-testosterone neurosignatures to relieve some stress by going for a run or hitting the company gym. This will help prevent them from getting over-amped and exploding with anger.

EXPLORING ESTROGEN

If you have a high-estrogen neurosignature, you may notice that you are highly intuitive. Exposure to more estrogen in the womb causes a fetus to grow more lateral connections between its brain hemispheres. This can lead to an ability to spot patterns in seemingly random data. Estrogen also facilitates development of "body loops," which are neural circuits that connect the brain to the skin, stomach, heart, and other organs. This leads to more "hunches," or "gut feelings."

High-estrogen neurosignatures also experience more activity in the mirror neuron system. This is a group of specialized neurons that allow us to learn

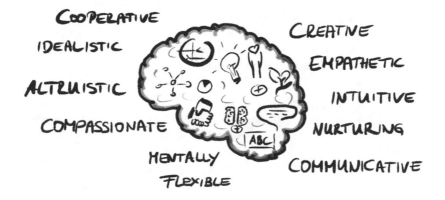

through imitation. Mirror neurons enable us to reflect body language, facial expressions, and emotions. They play an essential part in our social life. This may explain why people with high-estrogen brains are strong on empathy.

People with high-estrogen neurosignatures are interested in other people and seek to bond with them. "Tend and befriend" is the high-estrogen neurosignature mantra. They can be altruistic, but their altruism is more likely to involve supporting charitable causes than dashing into burning buildings.

⤘

Rumination is repetitive, obsessive thinking about the causes and consequences of a negative emotional experience.

⤘

People with this neurosignature can be "systems blind," meaning that they can struggle to focus on the details of a "big picture" that has captured their imagination. They are also prone to rumination and worry, which can lead to pessimism and unproductive self-criticism. Under stress, they may seek relief from this inner turmoil by gossiping or indulging in backstabbing behavior. Invite your high-estrogen employees into your office for a heart-to-heart when they seem stressed. Some one-on-one bonding will do them a lot of good.

⤘

Brain Boost—The research on rumination is extremely consistent. People who ruminate are much more likely to have, or develop, depression and anxiety. Think of rumination as problem-solving run amok. What you need is to get your mind off the problem.

To overcome rumination, engage in a fun, challenging activity that fully occupies your mind and prevents your thoughts from drifting back to the problem. Take a dance or yoga class, go to an exciting movie, or meet up with a friend to play chess. Give your mind something else entertaining and stimulating to focus on, and it will be easier to stop ruminating. Meditation and mindfulness training are also very helpful.

⤘

In 1831, Charles Darwin, twenty-two, was hired as the "naturalist" for the HMS *Beagle*. Darwin spent five years sailing around the world on this ship, visiting South America, Australia, and the southern tip of Africa. At each expedition stop, Darwin studied and cataloged local plants and animals.

Darwin exhibited the traits of a high-estrogen lateral thinker when he began noticing three patterns emerging from his notes: species vary globally, locally, and over time. He developed these observations into his renowned theory of evolution by natural selection.

Even though he gave us "survival of the fittest," Darwin was a gentle, loving family man, beloved by his wife, children, and friends. He was humble and self-effacing. Darwin even put off publication of his famous book, *On the Origin of Species*, because he didn't want to upset other scientists by contradicting their theories. Luckily, he was eventually talked into publishing it, and this foundation of evolutionary biology was published in 1859.

Estrogen at Work

High-estrogen executives bring intuition, empathy, and creative lateral thinking into the workplace. They seek to create cooperation and harmony, and have a gift for diplomacy. These traits make them excellent team leaders who create a positive, encouraging workplace. They may struggle at times to earn the respect of high-testosterone or high-dopamine leaders who mistake their strengths for weaknesses. An experienced high-estrogen leader usually can figure out, though, how to motivate and earn respect from colleagues.

High-estrogen neurosignatures gravitate toward positions in human resources. I know a male high-estrogen HR leader. He has created an exceptionally family-friendly and inclusive workplace that is attracting talent to his company like a magnet.

Money and status aren't as important to high-estrogen people as having a positive impact on the world. They are often activists, promoting charitable causes. They tend to have strong verbal skills and are adept at writing, giving presentations, and learning languages.

Arianna Huffington, for example, has built an incredible career on her ability to connect strongly with people on an emotional level through her books and appearances. She founded Thrive Global, her initiative "to end the burnout epidemic" by encouraging companies to focus on employee well-being.

On the flip side, high-estrogen neurosignatures can be "systems blind" and neglect critical details of a project. Pair them with high-serotonin types who will delight in buttoning up the details.

A healthy work/life balance and lifestyle are important to people high in estrogen. They will gravitate toward brain-friendly workplaces that provide paid family leave and encourage employees to exercise and eat healthily.

BENEFITS OF UNDERSTANDING
YOUR NEUROSIGNATURE

Isn't it cool to discover your own neurosignature? Understanding neurosignatures also improves our respect for clients and team members and reduces the tension and frustration that can build up when we don't understand each other. It's really helpful in our personal relationships, too.

In the next chapter, you'll meet CEOs who are applying brain-friendly strategies such as shorter work days and switching from hustle culture to outcome culture—with exciting results.

THE BRAIN-FRIENDLY INTERVIEW

Dr. Scott Barry Kaufman, author, scientist, host/creator of The Psychology Podcast

Kaufman was named by *Business Insider* one of "50 groundbreaking scientists changing the way we see the world." He hosts *The Psychology Podcast* and has produced nine fascinating books exploring the mysteries of creativity, intelligence, and talent, as well as articles for *Scientific American, Psychology Today, The Atlantic, Harvard Business Review*, and more. Kaufman holds a PhD in cognitive psychology from Yale University.

Classified "special ed" as a child, Scott makes a powerful case in his books for neurodiversity and bright, creative students with learning difficulties, whom he describes as "twice exceptional."

> **Friederike:** I love your work, because I strongly believe that we need to understand and respect neurosignature diversity.
>
> **Scott:** So, does testosterone explain the asshole boss?
>
> **Friederike:** Ha. Yes, it can. Sometimes the high-testosterone/high-dopamine neurosignature, which can occur in both men and women—though it's more predominant in men—can push someone in that direction, though certainly not always.
>
> **Scott:** This makes me think of *Why Do So Many Incompetent Men Become Leaders? (and How to Fix It)* by Tomas Chamorro-Premuzic. He argues that the way to fix this problem is not by training women to become more masculine at work but, rather, to appreciate the different qualities they bring to the workplace.
>
> **Friederike:** Yes! That's exactly what I'm saying—capable, competent people drop out when the workplace becomes dominated by one type of person, to the detri-

ment of the company. Do you have any thoughts on how we can overcome this problem?

Scott: Yes, through my work on neurodiversity and especially how we can create school systems that appreciate different kinds of minds. We can extrapolate some of that into the workplace as well. You need to have enlightened leadership that allows for people to question authority figures and be able to speak up. You also have to make sure there's a really good fit between the job and what the person wants to do—in particular, by giving people opportunities to do job crafting.

Friederike: What is "job crafting"?

Scott: It's a technique that allows people to reframe their current jobs more in line with their unique ways of thinking and their values and aspirations in life. Let's say, for example, that you're a teacher with a gift for opera—and you've never been able to fully embrace your love for opera in your life. You become the opera-singing teacher! You craft your job around who you really are, around your unique gifts and passions.

Friederike: Wow, I love that!

Scott: Job crafting can play a big role in helping us appreciate the neurodiversity that surrounds us and that actually exists in the workplace. It involves appreciating the unique skills and perspectives that a person may bring to a "generic" job.

Friederike: In a sense, I'm talking about "crafting" the workplace itself, in order to enable people to bring more of themselves to work and be appreciated for their neurosignature diversity.

As a child, you were classified as "special needs." How did you overcome that early stigma? It must have been so frustrating.

Scott: I had an auditory difficulty when I was young due to a lot of fluid in my ears. That made it hard for me to process things, and I was viewed only through that singular lens. The educational system failed to see the whole child and interpreted my deep imagination and daydreaming as an indication of stupidity.

I was kept in special education until ninth grade, when a special ed teacher asked me, "Why are you still here?" That motivated me to fight my way out and see what I was capable of achieving in life. Extrapolating that to the workplace, we do a lot of things that kill creativity in employees, because leaders are ignoring their gifts.

Friederike: How so?

Scott: I would argue that dopamine is underappreciated. I have dopamine up the kazoo. That was a big part of why I struggled in school because I was curious about everything and questioned everything. I also loved to run around the classroom in superhero capes while we were supposed to be listening to the teacher read, which did not go over well.

But I was genuinely curious about the material, and I wanted to go fifty thousand steps beyond the material and understand the point of what we were learning. When we were studying American history, for example, I asked, "What about the indigenous people? Why aren't we learning their perspective?" The response was basically, "Shut up, Scott." I definitely got overlooked as a kid for my inquisitiveness, creativity, and imagination.

Friederike: We could say that you were stuck in a high-serotonin environment that valued rules above creativity and exploration. High-serotonin teachers who value order and structure may struggle to relate to a child with a high-dopamine neurosignature, which tends to be very creative and energetic.

Scott: Oh, interesting. That could be part of the story, for sure. Too many school environments are geared toward rewarding students for following instructions and punishing them for challenging the instructions.

Friederike: You've written extensively about people who are "twice exceptional," learning disabled yet gifted, for example. How does neurodiversity play into a brain-friendly workplace?

Scott: Many people might have a disability they viewed as self-limiting, yet they also have extraordinary strengths and talents. The neurodiversity movement is about recontextualizing some "disabilities" or "weaknesses" as strengths.

The brain has wonderful compensatory capacities, and when we neglect some capacities, the brain develops and restructures in ways that enable us to get even greater capacity out of other aspects. People on the autism spectrum are great at telling you the truth, for instance. I love having friends on the autism spectrum, especially when I want to know the truth. I don't like having them as friends quite as much when I don't want to know the truth about myself! He he; just kidding. Also, for example, many people with dyslexia are gifted entrepreneurs and artists.

We think about talent wrong in our society, and we have very narrow notions about what constitutes a talent. We leave out a lot of people who have ways of seeing the world that would be very beneficial to a project, especially a creative project.

Friederike: Do you feel hopeful that neurodiversity will begin to be accepted into the workplace?

Scott: I do feel hopeful. There are definitely companies out there that very much care about this. I do wish that neurodiversity were taken just as seriously as other forms of diversity, however. Racial diversity is important and getting a lot of attention right now. I hope neurodiversity will have that kind of moment as well.

Friederike: So true! A company might have excellent racial and gender diversity programs, but if it is only hiring one neurosignature, it is failing to achieve genuine diversity—diversity of thought.

Scott: Yes! Let's not forget neurodiversity; not everything is just skin deep.

3

Outcome Culture

Culture eats strategy for breakfast.

—Peter Drucker

In 1914, Henry Ford took a huge gamble that transformed the lives of American workers. At that time, factory workers toiled up to sixteen hours per day, six days a week, with no paid holidays or vacation. But Ford Motor Company's new technology—the assembly line—was providing a massive increase in productivity. Under pressure from labor unions, Ford doubled his workers' minimum hourly wage from $2.34 to $5 and cut their schedule to eight hours a day. In 1926, Ford Motor Company became one of the first American companies to commit to a five-day, forty-hour week.

Ford bet that by giving his employees more time and money, he would attract the smartest, most innovative workers—and he was right. He also bet correctly that he would reduce workplace accidents and other problems brought on by fatigue. Ford Motor Company boomed, grabbing 61 percent market share in just seven years. A hundred-plus years later, Ford is still one of the world's top ten automakers.

Today, our new "assembly line" is computers, software, and the internet that connects them. We're in an era of monumental gains in worker productivity that have made corporations more gigantically profitable than ever. But most of us are working more hours than ever before.

Now, some innovative business leaders are making the same brain-friendly bet on "outcome culture" that Henry Ford did: focus on workers' outcomes instead of on how much time they spend at work.

FIVE-HOUR WORKDAY AT TOWER PADDLE BOARDS

Stephan Aarstol founded Tower Paddle Boards in 2010. In 2012, he pitched his stand up paddle boards on the TV show *Shark Tank*. Aarstol landed one very powerful shark, billionaire Mark Cuban. Cuban invested $150,000 for a 30 percent stake in Tower. At the time, Tower had only $100,000 in annual sales. By 2018, the company had reached a milestone of $30 million in revenue, making it one of the show's biggest success stories.

OUTCOME CULTURE

OUTCOME

The most surprising contributor to Tower's growth was Aarstol's radical decision to cut his employees' workday to five hours. He presented this as a "summer hours" pilot. He also offered employees a 5-percent profit-sharing plan.

"I told my employees I wanted to give them two things," Aarstol told *Fast Company*.[1] "First, I simply wanted to give them their lives back—so they'd have a pass to walk out each day right at one p.m. as long as they proved highly productive. Second, I wanted to pay them better for the more focused effort that would take. Their per-hour earnings were set to nearly double overnight: we'd be rolling out five percent profit-sharing at the same time."

Each employee needed to figure out how to be nearly twice as efficient and productive. "We had a high bar of productivity to clear before this, and that didn't change," Aarstol explained. "I told them they just needed to figure out how to do it all in just five hours now—but there'd be support. We'd *all* need to figure it out and were in this together. If anybody couldn't, though, they'd be fired."

Aarstol thought his company's productivity might decline until employees adjusted to the change, but "the reality is that we didn't take a hit at all. Our annual revenues for 2015 were up over 40 percent.... There's no reason virtually any company that employs a large chunk of knowledge workers can't cut its hours by 30 percent and still succeed."

The summer pilot went so well that Aarstol extended the five-hour workday. In 2016, Tower Paddle Boards showed an astounding three-year growth of 1,850 percent and was recognized as the fastest-growing private company in San Diego. Tower made the *Inc.* 500 list of America's fastest growing companies in 2015. By 2018, Tower had earned more than $30 million in revenue.[2]

⁓⊃⁓

Brain Boost—Did you know that by trimming your workday to five hours, for example, you may find it easier to concentrate? In *Scarcity: Why Having Too Little Means So Much*, Sendhil Mullainathan and Eldar Shafir explain that having less time creates heightened productivity periods called "focus dividends." They argue, "When scarcity captures the mind, we become more attentive and efficient."[3]

⁓⊃⁓

Tower's short workday also attracted talent. "I've had incredibly high performers at local companies send us résumés completely unsolicited," Aarstol noted in his book *The Five-Hour Work Day: Live Differently, Unlock Productivity, and Find Happiness*,[4] adding, "We've been able to recruit extremely talented people." He also acknowledged, though, "After we went to the five-hour workday, we were getting two new types of people: talented people who love the five-hour workday for the right reasons and lazy people who want to do as little as possible."

Tower began requiring job applicants to submit a three-minute YouTube video. That made it easy to spot, Aarstol wrote, "those who were basically just slobs, sitting on the couch saying, like . . . 'Duuude . . . I'd love to only work five hours a day. That would be totally awesome!'"

❧

Outcome culture focuses on employee results, not on how many hours they log at work. It removes time-wasting at work in favor of concrete, measurable results.

❧

A FOUR-DAY WEEK AT MICROSOFT JAPAN

I can practically hear you thinking, *Yeah . . . a shorter workday might work for a groovy company that produces paddle boards for beach bums—but for the rest of us? Come on.*

Well, in the summer of 2019, Microsoft ran a four-day workweek pilot called the "Work Life Choice Challenge." It boosted sales by nearly 40 percent.[5] Forty percent! I just had to repeat that.

Microsoft Japan closed its offices every Friday that August. Full-time employees received the same pay they had been getting for a five-day week. Microsoft Japan also imposed a thirty-minute time limit on meetings and encouraged remote communication over face-to-face meetings.

The company reported that sales increased by 39.9 percent compared with August 2018. This move also saved Microsoft Japan money in surprising ways. The number of pages printed decreased by 58.7 percent, and electricity consumption dropped 23.1 percent, compared with August 2018.[6]

Microsoft Japan plans to continue testing four-day workweek pilots at different times of the year. Other companies experimenting with four-day workweeks include Shopify, Shake Shack, Elephant Ventures, and Perpetual Guardian.

PHONY PRODUCTIVITY

Sadly, most corporate workers are trapped in "hustle culture," which equates extra-long hours with productivity. They can only dream of a forty-hour work-week. Sixty- to eighty-hour weeks are the norm for many corporate managers and executives.

Our brains are not designed for this. People are only truly productive on average three hours during an eight-hour workday. Working more than eight hours does not improve their productivity.[7]

According to the Bureau of Labor Statistics, the average American works 8.8 hours every day. Yet a study of nearly two thousand office workers revealed that people waste hours at work on the following:[8]

- Reading news websites: 1 hour, 5 minutes
- Checking social media: 44 minutes
- Discussing nonwork-related things with coworkers: 40 minutes
- Searching for new jobs: 26 minutes
- Taking smoke breaks: 23 minutes
- Making calls to partners or friends: 18 minutes
- Making hot drinks: 17 minutes
- Texting/instant messaging: 14 minutes
- Eating snacks: 8 minutes
- Making food in office: 7 minutes

I have coached many high-level executives. They admit to me that the pressure to put in long hours incentivizes them to "pretend" to be productive at work. They may have already finished their projects and would benefit from going home to refresh and recharge. But hustle culture dictates that they log extreme hours to be considered for bonuses and promotions.

One of my coachees wrapped up a key project nine days before she was due to take her required vacation. Rather than talking to her boss about leaving for vacation earlier or taking on a new project, she sat at her desk for nine days pretending to appear busy. She told me she felt guilty and stressed-out the entire time. Companies are rewarding time wasting at the expense of genuine productivity and workers' well-being.

I'll never forget attending a "female executives" luncheon hosted by one of the few female partners of a consulting firm where I was working. We all were working eighty hours per week and traveling around the world on no sleep. As we sat around a table adorned with fine china and floral centerpieces, the notoriously hard-driving partner regaled us with the story of a young woman on her team whom she had discovered sleeping underneath her desk.

"So unprofessional!" she exclaimed, as the rest of us exchanged bemused glances. All I could think was, *she should feel ashamed that her team is so exhausted.* Today, she's head of a prominent HR company.

⤙⤚

Mind Bender—Office workers waste time on "shallow work," says computer science professor Cal Newport. He defines shallow work as lightweight tasks such as responding to e-mail or tinkering with social media. We like to use it to avoid "deep work," which Newport defines as "focusing without distraction on a cogitatively demanding task."[9]

Shallow work is tempting, in part, because it's rich in the personal interactions that humans crave, yet it's deep work that truly makes us feel satisfied and accomplished. A shorter workday can motivate people to shut off distractions and dive into deep work, so they can go home sooner.

⤙⤚

WE'RE WIRED FOR BURSTS, NOT SLOGS

The human brain is not designed to be fully focused for eight hours in a row. We are wired to be intensely focused and productive for around three hours, at most. After that, we need to take a break to replenish our neurotransmitter levels. Attention span, focus, willpower—these are all qualities that only function for brief periods of time. They are not meant to be used for eight hours straight.

The average adult has a maximum attention span of about twenty minutes. We can refocus our attention on the same activity repeatedly—when we watch movies, for example. But it's normal for attention to lapse. To explain why humans are wired like this, I need to take you back a few millennia.

For most of human history we worked far less than we do today, according to anthropologist James Suzman. For roughly 95 percent of human history on earth, human beings were nomadic hunter-gatherers. Suzman estimates that they worked around fifteen hours a week.[10]

Our ancestors had to be hyper-focused while stalking and killing prey. After the thrill of the hunt, they'd come home to feast and relax. I like to call this pattern "cycling" and our brains still need it. We are not supposed to be "on" for the entire day without a break.

WE'RE WIRED FOR BURSTS, NOT SLOGS

Mothers in hunter-gatherer tribes worked with their children close by. They carried babies in slings and watched over young children while picking fruit and gathering nuts and vegetables to cook around the fire. Work and family life were intertwined.

"Our hunter-gatherer ancestors," Suzman reports from his decades-long studies, were "well fed, content, and longer-lived than people in many agricultural societies, and by rarely having to work more than fifteen hours per week had plenty of time and energy to devote to leisure." Our ancestors spent that leisure time, Suzman says, "on purposeful activities such as making music, exploring, decorating their bodies, and socializing."[11]

Around twelve thousand years ago, humans began cultivating wild crops such as peas, lentils, and barley, and herding wild goats. This enabled people to develop permanent settlements. But farming families still worked far fewer hours than your average corporate executive today. Work followed crop cycles, so winters provided lots of down time. English peasants worked around

120–150 days per year, according to *The Overworked American: The Unexpected Decline of Leisure* by Juliet Schor.[12] Medieval France had ninety vacation days per year—not counting the weekly Sabbath or the winter break.

Men, women, and children worked together on whatever tasks needed to be accomplished. "Home" and "work" were in the same place. Our brains evolved in this family/tribe-oriented environment.

Child-free corporate workplaces are actually relatively new. They didn't become dominant until the early 1900s. It was only during the industrial age that people began working extreme hours in factories, away from their families. When the forty-hour workweek finally became U.S. law in 1940, it was a huge relief to millions of harshly exploited workers. But prior to the industrial age, most people worked fewer than forty hours per week, and parenting was interwoven with work.

❧

Mind Bender—Corporations took hold in the United States in the 1800s because small, family-owned farms and other businesses needed capital in order to expand. The first American corporations were developed in the 1790s and became key institutions in the young nation's economy. Although corporations existed in Europe in the early nineteenth century—particularly in Great Britain and the Netherlands—no country took to corporate development like the United States.

❧

LONG HOURS: BAD FOR PERFORMANCE, WORSE FOR HEALTH

My theory is that corporate workplaces push their execs to put in extreme hours because the high-testosterone/dopamine neurosignature is overrepresented at the top. People with this neurosignature love constant activity, can get by on less sleep, and have the stamina to keep going when other neurosignatures are about to collapse. Nonetheless, their health suffers, as evidenced by the high incidence of heart attacks, strokes, and other health crises among CEOs and other top-level executives.

A World Health Organization study released in May 2021 found that 745,000 people died in 2016 from stroke and heart disease as a *direct result of working more than fifty-five hours per week*. Researchers concluded that people who work more than fifty-five hours per week increase their risk of stroke by

35 percent and heart disease by 17 percent, compared to people who work thirty-five to forty hours per week.[13]

The study attributed this increased risk partly to the stress associated with long hours and partly to terrible habits people adopt when they're crushed by work. These include smoking, drinking, not getting enough sleep or exercise, and eating poorly.

Most neurosignatures don't function well on insufficient sleep. Our productivity takes a hit. We will suffer resentfully in silence—or spend twenty-six minutes per day looking for a new job. As a result, companies that worship hustle culture are losing diversity and talent. Women, in particular, need on average a half hour more sleep per day than men.[14] Companies that push extreme hours may be inadvertently pushing out female talent.

Managers mistakenly assume that requiring employees to put in more time at work leads to more productivity and profit. But corporations are not hiring expensively educated young men and women to bolt wheels onto a car all day long. Today's corporate jobs involve thinking, planning, and forecasting. Companies are hiring smart people to innovate and solve problems—to have "aha" moments that can save them millions of dollars, or lead to a best-selling new product.

Here are some brain-friendly ways to improve productivity:

- Enable employees to get enough sleep.
- Provide them with time and incentives to exercise.
- Provide healthy meal and snack options.
- Create a quiet, peaceful environment.
- Allow them to turn off phones and e-mail, so they can dive into deep work.
- Encourage them to get up and take breaks—like brisk walks around the block—to stimulate the flow of energizing dopamine in their brains.

THE HAPPINESS IMPACT

Hustle culture also makes it tough for employees to accomplish anything outside of work, including raising children. This traps the majority of women on the "mommy track," a career path for women who opt to sacrifice promotions and pay raises in order to devote more time to raising their children, while men are ushered into executive suites. Gender diversity initiatives will keep failing, wasting millions of dollars. Companies will continue to lose out on female insights, intelligence, and innovation.

On the flip side, having time to pursue your passions, nurture your friendships and family, eat right, and exercise gives you more emotional and physical energy to do your job well. I call this the "happiness impact" on productivity.

My client, Riaz Shah, a senior partner at EY (formerly Ernst & Young), is an incredible example of the power of the happiness impact. Shah is responsible for the learning and development of more than 340,000 people at EY. Nonetheless, starting in 2016, he began cutting back his hours in order to fulfill a promise he had made to a dying young friend to establish a free school in London for disadvantaged children.

Over eighteen months, Shah cut his hours by 50 percent. He told me that he used that free time to build a school that provides free top-notch education for low-income children, with a warm, supportive environment that brings out the very best in them. During this reduced working time, Shah focused on his new mission. Three years after opening, the school was awarded an outstanding rating by government inspectors, rare for a new school to achieve.

Shah returned to full-time work with renewed vigor and a commitment to democratizing education. He was inspired to create the world's first fully accredited corporate MBA program, which is free to all EY employees.

Shah continues to advise several social enterprises, including one that helps homeless people become coding professionals. "My life has been profoundly enriched by my decision to work less and give more," Shah tells me. "To my surprise, I am more productive at work than ever, because I feel happy and fulfilled." Shah adds that he has inspired some high-level colleagues at EY to follow his example.

❧

Mind Bender—Teleworking may sound like a promising alternative to hustle culture, but the 2020 lockdowns proved that it's not. A WHO study found that during the shutdown, teleworkers in the United States, United Kingdom, Austria, and Canada added 2.5 hours on average to their workdays, typically wrapping up around 8 p.m.[15]

"Teleworking has become the norm in many industries, blurring the boundaries between home and work," says WHO director-general Dr. Tedros Adhanom Ghebreyesus. "No job is worth the risk of stroke or heart disease. Employers and workers need to work together to agree on limits to protect the health of workers."[16]

❧

MILLENNIAL AND GEN-Z WOMEN SPEAK OUT

Millennial and Gen-Z women are increasingly vocal about feeling trapped in hustle culture. Branding and live events coordinator Kate Flowers, thirty-two, told feminist/pop culture blog *Jezebel*, "Ninety percent of my identity is my job." She said that talking with her equally ambitious friends was like "the work Olympics: We're like, 'I'm more stressed out,' 'I'm busier,' 'Well, I got shingles from work.'"[17]

Publicist Danielle Jackson, thirty-three, often posts Instagram stories showing herself waking up at 5 a.m. and working well into the night. "I've been a sucker in buying into the whole 'hustle culture' thing," Jackson admitted to *Jezebel*. "I had this image in my head I was trying to live up to of what success looks like, and it was a woman pounding the pavement in high heels, always grinding, always on the phone."[18]

Young female executives strongly identify with their work and want to succeed—but they're fed up with the pressure to put in extremely long hours in order to prove their worth. Many are abandoning corporate life, taking valuable gender and neurosignature diversity with them. As Sarah Jaffe, author of *Work Won't Love You Back*, puts it, "The reckonings people are having with work are happening everywhere. What we do with them is the next question."[19]

EUROPE'S SHORTER WORKDAYS

The United States lags the growing number of countries getting on board with shorter workweeks. France, for example, cut its workweek from forty to thirty-five hours in 2000, yet consistently appears near the top of worker productivity lists.[20] The French thirty-five-hour workweek was originally introduced as an economic measure to cut unemployment. It is highly popular with workers and a key factor in the healthy work/life balance that French people enjoy.

In the Netherlands, women average twenty-five work hours a week, and men average thirty-four hours a week. This works out to roughly a four-day workweek, overall. Yet, Dutch productivity is among the highest in the world. Productivity is so high in the Netherlands that only 0.4 percent of employees work more than fifty hours per week, according to the World Population Review.[21]

In addition, workers in the Netherlands receive spring "vacation bonuses" from their employers that must be at least 8 percent of the employee's gross wage of the previous year, according to Dutch law.[22] This money materializes in employee accounts just before the summer holidays, and employees are expected to spend it on plane tickets, surfing lessons, and piña coladas.

When people work less and earn more, productivity, profit, and satisfaction rise. In addition, shorter workdays attract top talent, if you know how to screen for it. Switching to outcome culture is a powerful solution for so many workplace problems. Benefits include:

- less attrition
- more engaged employees
- fewer sick days because people have time to take care of themselves
- more time spent reading and learning
- improved neurosignature diversity, leading naturally to greater gender and racial diversity
- happier parents and children

My neighbor is a CEO who runs a marketing firm. He noticed during the 2020 restrictions that his employees were actually more efficient when they were working from home. Paul made the radical decision to cut their workweek by giving them Fridays off at equal pay—and has nothing but great things to say about it. "My employees who are parents with young families have especially appreciated this," Paul says. "Honestly, the quality of everyone's work is just as good, if not better. My company has been really flourishing ever since I did this."

❧

Mental Break—New Zealand financial services firm Perpetual Guardian implemented a shortened workweek in 2020 that was well-received by its 250 workers. Company founder Andrew Barnes said, "This is about our company getting improved productivity from greater workplace efficiencies. There's no downside for us."[23]

❧

AD AGENCY GOES TO FIVE-HOUR DAY

In 2017, the Rheingans Digital Enabler ad agency successfully introduced a five-hour workday. CEO Lasse Rheingans founded his own firm after leaving another agency where the brutal schedule made it impossible to balance work with his young family. "In agency business," Rheingans told *Business Insider*, "it's the norm to leave only when it gets dark."[24]

Millennial men are becoming increasingly vocal about not wanting to be robbed of fatherhood by hyper-demanding jobs. At his own shop, Rheingans decided to take off two afternoons a week to spend with his children. Surprisingly, he noticed that he was still getting all of his work done—in less time.

The biggest time suck in his work life, Rheingans realized, was meetings—endless, boring, life-draining meetings. This is a common complaint. At my keynotes, I like to ask my audience of top executives to name their most boring experiences. No matter where I am in the world or to which company I'm speaking, the answer is always the same: meetings, the biggest time wasters in the corporate universe.

First, Rheingans cut all meetings to fifteen minutes. Every morning at Digital Enabler starts with a meeting to discuss the day's tasks—but it's conducted standing up, with no private conversations allowed. Tasks are quickly confirmed and delegated, and then each team is off to work.

A hush falls over the office. Smartphones are locked away. Social media activity is forbidden during the five-hour day. So are personal calls and e-mails, unless absolutely necessary. Silence is expected and appreciated, as it enhances concentration. Employees who need music to concentrate use headphones.

Employees are expected to meet the same outcomes they were achieving in a day eight hours or longer. They earn the same salaries and vacation pay that they did previously. If they want to stay longer than five hours, they won't be paid for the extra time.

Rheingans noticed right away that conflicts were resolved more quickly, and chitchat was replaced with productive, necessary conversations. "People stay focused, because they don't want to waste time. This is a constant learning process that never stops," Rheingans explains. "In an eight-hour day you can mask problems and cheat yourself. This simply isn't possible within a five-hour day. It's merciless. It highlights exactly which areas aren't working and what to take care of—it's like holding a magnifying glass to every flaw."[25]

Rheingans Digital Enabler Web developer Luca Anzaldo, who used to spend at least nine hours per day at his previous job, told *Business Insider*, "For me, it's perfect—I like to focus for five hours, then go do something else, rather than constantly getting coffee and chatting."[26]

Rheingans was so pleased he decided to make the experiment permanent. "In my experience, there is nothing to gain from working longer," he told the *Initiative Chefsache*. Rheingans is also pleased that the shorter workday is helping female employees escape the dead-end mommy track. "In our company, both men and women work five hours a day," he notes. "Women who work part-time due to personal reasons are no longer perceived, therefore, as less valuable. We have revolutionized the classical distribution of gender roles, since men also take time now for their families in the afternoon."[27]

⚛

Brain Boost—At Rheingans Digital Enabler, employees loved the five-hour workday but missed the small talk that used to make them feel like a friendly team. Some employees started a non-mandatory Friday afternoon social during which they cook a meal together and catch up.

⚛

THE PARETO PRINCIPLE

Here's the core message of outcome culture: figure out how to spend less time achieving greater productivity, satisfaction, and joy. It may help you to use the Pareto Principle, also called the 80/20 rule, which posits that 80 percent of outcomes are driven by only 20 percent of effort. The Pareto Principle dates back to 1906, when famed Italian economist Vilfredo Pareto observed that 80 percent of Italy's land and wealth was owned by just 20 percent of its population.

Let's say you have a client roster that's a mile long. If you dig in, you may notice that 75–80 percent of your revenue is coming from just five or six clients. What if you focused your time and energy on those five clients instead of running yourself into the ground trying to manage your entire client list and feeling constantly overwhelmed? You would spend less time yet achieve greater results.

On the other hand, if a difficult client who needs loads of handholding is taking up 80 percent of your time, energy, or resources but supplies only 20 percent of your business, get rid of that client. Otherwise, you've stamped yourself a one-way ticket to burnout.

So, ask yourself: What 20 percent of your day is producing 80 percent of your joy? What 20 percent of your activities produces 80 percent of your energy? What 20 percent of your friends and family provides 80 percent of the love and support in your life?

SEVEN-STEP BLUEPRINT FOR TRYING OUTCOME CULTURE

When things aren't going well, most companies introduce yet another "training" for their employees. Instead, look at how you can change the workplace to improve results. It will always be easier to change the workplace than to change people.

Before you make these changes, however, explain to your team what you are doing and why. Share examples from other companies where outcome culture has been successful. If people understand the benefits of this culture shift, they'll be more likely to hop on board with enthusiasm.

⤳

It always will be easier to change the workplace than to change people.

⤳

Here are seven simple steps for piloting a shorter workday or workweek:

Step 1: Start with a Pilot

Starting with a small pilot program enables you to keep control of the "experiment." If it doesn't work out, you can reverse it with minimal employee grumbling.

Unilever began a four-day workweek pilot in December 2020. The food and consumer-staples giant chose its New Zealand branch as the test case. Eighty-one employees moved to four days per week without a drop in pay. Managing Director Nick Bangs said, "We hope the trial will result in Unilever being the first global company to embrace ways of working that provide tangible benefits for staff and for business."[28]

Step 2: Establish Ground Rules

Establish rules that support productivity, such as:

- no social media activity during office hours;
- turn off smartphones during office hours;
- keep small talk to a minimum;
- no personal calls or e-mails during office hours; and
- be quiet in workspace areas designated "quiet space."

Establish quiet, distraction-free workspaces that encourage concentration. Pro-vide separate common areas where employees can talk without disturbing their colleagues. Open-space offices may not work unless employees can commit to being quiet and respectful of others.

⌇

Brain Food—If you're going to try a shorter workday, make sure you fuel it with a good breakfast. Berries have a very positive impact on brain function—toss some fresh blueberries or strawberries onto your oatmeal or whole-grain cereal, or into your morning smoothie. "Recent clinical research has demon-strated that berry fruits can prevent age-related neurodegenerative diseases and improve motor and cognitive functions," reports *Neural Regeneration Research.*[29]

⌇

Step 3: Measure Outcomes

Communicate that this is not about reducing salaries or benefits, nor is it about reducing expectations. Employees who prove incapable of delivering agreed-upon outcomes will be let go.

Track key performance indicators (KPIs): productivity, revenue, client sat-isfaction, employee and client retention, and sick days. If the KPIs are good, you have the numbers to support a bigger rollout. If they aren't, you can either adjust or return to the way things were before the pilot.

Unilever enlisted University of Technology-Sydney to help track outcomes and evaluate the four-day workweek pilot. After one year, the company plans to assess the pilot and decide whether to roll it out to more than 150,000 employees around the world.

Step 4: Limit Meetings

Pointers for transforming meetings into useful, productive events:

- Schedule meetings for fifteen minutes or less.
- Only invite people who will add value to the meeting. Don't invite people just to be "inclusive."
- Empower your employees to leave a meeting if they realize that their pres-ence will not add value or the meeting is a waste of their time.
- Use an egg timer to give each speaker two minutes max.
- Provide every meeting participant with a concise agenda.

- Schedule meetings in the mornings, so that employees can leave for the day when they finish their work.
- If the meeting can be replaced with an e-mail, do so.

⸻

Mind Bender—Executives spend on average twenty-three hours a week in meetings, according to an MIT Sloan Management Review.[30]

⸻

Step 5: End 24/7 Availability

Stop requiring employees to be available via e-mail or text 24/7. It's invasive, disruptive, and not nearly as necessary as we think it is. Instead, communicate clearly to clients when your employees are available and exactly how to reach them. Establish similar clear boundaries for internal communication between employees and their higher-ups or subordinates.

When Stephan Aarstol moved Tower Paddle Boards to a five-hour workday, his biggest concern was losing half his business by cutting hours in half. Instead, the company found that it received the same number of customer calls in fewer hours—and that sales rose.

⸻

Brain Boost—One potential drawback of a short workweek or workday is that if someone on a team gets sick, other team members may have to cover that person's workload as well as their own. There is little buffer in a hyper-efficient workplace. You can solve this problem by cultivating a network of freelancers who can step in to help when needed.

⸻

Step 6: Use Tech to Boost Efficiency

Automate anything that can be automated. This is key to achieving greater productivity in less time. Use packing and shipping software to reduce warehouse time. Create video tutorials on your customer service page or FAQ to help customers find answers without having to reach out to your staff.

What's exciting about working less is that it will drive your company to innovate and use technology to do some heavy lifting so that outcomes don't suffer.

Step 7: Be Flexible

Be flexible with employees regarding their hours. Let them know that sometimes they will have to step up and put in extra hours—during a seasonal crunch, for example. That is part of the deal they are making with you for shorter hours overall. Their salaries are tied to outcome, not to hours.

Your high-testosterone performers may enjoy putting in longer hours. Your high-estrogen neurosignatures may prefer to spend time with family. Don't guilt-trip or penalize anyone as long as outcomes are met. Set your expectations for deliverables clearly, but provide employees with lots of flexibility in meeting them.

UP NEXT: LEARNING TO FOCUS AND FLOW

Imagine if your workplace did trade hustle culture for outcome culture—and a shorter workweek. Sounds fabulous at first, but then you may begin to feel uneasy. What would it mean to make every hour at work count? If you only have thirty hours to get done what you used to do in forty, that will cut into your time spacing out during meetings or surreptitiously checking Instagram while a colleague drones on via conference call. How's that any fun?

Becoming more focused at work so you accomplish more in less time may sound scary, but it's really fun and rewarding. We'll explore just how to do this in the next chapter, "Fun, Fear, and Focus."

THE BRAIN-FRIENDLY INTERVIEW

Stephan Aarstol, CEO, Tower Paddle Boards and Tower Electric Bikes

In 2012, entrepreneur Stephan Aarstol pitched his company to the ABC show *Shark Tank* and landed Mark Cuban as an investor. In 2015, Aarstol shocked the business world when he instituted a five-hour workday at his young company, Tower Paddle Boards. That year Tower ranked #239 on the Inc. 500 list of America's fastest-growing companies. With more than $30 million in sales to date, Tower is one of *Shark Tank*'s biggest success stories.

Meanwhile, Stephan's popular book, *The Five-Hour Workday: Live Differently, Unlock Productivity, and Find Happiness*, has spread his influential ideas about how working less can make a company more profitable.

Friederike: I've read your entire book cover to cover. I love it. Have you noticed whether reducing work hours improves gender diversity?

Stephan: Gender diversity has never been a problem for our company, so I don't know. We have predominantly female executives and more female than male employees. I like to hire right out of college because internet marketing is constantly evolving, so I want people who are still in learning mode. We look for the highest GPAs, because the people who have been most successful at Tower are those A-plus students. They make incredible workers. I'm always looking for the smartest of the smart, and, honestly, women in that category have fewer opportunities than their male peers, so we have more opportunity to hire the smartest of the smart among women.

Friederike: How has the shorter workday improved your life as a single dad?

Stephan: When I started the business as a solo entrepreneur, I set my own hours. Sometimes if my son had a baseball game or whatever, I felt like I could leave at one or two in the afternoon to make it, and sometimes I felt like, "No, I gotta work; I'm gonna skip that game." There was always this conflict in my mind.

I was hustling to get the company up to speed, but then we were so successful in 2014 that I started giving myself a more flexible schedule. Now that I had employees, though, I felt guilty leaving the office while they were all still grinding away.

That got me thinking that maybe we didn't have to maintain the stereotypical "grind" startup culture. Maybe I could hire really smart people and try giving everyone the same schedule as mine. If we were all walking out at 1 p.m., there was no reason I couldn't be at every baseball game. There was no conflict in my mind anymore.

Friederike: What has been the largest benefit of the five-hour workday?

Stephan: The shorter workday fights burnout, and that's important. When you compress your time, it forces you to focus, and then it frees up time to rest. Without that constraint, the tendency for people like me is to burn yourself out working day and night. If you don't rest, and you just keep grinding, you become less efficient, less effective.

Friederike: So, with the shorter workday, you reap focus dividends, and you also build in time for what I like to call "strategic rest."

Stephan: Yes, for sure. But the weirdest lesson I learned is that people don't care about money, and they don't care about the shorter hours. They care about alignment with purpose.

Friederike: What do you mean?

Stephan: We did the five-hour workday, and it was going great. But then I suddenly lost about half my employees. What we realized was that the five-hour workday had broken our company culture. The employees were happy, the company was productive, everything was going fine. But people were far more willing to leave this company than they had been before, because our employees were no longer building the kind of intense bonds with each other that happens in a startup, when you're working in the trenches. It's almost like the bonding experience of going to war together, right? When people leave a company, they're leaving the people they work with. When we switched from an intense startup culture to a culture where people were coming in, working very intently and not chitchatting or socializing with each other, the bonds were far less strong. It became easier for people to leave.

Friederike: How did you respond?

Stephan: We had created a company culture of efficiency and identifying productivity tools, but we lost that bonding. So, I decided we would only have the five-hour workday four months out of the year, from summer to fall. The rest of the year, we returned to startup hours. This gives us the productivity benefits of the five-hour workday, because during that period our employees have to think really hard about how to get their work done and orders filled in less time. Yet, we also now gain some of those startup culture benefits again.

I ran into a lot of entitlement and disappointment from the employees when I did that, so now I've tied the five-hour workday to our revenue. We will do it part-time, *if* we're increasing revenue. They know now that it's a privilege we have to earn together. It's a live experiment that we're conducting here. We're trying to fix what doesn't work and keep what does.

Friederike: That's incredible.

Stephan: If we increase revenues, then the shorter workday becomes a company bonus that the whole team is working together to achieve. In that way, we are mitigating the entitlement issue and improving our company culture, because the startup culture is a shared struggle, right? The five-hour workday? Not so much of a struggle.

4

Fun, Fear, and Focus

Instead of focusing on how much you can accomplish, focus on how much
you can absolutely love what you're doing.

—Leo Babauta

I was a bundle of nerves. I was about to give my first-ever TEDx talk, "The
Neurochemistry of Peak Performance." I had rehearsed a million times and sent
my technical requirements to the TEDx team well ahead of time. "It's going to
be great," I kept muttering as I entered the theater clutching my iPad. I couldn't
wait to see my presentation fired up on the huge screen above the stage.

A scruffy tech guy ambled over to me with some cables. None of them fit
into my iPad. "No worries," he said. "Give it to me. We'll get it connected and
set up on stage for you. Go backstage and relax." I reluctantly surrendered the
tablet and made my way backstage.

Twenty minutes later, I stood in the wings waiting. I was so relieved to see
my trusty iPad on the lectern. I took a deep breath and strolled confidently onstage, launching into my introduction. The audience laughed at my jokes and
seemed truly engaged by my brilliant insights. I picked up my iPad and began
to draw my first graph with my iPad pencil. Nothing appeared on screen.

Oh, my God, I thought, keeping a smile frozen on my face. I tried again.
Nothing. I was acutely aware of the spotlight shining on me and a thousand
people staring up at me. I felt like a deer in the headlights of a Mack truck.
Then, somehow, I snapped out of it.

"OK, we will do without this," I announced. "Sometimes," I continued, "our brains are so bored that we will not go into peak performance, because the brain is a lazy couch potato. It won't go into peak performance when we're sitting in a boring meeting, for example. And sometimes, we're so stressed out that our minds go blank, like mine just did!"

The audience laughed—with me, not at me. In that moment, my vulnerability and willingness to roll with the technical punches seemed to conquer my audience's collective heart. To my surprise, I found myself in a state of peak performance. Jokes, spontaneous ideas, new insights and connections flowed through me effortlessly as I worked the stage. Honestly, I had been so over-rehearsed for my talk that I think I was a little bored with it. The jolt of my technology's failing gave me just the right zing of adrenaline to get me into "flow."

Afterward, a TEDx organizer from a different city approached me. "Did you stage that tech failure thing with your iPad to make your point?" he asked. "No," I told him, thinking, *but I wish I had.*

⁓

Peak performance is the joyful experience of performing at your maximum ability. Your brain releases a delicious cocktail of neurochemicals that help you become completely, effortlessly absorbed in what you are doing. You feel fully present and are loving life. You may even lose track of time. Research indicates that when we are in this state of mind, we are *five times* more productive.[1] This state is also called **flow**.

⁓

THE RIGHT MIX

My TEDx snafu threw me into peak performance because my high-dopamine neurosignature makes me a sensation seeker who loves novelty. I like roller coasters. My technical difficulties that day provided just the right burst of fear to sharpen my focus.

My neurosignature is also high in estrogen/oxytocin, which means that I love to connect with people. Without my iPad to fall back on, I had to relate emotionally to my audience. I knew that to survive losing my presentation, I would have to build a relationship with them—and fast. That was fun for me. When I shared my real feelings with the audience, and people responded positively, I felt energized and happy.

But here's what's key: that combination of fun and fear was the right mix for *my* neurosignature. Someone with a neurosignature high in serotonin might have found that level of fear on stage crippling, not exhilarating. She probably wouldn't get on the latest roller coaster at the amusement park either. I am not better than she is. We simply have different neurosignatures. We each need different mixes of fear, fun, and focus to get into peak performance and perform at our best.

WHAT IS FLOW?

Peak performance is also called "flow." Flow is a state of mind in which you feel fully immersed in an activity with a feeling of energized focus. Some call it "being in the zone." Flow can happen to an individual and to a group—more on that in chapter 10.

Most of us recognize the heady feeling of performing at our peak. Time becomes irrelevant, doubt and self-consciousness evaporate, and we feel completely immersed in the task at hand. It's like falling in love with whatever you're doing. For a brief, magical time, your work becomes the center of your universe.

In the flow state, you are five times more productive, according to research from McKinsey & Co.[2] Imagine being able to reach this state whenever you want. Forward-thinking companies such as Pixar Animation Studios and SAP recognize that teaching employees to get into flow is far more important to productivity than the number of hours they spend at their desks. Companies seeking to exchange hustle culture for outcome culture need to teach employees how to access flow so they can accomplish more in less time.

❧

Brain Food—Anandamide is a neurotransmitter that binds to the same receptors in our brains as marijuana's psychoactive compound THC. The word "anandamide" derives from the Sanskrit *ananda*, which translates to "bliss" or "joy." Eating apples, blackberries, and dark chocolate all increase our production of anandamide.

❧

YOUR BRAIN ON FLOW

Strange things start happening in your brain as you enter the flow state. First, your prefrontal cortex—the seat of your "inner critic"—becomes deactivated. Self-doubt and insecurities evaporate.

Next, your right parietal lobe is deactivated. This part of your brain defines your individual "self" as different from other "selves." This is why in flow state, climbers say they become "one with the mountain," and surfers feel "one with the wave, dude."

Your brain starts kicking out powerful neurotransmitters. Bursts of dopamine and norepinephrine give you laser focus and make you feel excited and upbeat. Anandamide starts pumping, helping you focus intently and enhancing your ability to "think outside the box" and brainstorm. Anandamide boosts lateral thinking—our ability to make far-flung connections between disparate ideas. This is why during flow you may experience enhanced pattern recognition and have "aha" moments of insight. Your endorphins rise, increasing feelings of pleasure that further motivate you to stay in this delicious state of flow.

❧

Norepinephrine (NE), also called noradrenaline, acts as both a stress hormone and neurotransmitter. Increased NE activity enhances formation and retrieval of memory and focuses attention.

NE also makes you feel happy. Caffeine raises NE activity in the brain, and some recreational drugs artificially boost norepinephrine and dopamine brain activity, inducing euphoria.

❧

Finally, as you begin to emerge from the flow state, serotonin and oxytocin are released, promoting feelings of well-being. If you've been working in a team that has collectively entered group flow, you will bond and feel great about each other as you come down from the high of having experienced extraordinary performance and productivity together.

❧

Mind Bender—My clients love to ask me if they can "take a pill" to boost their neurotransmitters and get into peak performance. My answer is always "Noooooo!" The brain is a complex, interwoven system. If you artificially raise the levels of one neurotransmitter, you might dampen another, with unforeseen and unpleasant consequences. Natural is always best.

⟨≋⟩

FLOW OPENS YOUR MIND

Not only does flow feel good, but it's a highly productive state that also opens your mind. Losing your sense of "self" during flow makes you more open to ideas from other people that you may have resisted previously. Flow expert Steven Kotler often points out that being able to entertain opposing ideas and engage in lateral thinking spikes innovation at companies.[3]

Guess who is extra-good at this? People with high-estrogen neurosignatures. Neuroscientists using diffusion tensor imaging (DTI) have discovered that women have more lateral connections across the brain's two hemispheres, which may help explain why women tend to excel at lateral thinking.[4] Hiring more women and respecting their thinking styles is a great way to add valuable lateral thinking to the workplace.

If you have a high-testosterone neurosignature, you may sometimes feel impatient with your more ruminative high-estrogen colleagues. I get that. My husband has learned to tolerate my high-estrogen brain's tendency to wander through my inner shopping mall of ideas, dragging his high-testosterone brain along reluctantly. He understands that I do eventually get to the point—and it's often a good one, because I have been sifting through opposing ideas looking for insight.

⟨≋⟩

Mental Break—When we are stressed out, our brain produces small, fast beta waves. In the flow state, the brain switches to larger, slower alpha waves. This creates a pleasant, dreamy state of mind. Next, as we sink deeper into flow, our brain elicits a mix of alpha and slow, relaxing theta waves as we sink deeper into flow. Theta waves set up the brain for gamma oscillations, the fastest and most subtle brain waves. Gamma waves can lead us to aha moments and creative insights.

⟨≋⟩

TRIGGER FLOW WITH FUN, FEAR, AND FOCUS

In the previous chapter, we learned that some companies—and countries—are abandoning hustle culture for outcome culture. They're using shorter work hours to enhance productivity and employee satisfaction—with great results. The time pressure created by shorter work hours can result in super-productive "focus dividends" as employees buckle down to get "deep work" done so they can go home earlier.

But how will you achieve more in less time? Isn't flow some weird phenomenon that just happens once in a blue moon, if you're lucky?

Here's the biggest secret I can give you: you can trigger the hyper-productive flow state *systematically*. Highly successful people set up their lives around this fact. I teach my clients how to get into flow so they can reap focus dividends whenever they need them. Anyone can do it.

Three neurochemicals contribute to the unmistakable feeling of flow: dopamine (fun), norepinephrine (fear), and acetylcholine (focus). Actually, you really just need two—fun and fear. Find the right level of fun and fear, and focus will follow naturally. Let's explore how to use fun, fear, and focus to hack your brain and enter the flow state anytime you want.

FUN? AT WORK?

Let's start with fun. Why should you have fun at work? Aren't you being paid to work, not to have fun?

When you're having fun, your brain releases dopamine, a major brain booster. When your brain is flush with dopamine, you think faster and learn faster. This is fantastic for your performance at work. Remember my colleague who made everybody laugh? Keep those folks around because laughter provides bursts of dopamine, and dopamine makes it easier for you to focus.

One day, I was scheduled to give a fun, fear, and focus keynote to some very senior executives. I could practically hear their inner groans as I began to set up my laptop in the conference room where we had assembled for my "peak performance" talk. I'm sure they were expecting a tedious PowerPoint presentation that would drain away their morning.

After briefly introducing myself, I turned back to my computer. Out of the corner of my eye, I saw them all grab their phones and begin scrolling and tapping furiously.

I suppressed a grin. They had no idea what they were in for. Stephen Brown was about to shake things up.

Stephen is a laid-back bearded fellow, nearly always clad in a hoodie and jeans. When he lumbered in with a huge bag over his shoulders, the executives glanced up briefly before returning to their phones. They probably assumed he was my driver, or that I always walk around with a man who carries heavy things for me.

Actually, Stephen is the founder of Firewalking International. He's an extremely successful certified master fire walker who leads empowerment seminars and team-building experiences across the globe. Stephen developed a special routine for corporate settings where small fires might be frowned upon.

Stephen put down the bag, took out an empty wine bottle, and smashed it on the floor. Bang! He took out another wine bottle and smashed that to the floor. Boom!

The executives nearly dropped their phones. I stood calmly, trying not to laugh as they stared at Stephen, dumbfounded.

Smash! Another wine bottle hit the floor. Stephen continued smashing wine bottles until the floor was covered in broken glass. "Hi there, folks," he drawled. "It's time for you to get up and walk around the room." The executives stared at me as I kicked off my shoes.

"Come on," I said. "Please remove your shoes." More stares.

"He's serious. Let's go; follow me," I commanded. I started to pick my way around the room in my stocking feet as Stephen demonstrated how to gently, carefully walk on glass. Soon all the execs were laughing and grabbing onto each other as they followed me around the room, walking on broken glass. A little fear plus a little fun, and suddenly we were all fully focused on the task at hand.

❦

Brain Boost—Surprise and novelty raise our dopamine levels. Every time you feel surprised, your brain releases dopamine. Every time you see or experience something new, your brain reacts by releasing dopamine.

❦

QUICK DOPAMINE BOOSTS

Here are four quick ways to raise your dopamine levels at work:

1. Shorten meetings dramatically. Nothing reduces dopamine output more than having to sit through a long, boring meeting.
2. Get exercise. Focus intently for forty-five minutes, then get up and exercise for fifteen minutes. Take a walk outside; hit the gym, and do squats—whatever it takes to get a boost.

3. Keep a YouTube playlist of your favorite comedians. Take five minutes to watch something that cracks you up.
4. Hire optimistic, positive people. When conducting job interviews, screen for complainers or other "energy vampires."

YOU HAVE TO LOVE YOUR JOB

I must offer one caveat, though. None of this works if you hate your job. I know it can be tough to find work you truly love. But it's no coincidence that most successful people love what they do. They are riding that dopamine train—having fun at work and feeling stimulated by the challenges they encounter.

When you hate your job, your brain is starving for dopamine. You feel like you're dragging yourself through your workday—because you are. Without the kick of dopamine provided by genuine enjoyment, it's impossible to get into flow and to reach your potential.

The best brain-friendly advice I can give you is to find a job and workplace that appeal to you. You'll get bursts of dopamine that will raise your performance. Until you find that job, practice having more fun on evenings and weekends. You'll notice the good it does your brain.

One more thing: highly skilled people enter flow more easily. If you want to experience flow at your job, work on improving your skills. Professional athletes and artists experience flow because they love what they do *and* they work hard to expand the limits of their abilities.

FUN IS IN THE MIND OF THE BEHOLDER

What one person thinks is fun may drive another neurosignature right up the wall. If something your friends think is fun does not entertain you in the slightest, nothing is wrong with you. You need to find what gives *you* that dopamine kick.

Recently, some girlfriends were raving about how yoga had changed their lives by calming their minds, improving their posture—and toning their legs. Sign me up!

I eagerly followed their yoga-toned legs to my first class. It was quite possibly the longest sixty minutes of my life. All I could think was, *When can I stop holding these boring poses and listening to this boring music?*

Remember, I'm a high-estrogen/dopamine neurosignature who loves roller coasters. I needed to go for a pounding run afterward to get rid of all the stress hormones I had accumulated in yoga class.

Then there's my disturbingly calm and self-possessed six-year-old, Benita. The other day I was picking her up from school when her classmate's mother walked up and asked, "Benita, are you coming to Tommy's birthday party this weekend? He's so excited about it!"

Benita replied, "I'm awfully sorry, but I won't be able to attend. I have an appointment."

The mother gave me a wink. "Oh, my, an appointment! What kind of appointment do you have, Benita?"

"I have an appointment with my room," Benita stated. I stifled a giggle as the other mother struggled to formulate a response.

For many children, a weekend birthday party is something they look forward to eagerly all week. All they can think about is cake and balloons and charging around, hopped-up on sugar, with their friends. For my daughter, the highlight of her weekend is spending hours in her room doing arts and crafts. She's an artist who loves nothing more than to create a fancy purse for me out of paper, glue, and glitter, or a toy for her younger brothers and sister.

Trust your instincts, respect your neurosignature, and do what you love.

❦

Mental Break—Being kind to yourself is key to achieving flow. As cognitive scientist Dr. Scott Barry Kaufman explained to me, "When my clients are struggling to get into the flow state, it's usually because they're being too self-critical. They're not showing themselves compassion or allowing themselves to ease in slowly.

"I try to remove time constraints that people place on themselves. We might try role-playing, so they can at least fool themselves into thinking that they're not under pressure. You want to get that prefrontal cortex to reduce its activity, so it's not so self-critical. You want it to become immersed and at-one with what you're doing."

❦

HITTING YOUR OPTIMAL STRESS POINT

We need to experience fun to get into flow—but, as Stephen Brown's glass walk so beautifully illustrates, we also need a *soupçon* of fear. Surprisingly, our best performance does not take place when our skill level is perfectly in line with the task before us. We perform at our best when we feel *slightly over-challenged* and a little scared. If you're worried that maybe you can't pull off that presentation, boy, will you focus.

WE NEED TO BE SLIGHTLY — OVERCHALLENGED

NOREPINEPHRINE

When you feel challenged, your brain releases the positive "fear" chemical norepinephrine. You know that exhilarating rush after you dive into a cold pool or plunge into a snowbank to cap a steamy sauna? That's norepinephrine. It gives you a delicious kick right after you've done something a bit scary.

Norepinephrine makes you think faster. It helps you rise to a challenge. Remember, the brain is a lazy couch potato. It won't go into peak performance unless you're afraid of something—like bombing at your TEDx talk when your iPad stops working.

If you aren't feeling any fear at work, you'll get bored and won't be able to focus. On the other hand, if you feel too much stress at work, you'll become overwhelmed. Your higher-order thinking will shut down as your brain races like a hamster on a wheel.

We each have an "optimal stress point" at which we feel challenged and focused but not overwhelmed. If you learn to consistently hit your optimal stress point, you will experience much higher performance than someone who is bored *or* someone who is stressed out.

The chart below illustrates this fascinating correlation between performance and stress. As you can see, having no stress is not where optimal performance lies. Your performance also drops like a stone when you are too stressed. Your peak performance is at the curve's apex.

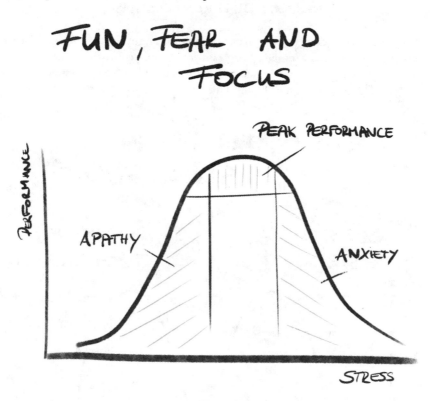

YOUR NEUROSIGNATURE ON FEAR

One size does not fit all when it comes to finding the level of fear that optimizes *your* performance. Check the chart below. Again, the apex of the curve is "peak performance." This chart illustrates that if your neurosignature is high in estrogen and serotonin, you will reach peak performance at a lower stress point than people with high-testosterone or high-dopamine neurosignatures. They, in contrast, need more stress than you to boost them into peak performance.

As we've learned previously, high-testosterone/dopamine neurosignatures can thrive in high-stress environments that make the rest of us want to kill ourselves, or at least take a long nap. This chart shows exactly why. Their brains need more fear to reach flow.

RESPECT DIFFERENT BRAINS

If you manage a team, this optimal stress point is an invaluable concept. You may now understand why some people on your team are thriving while others are caving. High-testosterone neurosignatures thrive on levels of stress that high-estrogen people find draining. This has nothing to do with talent, skill,

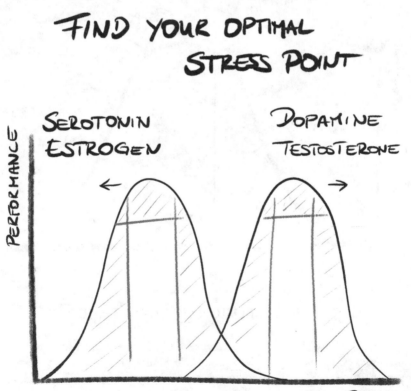

FIND YOUR OPTIMAL STRESS POINT

SEROTONIN ESTROGEN

DOPAMINE TESTOSTERONE

PERFORMANCE

or productivity. It only has to do with how different neurosignatures process stress. You aren't "better" if you can handle more stress than your colleague—you're just different.

Different neurosignatures also need different settings to achieve flow. Some people need a quiet private office with a closed door in order to reach peak performance. Others get into flow more easily tapping on their laptops in a bustling open space.

You can boost your team into flow by respecting each person's neurosignature and adjusting stress levels accordingly. I hope this information also provides ammunition you can use to combat bosses who think that putting all employees under extreme stress will result in peak performance.

⟨☞⟩

Mind Bender—As we get older, we biologically have lower stress tolerance, but we compensate for this with experience. We learn to manage anxiety and fear better and get better at maintaining optimal stress levels for peak performance.

⟨☞⟩

MY BOSS, THE BEAR

I once had a boss who drove me nuts. We regularly took predawn flights in order to arrive at client offices as soon as they opened so we could set up our presentation. Yet, my boss would never start reviewing our PowerPoint until the night before we were to fly out.

I always sent him my draft weeks ahead of time. It sat in his inbox. He showed zero motivation to dig into the deck and polish it, even though our clients represented hundreds of thousands of dollars in billing. The stakes were high. I would be a wreck with worry, whereas he was cool as a cucumber.

Invariably, around 8 p.m. the night before our big presentation, my boss would pop into my office with a huge grin on his face and exclaim, "Let's go through the deck together." He was like a starving bear that had emerged from hibernation. I could almost hear him roar. Suddenly, he was full of ideas for changes we should make to our slide show.

I was really starting to get angry. I had worked so hard to prepare our presentation well in advance. Now I was expected to pull an all-nighter, cramming last-minute changes into it, and then hop a jet on no sleep to go see our client?

I finally sat my boss down and explained "fun, fear, and focus." I even drew him the performance/stress graph. I explained that pulling an all-nighter was exciting for his high-testosterone/dopamine brain. It provided the perfect kick of fun and fear that he needed in order to focus. He also functioned just fine the next day on little to no sleep.

But this approach was stressful and exhausting for my high-estrogen/dopamine neurosignature. If he wanted me at my best for the presentation, I would have to skip the last-minute bull session and get a good night's sleep. In the end, we agreed that he could stay up all night tweaking the deck to his heart's content—alone. In return, I promised to roll with his changes during the presentation.

I also admitted that the red-eye flights were killing me. We negotiated that I would fly out the night before, check into my hotel room, and get a good night's sleep. I would get up early and head to the client's office to prepare the conference room for our presentation. This worked out great for us both.

The moral of the story? Stand up for what *you* need to reach peak performance.

ACh: THE HOLY GRAIL OF FOCUS

I encourage you to play with fun and fear until you figure out what magic combination helps you focus. When you are focused, your brain releases acetylcholine (ACh)—the "focus" neurochemical. ACh is like a spotlight. It highlights your most important thoughts while placing everything else that might normally distract you in the dark. Without fear and fun, your lazy couch-potato brain will not bother to produce ACh. You'll never reach focus.

If you are struggling to focus at work, ask yourself: Am I at the right level of fear? Am I having the right amount of fun? If you get fear and fun right, ACh will flow naturally.

You'll also find yourself sliding into flow more often. It's rather like meditation. You can't actually practice meditation. What people practice when they sit still, close their eyes, and focus on their breathing is concentration. Eventually, steady concentration allows the mind to slip into the blissful state of meditation. Flow is similar. If you get focused, you may slip into the blissful state of flow. When that happens, work may become truly joyful.

❧

Mental Break—People who practice meditation also become better at getting into flow. "Being able to achieve even a bit of focus is essential to achieving goals," notes Headspace cofounder Andy Puddicombe, "but being able to maintain focus and stability of mind can be challenging. That's where meditation and mindfulness come in. A mind trained to be more present and at ease with itself—calmer, clearer, and content—is more likely to experience the flow state because we are training in non-distraction and focus."[5]

⤬

HOW PHONES STEAL OUR FOCUS

Imagine Serena Williams pulling out her phone and texting during her Wimbledon finals match. It's laughable, because she's so fiercely focused while competing. Half the stadium could collapse, and Williams would still slam that volley back to her opponent. Yet, in the business world, highly professional, accomplished people allow their phones to distract them constantly.

We check our phones on average 110 times per day.[6] This makes parts of our brains shrink, in particular the anterior cingulate cortex—the very brain area that is vitally important to the ability to focus. Being online constantly can temporarily reduce your IQ by roughly ten points.[7] You may struggle to focus because you can't put down your phone. But why?

People use their smartphones as escape mechanisms when they feel bored (not enough fun) or stressed out (too much fear). Consider this an easy "tell." If you're checking your phone, you're not accessing the flow state. Your brain cannot do two things at once efficiently. You may think it can, but studies find that when we multitask, we make 50 percent more mistakes and take 50 percent longer to complete a task.[8]

WHY ARE WE ADDICTED TO OUR PHONES?

We become addicted to our phones because, as renowned Stanford professor and neuro-endocrinologist Robert Sapolsky explains, "Maybe is addictive like nothing else." Every time you get a notification on social media, you get a little burst of dopamine due to the *possibility* of a rewarding interaction with another person. Sometimes you get that reward, and sometimes you don't. Dopamine, Sapolsky explains, "is not about pleasure; it's about the anticipation of pleasure. It's about the pursuit of happiness, rather than about happiness itself."[9]

Nothing drives goal-directed behavior more, Sapolsky notes, than intermittent reinforcement. When we're bored at work, we pick up our phones, looking for stimulation. When we're stressed at work, we pick up our phones, looking to escape into a carefree world for just a few minutes.

Every time you indulge, you feed your tech addiction. Human attention spans are declining because our brains are plastic. We're constantly multitasking, distracted by e-mail and social media. Your plastic brain thinks, *I never need focused, prolonged attention, right? So why should I develop that skill?*

If you want to improve your attention span, turn off your phone and put it in a drawer. Check it once per hour, if you must, for five minutes, and then turn it off again. Some companies that have switched to outcome culture, such as Rheingans Digital Enablers, have employees lock away their phones as soon as they walk through the door.

⌦

Brain Boost—Establish short time windows during which you turn off your phone. Rather than telling yourself, "I will spend less time on my phone," create a simple when-then connection—for example, "When it's dinnertime, then I'll turn off my phone," or "When I have to do deep work, then I'll turn off my phone for forty-five minutes." This simple technique is called an implementation intention. Give it a try.

⌦

A MEETING OF ONE

You already know I'm not a fan of meetings, but there is one meeting I do love. I call it "a meeting of one." This is a meeting you schedule with yourself. During this meeting, consider yourself off limits to the demands of others. Turn off your phone and, if you have a door, close it.

The goal is to consciously set aside time to move into deep work and a state of flow. If you have to put together an important presentation, or you need to solve a critical problem, schedule that "meeting of one" with yourself.

Some companies have begun to do this as a team. They have "Focus Fridays," during which no meetings are scheduled. Employees get the gift of one uninterrupted day to truly focus. Granted, focusing can be tough if you work in an open office. When teams have too much open office space, communication decreases. Why? Because people are hiding, trying to get away so they can focus. According to a Harvard Business School study, "removing spatial boundaries [in the open workspace] can actually decrease collaboration and collective intelligence."[10]

STRATEGIC REST

As you get better at entering the flow state, you will require what I call "strategic rest." The flow state is very energy intensive. During flow, neurotransmitters zoom through your brain, raising your performance to its peak. After you come out of flow, schedule a rest period in order to replenish your neurotransmitters and restore your neurobalance.

Strategic rest keeps your high performance sustainable. By recovering after an intense period of peak performance, you'll be primed to reach your peak more easily next time. Athletes don't train 24/7. They schedule in recovery periods, which maximizes their results.

Unfortunately, most of us in the business world fail to do this. We feel guilty or lazy if we take any down time. We carry on, becoming increasingly depleted and exhausted, and then wonder why we feel lousy and can't concentrate.

Never feel guilty about strategic rest; it's part of the flow cycle. It's not lazy to take time to recharge. If you want to perform at your peak regularly, it's necessary. People who are serious about rest outperform the rest.

I always book a spa appointment after I deliver a keynote speech. Speaking to an audience for forty-five minutes to an hour requires me to get into flow and stay there. I'm also usually fatigued from traveling to the venue, meeting many people, and answering lots of questions. Making an appointment for a massage or sauna is how I build strategic rest into my calendar, because most spas require twenty-four-hour notice for a cancellation. Scheduling recovery time I can't wriggle out of ensures that I take it and replenish my brain.

In the next chapter, we'll explore how to get quality sleep and use healthy food and smart exercise to refresh and recharge. You'll learn exactly how to use strategic rest so you can operate in the flow state anytime you want.

THE BRAIN-FRIENDLY INTERVIEW

Dr. Janin Schwartau, global head of learning and transformation, thyssenkrupp

I met Dr. Schwartau in 2009 when I conducted a "sustainable peak performance" program for thyssenkrupp Academy, which she oversees. The academy is home to the company's learning and organizational development. Dr. Schwartau also serves as global head of learning and transformation for this German multinational conglomerate. She joined thyssenkrupp in 2008 after working on the initial concept for the academy as a consultant. Since then, she and her passionate team have developed thyssenkrupp Academy into a transformation driver within the company.

Friederike: In your view, what made the peak-performance program special? What impact has it had?

Janin: You translated brain science into practical actions for turning the workplace into a brain-friendly, productive environment. You explained brain theory on personal peak performance, and we explored ways of bringing the theory into our lives and work environment: We tried out easy-to-adapt sports, we experienced brain-friendly nutrition, we practiced mindfulness, neurofeedback, and emotional regulation. There was a lot for everyone to take home.

Friederike: I remember we had some participants who were less than enthusiastic about the sports segment.

Janin: We had a sixty-year-old participant who said, "If God wanted me to move fast, he would have given me wheels." He had never done sports in his life. By the end of the program, he was so inspired that he took up jogging. He followed the recommendation to start with just two minutes, stop and rest, and then do two minutes again. He's become a dedicated jogger.

You also built regular "walking outside breaks" into the program, and we really became aware of the energy boost that gives you. Since then, that's something my team has incorporated in daily work life: when we do one-on-one meetings, or even two-on-one meetings, if the weather permits, we hold them while walking outside.

Friederike: Did anything have a special impact on your life?

Janin: Yes, how meditation affects your brain positively in so many ways. After your program, I took an MBSR [mindfulness-based stress reduction] course. That has been one of the best things I have done for myself personally. I learned that I had an issue with being overly focused and, at a time when meditation was not as broadly practiced as today, I would never have thought of meditation as the solution. Meditation has improved my sleep, my well-being, my relationships, and truly changed my life for the better. Ever since, I have been passing on this experience to friends, clients, and top managers. Many have checked it out, perhaps thinking, *Well, she's a rational, efficient type of person, and she meditates . . . maybe there is something to this.*

We started a mindfulness initiative for my team that builds on MBSR but adapted for work issues. We went through the program and created a daily meditation routine as a team. We bought meditation cushions, and every day at a quarter to twelve, we meet in the library for a ten-minute meditation. Of course, not everybody was ready to take this on, but a lot of people have made it part of their lives. We then started offering the program to employees and teams across our company. It has become a popular offering that is more relevant now than ever.

Friederike: How did you address thought diversity at thyssenkrupp?

Janin: When we redesigned the office space for the academy, we wanted it to accommodate how people with different types of brains prefer to work. So, when designing it, we asked each employee, "How would you like to work?" We designed different zones to accommodate different working styles. We have an open space, we have very quiet areas, we have places where people can casually meet and communicate, and we have places where people can collaborate more formally.

We also asked, "What kind of environment do you want?" It turned out to be quite colorful but not overstimulating. We have different zones that reflect nature: the ocean, the forest, the savannah, and so on.

Friederike: Wow! How did people respond to the new space?

Janin: It was amazing. To me, everything changed when we redesigned our office space. When the walls came down, we saw an instant shift in team dynamics: people started to work together who never worked together before. Before, we were working in silos, but the new office encouraged a lot more interaction, and it was a totally different feeling. The team really came together; it started to feel more like a group of friends. I always say that coming into the office is like coming into a living room with friends. It's just a great feeling.

We have one area that we call "the beach." There's a surfboard hanging on driftwood walls, and people sit around one big table with their laptops—a typical startup atmosphere. Many of us love this area; for others, it's too casual. So, we also provide closed office spaces with separate desks and monitors for people who prefer that kind of environment. Fascinatingly, the most unwanted space type during the planning phase—the open space—is now the most popular spot. People love to go there.

Friederike: You offer schedule flexibility as well, correct?

Janin: Yes, within my team. We let every person create his or her own schedule. Some people work nine to five. Others like to work at night and start later in the day.

Friederike: Did anything change based on the "brain food experience" during our program?

Janin: Definitely! We all noticed during the program that we felt so much better, and I wanted to take that back to the office. During seminars and events, you are fed all day long, and much of the food is quite sugary. In your program, we experienced the effects of eating nuts, fruits, and other healthy snacks and meals. It was a revelation to realize you could eat all day long and actually feel good. Today, we try to provide brain food in the office and our programs as much as we possibly can. Keep the cake to a minimum.

5

Nurture Your Neurobalance

Let her sleep, for when she wakes, she will shake the world.

—Napoleon Bonaparte

Want to know what brilliant brain-friendly preparations I made before sitting down to write this chapter? After a good night's sleep, I went for a brisk power walk in the beautiful forest near my home, soaking up fresh pine-scented air and catching some rays. When I came home, I grabbed a handful of my favorite snack: cashews and dried cranberries. I munched on them as I settled at my desk and began reading over my notes.

You might be thinking, *You're a neuroscientist! That's all you got? That's all you do to prepare for your so-called deep work?*

Well, yes. If you sleep well, exercise, and eat right, you will achieve your optimal neurochemical balance. Nurturing this neurobalance will make it much easier for you to enter the flow state and reach peak performance.

Exercise, for example, boosts dopamine, which helps you to think better, learn better, and be more innovative. If you're ever stuck on a problem or feel fidgety and agitated while working, get up and go for a walk. Better yet, hit the gym. Fifteen minutes on an elliptical machine or pounding weights will get brain chemicals surging that will help you focus and get into flow when you sit back down.

If you want to gain control over your mind, use your body. Most people attempt to use their minds to control their minds. Meditation, for example, is a wonderful practice but takes time to master, and many people find it challenging. Using your body to positively affect your brain, in contrast, works fast. In this chapter, we'll dive into this powerful body-brain connection. You'll discover how to hack it to reach peak performance. This will boost not only your mental performance, but also your health and well-being.

We'll also explore brain-friendly companies such as Patagonia and thyssenkrupp that integrate physical exercise and adequate rest into their workplaces. They're doing this because it increases productivity, diversity, and talent retention.

THE FITNESS-FOCUS LINK

Most people think they should go to the gym to exercise their bodies and do crossword puzzles to exercise their minds. This mind/body split is based on

the false premise that exercise does not directly benefit the brain. Actually, new studies prove that it does—significantly.

After aerobic exercise, sedentary men showed significantly improved cerebral blood flow, associated with better memory and overall better brain performance, according to a recent study.[1] When researchers at Stanford took blood from mice that were running around like gangbusters and infused it into a group of sedentary mice, the results were mind-blowing. The couch-potato mice promptly exhibited far less acute brain inflammation in their bodies—and their brains. "These findings," the researchers write, "demonstrate anti-inflammatory exercise factors that . . . benefit the brain, and are present in humans who engage in exercise."[2]

Evidence is also growing of a strong link between exercise and academic performance in children. The Centers for Disease Control reports that "physical activity can have an impact on cognitive skills and attitudes and academic behavior, all important components of improved academic performance."[3]

Forward-thinking schools are investing in making sure that students get a move on. At the International School of the German-American Institute in Heidelberg, for example, students can take swimming lessons and have a thirty-minute group gymnastics session every morning. Classrooms provide furniture that enables students to sit in different positions and even stand during classes. As the German-American Institute's vice president, Ingrid Stolz, told me, "It's so surprising how easily these changes can be done. People always think it costs tons of money to integrate exercise into the children's schedule, when in reality anyone could do it—even on a small budget."

Despite this powerful link between focus and exercise, "wasting" time at the company gym is still frowned upon in some workplaces. Executives are encouraged, instead, to ignore the body's need for exercise, healthy food, sunshine, and rest. These employees pour excessive amounts of time into their work with diminishing returns, because they're exhausted and out of shape.

This approach also destroys thought diversity at a company, because people with high-testosterone/dopamine neurosignatures are most likely to neglect their health and push themselves too far. Other neurosignatures are more likely to drop out of an extremely unhealthy workplace.

⌒≈⌒

Brain Boost—If you want employees to exercise at work, because it's good for their brains and productivity, replace escalators with stairs. If you want them to eat well, provide healthy snacks and lunch options.

This approach to encouraging change is called "nudging." It was coined by behavioral economist Richard Thaler, who won the Nobel Prize for Economics in 2017. Thaler's research proved that change is best achieved by simply setting up an environment that encourages people to naturally behave in the way you want. "If you want people to do something, make it easy," Thaler says. "Put the fruit by the cafeteria checkout."[4]

Grocery stores use nudging (for evil) by placing magazines and candy near the cashier to tempt bored people in line to spend a few more bucks.

<hr>

LET MY PEOPLE GO . . . SURFING

Brain-friendly companies understand that employees are not only healthier if they exercise, but they are also more productive. Patagonia proactively encourages employees to embrace sports and have fun—at work! Patagonia's founder Yvon Chouinard wrote a much-beloved book, *Let My People Go Surfing: The Education of a Reluctant Businessman*, also known as the spiritual manual of Patagonia.

"Work has to be fun," Chouinard wrote. "Our policy has always allowed employees to work flexible hours, as long as the work gets done with no negative impacts on others. A serious surfer doesn't plan to go surfing next Tuesday at two o'clock. You go surfing when there are waves and the tide and wind are right."[5]

Patagonia takes work/life balance to new heights. At company headquarters in Ventura, California, the daily wave report appears each day on a whiteboard. Employees check it as they walk by colleagues tapping on their laptops on picnic tables under a grape arbor, snacking on organically grown goodies from the employee cafe.

"I'm so much more productive when I get into the water every day," retail marketing coordinator Danielle Egge told a reporter from the *Washington Post*, as she wrapped her blond hair into a bun and waded into the surf.[6] Even workers in Patagonia's Reno distribution center have free yoga, an organic cafe, free scooters and skateboards, and hiking trails out the back door.

Sure, an outdoor gear company such as Patagonia is a natural fit for encouraging sports, sun, and healthy snacks at work. But it's also very profitable. Patagonia has doubled in size and tripled in profits since 2008, hitting $800 million in revenue in 2019.

Patagonia's two-thousand-plus employees around the globe are fiercely loyal. Employee retention is fantastic, and turnover is minimal. Clearly, nurturing employees' neurobalance benefits Patagonia. But could it really work for your typical office-bound executive?

THE CASE OF THE TRANSFORMED EXEC

Adam Fetcher was a hard-charging workaholic who clocked insanely long hours as the Obama White House press secretary. Fetcher slept with his smartphone, responding to crises at all hours. He rarely slept or exercised.

"I put on extra pounds, eating cheeseburgers and drinking a little too much whiskey late at night," Fetcher told *Washington Post* reporter Brigid Schulte. "I felt that was the only way I could work in politics if I wanted to get ahead. I got caught up in being in the loop on everything, and it was hard to go offline for thirty minutes to go to the gym."[7]

When he was hired to head global communications at Patagonia, his fit new colleagues teased him that he wouldn't last a week. But Fetcher hung in there. He slowly learned to surf and rock climb. He took up biking and yoga. And he spent time with friends for the first time in years.

⤳

Brain Boost—Patagonia makes conscious efforts to get employees outdoors, connecting with nature. I spoke with Patagonia EMEA HR Director Evelyn Doyle about Earth University. This is a Patagonia program that "takes interdepartmental groups from across Europe out walking into nature to learn through, and with, nature," Doyle explains. Not only does Earth University enhance employee well-being, but it also encourages cross-department interactions that can lead to new product ideas and other developments.

⤳

What surprised Fetcher most was the positive impact this new lifestyle had on his performance at work. "I'm working hard by anyone's measure," he told Schulte. "But the work I'm putting into my job is a much higher quality than in the past," he said. "I have time to really consider my decisions before I make them. I'm not in a reactionary mode all the time."[8]

Corporate leaders who once dismissed Patagonia's attention to work/life details as goofy are taking notice. Other smart companies are encouraging employees to enjoy exercise at work for the boost in productivity and talent retention it provides. Google offers on-site fitness centers and provides more than two hundred exercise classes, including nerd-friendly options such as how to dance at a party. Employees also enjoy bocce courts, a bowling alley, and even pickup roller hockey games. At Clif Bar & Company, employees are encouraged to work out on the company's dime for a half hour every day.

⤳

Mental Break—Stanford economist Nick Bloom studied seven hundred firms around the world. "We find more productive, faster growing, and better managed firms offer their employees a more attractive work/life balance package."[9]

PLANET OF THE WEIGHT-LIFTING RATS

We significantly underestimate the positive impact that exercise has on our brains. Big Pharma has poured millions into curing dementia, for instance, yet so far, no drug beats exercise for slowing its onset. Regular dancing reduces the risk of developing dementia by 76 percent—twice as much as reading—according to the *New England Journal of Medicine*.[10]

The *Journal of Applied Psychology* reported recently on a study involving a tiny ladder and bags of weighted pellets gently taped to some rats' rear ends. The rodents received a Fruit Loop when they reached the top of the ladder. After a few weeks of weight lifting and ladder climbing, the rats' memory centers were positively teeming with enzymes as well as genetic markers known to kick-start new neurons and increase neuroplasticity.[11]

The rats not only gained stronger muscles, but they also showed an improvement in their ability to think. Although this sounds like the first act of a movie about musclebound rats taking over Planet Earth, it's a very encouraging indication of the power of exercise to stimulate the brain.

Maybe we could set up something similar in brain-friendly workplaces, only with a healthier snack as the reward. I can see Pauline from Accounting now, climbing that ladder in the hallway with a twenty-pound weight plate strapped to her behind, reaching for a granola bar dangling from the ceiling.

EXERCISE FIGHTS DEPRESSION

Exercise is a powerful fighter against depression because it prompts the release of mood-boosting dopamine. An NIH study of 150 adults over fifty with clinical depression found that, after sixteen weeks, the group given antidepressants and the group that participated instead in an aerobic exercise program experienced "essentially identical" improvement. The study concluded that "an exercise training program may be considered an alternative to antidepressants for treatment of depression."[12]

Absolutely do see a health professional if you suffer from depression. If you are taking antidepressants, never stop taking them cold turkey. Please check in with your psychiatrist if you are interested in adding exercise to your depression-fighting arsenal.

～✺～

Mental Break—EY Managing Director Julie Teigland travels the globe on an extremely demanding schedule. I see her at many events, and she always seems energized and upbeat. She never looks tired. I asked for her secret. "Before I have to speak to an audience," Teigland told me, "I love to get out and walk around the block for a couple minutes. And don't laugh, but I have one of those little under-the-desk pedaling machines. It really helps me keep my energy up."

～✺～

MORNING MUSCLES

When should you exercise? Whenever you can. But exercising before work is super-ideal in terms of prepping your brain to go into peak performance.

If you're low on time, or not a morning person, try walking or biking to work. If you have a lengthy commute, consider biking to and from your train or bus. Odds are, you can figure out how to fit in some exercise before you sit down at your desk.

On that walk or bike ride, your brain will receive an influx of dopamine, which makes you feel alive and happy. Dopamine is the "fun" factor in "fun, fear, and focus." When you hit your desk after exercising, you'll notice right away how much easier it is to focus.

Exercise also releases brain-derived neurotrophic factor (BDNF), which enhances neuroplasticity. This boosts your ability to learn and grow new neurons and connections between neurons. Working out also helps release built-up stress hormones that make us feel on edge and cranky. In short, exercise before work if you want to stroll into the office feeling good and ready to kick some cognitive behind.

In Japan, a calisthenic workout is broadcast to music on public radio early each morning. Some Japanese companies use this broadcast for company-wide morning workouts. My speaking agent worked in Japan in the 1990s and still fondly remembers getting together with her colleagues for those musical morning workouts.

Exercising to music stimulates the brain even more than exercise alone. Teams thrive on enjoyable rituals such as this.

❧

Neuroplasticity is your brain's ability to adapt, change, and learn throughout your life. Exercise helps to improve neuroplasticity and fights cognitive decline.

❧

SITTING IS THE NEW SMOKING

If you can squeeze some exercise into your workday, you'll be happier and more productive. Keep fun exercise gear in your office like resistance bands (which take up virtually no space), a kettlebell, a rebounder, an ab roller, or a balance board. Go for a brisk walk, grab some weights and do squats and bicep curls, or hit the floor for some push-ups. You'll be amazed at how much more energetic and focused you'll feel at work.

I encourage my clients to turn in-person meetings into walking meetings, and to walk when they are on Teams and Zoom meetings. According to a Stanford study, walking boosts creativity by 60 percent. The subjects who walked—indoors or outdoors—produced twice as many creative responses to solving a problem as those who only worked on it sitting down. Researchers found that walking forty minutes three times per week increased brain connectivity and cognitive performance.[13]

❧

Habit stacking involves grouping together small tasks into a routine and linking that routine to an already established habit—like your daily morning walk, for example.

❧

Walking is a great candidate for habit stacking. For example, how many calls do you take each day that could be combined with a regular walk? When I talk with my speaking agent once a week, we leave our offices and go for a walk outside during our chat. These are invariably our most productive and positive conversations and spark our best ideas. You could listen to voice mails during your morning walk to work, or enjoy a favorite podcast.

❧

Brain Boost—Fire up your focus with brief spurts of exercise throughout your workday.

- Turn your phone to "airplane mode" to block e-mails, texts, and other distractions.
- Set your phone's timer for forty-five minutes, and dive into your deep work.
- When the timer goes off, set it for fifteen minutes.
- Exercise for fifteen minutes.
- Repeat.

∽

THE BIKING MANAGEMENT GURU

My friend Jamie Anderson is a popular keynote speaker and organizational therapist dubbed a "management guru" by the *Financial Times*. As a teen, he was one of Australia's top young cyclists, then went on to build an extremely successful career in business management. By forty, Anderson was a top expert in strategic management, publishing in management journals and teaching at leading business schools. But something was missing.

"I asked myself, what does success really look like?" Anderson told me. "I realized how much I missed being an athlete." With the blessing of his wife and children, Anderson got back on his bike.

On training rides, "I started to realize that cycling and being a thinker were not in tension with each other," Anderson said. "They are actually fully compatible. Long hours on the bike give me time to think in blissful isolation. My best ideas come when I'm cycling through the wind and rain."

Anderson decided to reconfigure his career so that he could support his family and still train on his bike twenty hours a week. He channeled his energy into becoming a keynote speaker, wrote a successful book, and gave a series of popular TEDx talks. Anderson won a bronze medal at the World Masters Cycling Games in Italy, with his wife and children cheering as he zipped across the finish line.

Anderson has perfected blending sports with his career. He knocks off six to eight hours per week on his indoor bike during Zoom and Teams meetings with colleagues and clients. Anderson also handles simple tasks—from listening to voice mails to updating his calendar and answering e-mails—while pedaling vigorously on his indoor bike.

"I've delivered keynote speeches to global audiences while dressed in Lycra and pedaling away," Anderson chuckles. "Here's the thing," he adds, "a healthy body is not a luxury for knowledge workers. It's a necessity."

Brain Booster—Here are two simple, inexpensive ways to exercise *and* have fun at work:

1. Rebounders ($50–$150)—jumping on these mini-trampolines promotes bone density.
2. Desk Cycles ($50–$200)—Employees who pedaled fifty minutes per day burned more than five hundred calories a week. They reported feeling more alert and less tired, too.[14]

WIND DOWN WITH AFTER-WORK WORKOUTS

There is no "right" or "wrong" time of day to exercise. If evenings are best for you, go for it. Play basketball with your children or jump in a pool with them. Go for a leisurely walk or post-dinner bike ride with your spouse. Exercising in the evening is a wonderful way to connect with loved ones and get them moving, too.

Exercising after work is also a great way to release stress hormones that build up during your workday. My only caveat is to avoid exercising too late in the evening, as that could make it difficult for you to fall asleep. Build in some wind-down time to fully prepare for sleep.

Mind Bender—Short workouts are great. You can get a lot of exercise in just five minutes. Try this five-minute workout, and tell me you don't feel the burn:

- one minute of jumping jacks
- one minute of burpees
- one minute running in place
- one minute of squats
- one minute of stretching

STOP BRAGGING ABOUT NOT SLEEPING

My high-testosterone/dopamine clients love to respond to my urging them to get more exercise by enthusiastically setting their alarm clocks an hour earlier so they can get up and work out. Instead of sleeping six hours a night, they go for five. Soon, they call to tell me how exhausted they feel and complain that exercising is clearly terrible for their performance.

People—you are not superhuman! You need seven to eight hours of sleep per night. There's no getting around it. If you deprive yourself of sleep, you will walk around in a brain fog. You will have a very tough time hitting peak performance.

Sadly, it's trendy for corporate executives to brag about how little sleep they get. Former Yahoo boss Marissa Mayer claims she functions fabulously on four hours. Apple CEO Tim Cook says he hits the gym by 5 a.m. Fashion designer Tom Ford humblebrags in interviews that he can only sleep three hours a night because he's such a creative whirlwind.

I would love to change this ridiculous trend. Executives who deprive themselves of a decent night's sleep are wearing themselves out and destroying their ability to operate at their best. Ask any Olympic athlete—strategic rest periods are crucial to reaching peak performance. At a press conference, swimming great Michael Phelps described his post-meet routine: "I'm going to get a massage, I'm going to get in a fifty-degree ice tank, and then I'm going to go home and pass out."[15]

⁓⧉⁓

Mind Bender—An American Cancer Society survey of more than one million adults from 1959 to 1960 found that only 2 percent reported getting less than six hours of sleep per night. In contrast, a 2004 National Health Interview Survey found that around 30 percent of adults were getting six hours or less of sleep per night.[16] That's a twenty-eight percentage-point increase in sleep-deprived people.

⁓⧉⁓

TO SLEEP . . . PERCHANCE TO LEARN

If you want to be the smartest, sharpest exec at your company, get enough sleep. Much of our learning and processing of new information occurs in the brain while we sleep.

TO SLEEP...
PERCHANCE TO LEARN

We didn't know this until fairly recently. Scientists were perplexed by the purpose of sleep until an accidental animal study in 1991 illuminated how key sleep is to memory formation and learning. MIT professor Matthew Wilson was conducting a study with rats and a maze. His researchers attached electrodes to the rats' heads to record their brain activity while the rats ran mazes and solved problems.

One day, Wilson left the rats hooked up to the recording equipment after they finished running the maze while he sat at his bench working on some data analysis. "Suddenly," he told *MIT News*, "I could hear brain activity that sounded like the animal was running through the maze, but the animal was asleep." Wilson and his team were astounded to discover indications in this recorded brain activity that while sleeping the rats were running the maze patterns in reverse in their minds. The rats were memorizing maze patterns and learning them *while sleeping*.[17]

Mind Bender—Sleeping less than five hours a night reduces your life expectancy by around 15 percent, according to a Harvard Medical School division of sleep medicine analysis of data from several studies. For the standard life expectancy of seventy-eight years, that is nearly twelve years off your life.

⸎

Additional research has uncovered that our memories undergo "system consolidation" while we sleep. A 2013 study at the University of Zurich found that sleep "is a brain state optimizing memory consolidation." The researchers concluded that "sleep is mainly for the brain." They were also able to confirm that during sleep the brain is detoxified from free radicals and stress hormones such as cortisol.[18]

Neuroscientist and sleep expert Matthew Walker encapsulated this breakthrough research in his best-selling book *Why We Sleep: Unlocking the Power of Sleep and Dreams.* Sleep, Walker notes, enriches our ability to learn, recalibrates our emotions, restocks our immune system, fine-tunes our metabolism, and regulates appetite.[19]

⸎

If you want to be healthy, slim, productive, and a lifelong learner, get enough sleep.

⸎

SHRINKING HAMSTER TESTICLES

Taking melatonin to sleep or overcome jet lag is popular among some of my clients—until I share the tale of the Siberian hamsters' shrinking testicles. Stanford neurobiologist Andrew Huberman led an experiment that involved injecting Siberian hamsters with melatonin to observe its effect on circadian rhythms.

Huberman told the *Tim Ferriss Show* podcast, "these Siberian hamsters have testicles that, at least for hamsters, are pretty impressive." After dosing the hamsters regularly with melatonin, however, Huberman's team noticed a surprising complication. "Their testicles shrank to the size of a grain of rice," Huberman reported.[20]

One of the most powerful effects of melatonin is to suppress puberty. In young children, their strong natural melatonin rhythms prevent them from going into early puberty. As children approach puberty, melatonin levels decline, enabling estrogen and testosterone levels to rise and secondary sex characteristics to develop.

HOW TO KNOW IF YOU DON'T SLEEP ENOUGH

How do you know if you're sleep deprived? In his book, Walker suggests the following: "First, after waking up in the morning, could you fall back asleep at ten or eleven a.m.? If the answer is 'yes,' you are likely not getting sufficient sleep quantity and/or quality. Second, can you function optimally without caffeine before noon? If the answer is 'no,' then you are most likely self-medicating your state of chronic sleep deprivation."[21]

"Routinely sleeping less than six or seven hours a night demolishes your immune system, more than doubling your risk of cancer. There's been a remarkable lopping off of sleep time," Walker told *The Guardian* in 2017. "Longer commute times and longer hours are squeezing sleep almost like vice grips," he added.[22]

Sadly, I have seen many company trainings begin excruciatingly early—after attendees had to attend a company dinner that went late into the night. Even worse was the American company headquartered in New York City that bought a European company and required all the European employees to work on East Coast time. For the European employees, who were six hours ahead, this meant taking meetings with American counterparts late into the night. We need to get out the message that sleep deprivation is terribly counterproductive.

SLAVE TO THE RHYTHM

My executive client kept waking at 5:30 a.m. He couldn't bring himself to get up at that ungodly hour, but he couldn't fall back asleep either. He just lay there, miserable.

I proposed that we embrace his circadian rhythm, instead of fighting it. Your circadian rhythm is a natural, internal clock that regulates your sleep/wake cycle. We have very little control over our circadian rhythms. People are either night owls, morning larks, or intermediates. It's just the way we're wired by our genetics. About half the population are intermediates. They can shift their natural waking time or bedtime by an hour or so without too much difficulty.

I installed a light box next to my client's bed—and a well-stocked espresso machine. "When you wake up at five-thirty tomorrow morning," I told him, "all you have to do is hit two buttons to kick your system fully alive. Then, you'll have time to do your morning workout before heading to the office."

I knew the espresso would get him. Soon, he was bounding out of bed at five-thirty, getting in a solid workout, and feeling great all day.

If we want greater thought diversity and productivity at work, we must enable employees to create schedules that work with their circadian rhythms. At Patagonia, for example, employees set their own schedules. Morning larks scoot in early, get their work done, and go surfing. Night owls stroll in later—and stay later.

SLEEP HACKS

Between my own hectic career, and five children, I really have to make an effort to get enough sleep. Here are my "sleep hacks." Give them a try.

Morning Sleep Hacks

- Throw open the shades and get outside into the sun as soon as possible after you wake up. Sunlight gives you a cortisol and dopamine boost to start your day. It also prompts your brain to release serotonin, which transforms at night into melatonin, the "sleep hormone."
- If you drink coffee in the morning, consider waiting to consume it until an hour after you've gotten up. Some experts suggest that it's best to separate your morning cortisol/dopamine boost from your caffeine peak by holding off on that first cup of coffee for a little while.
- Work out, if possible. Morning workouts kick-start your circadian rhythm, making it easier to sleep at night. If you can work out in the sunshine, even better.
- Tackle difficult conversations in the morning, so that by the end of the day you have worked through your emotions and are ready to let them go.

Afternoon Sleep Hacks

- Take a nap. Twenty to thirty minutes of napping boosts neuroplasticity. Just don't sleep longer than thirty minutes, or you may have a tough time falling asleep that evening.

- Try to avoid caffeine after 2 p.m., however. I recommend boosting your energy with sunlight and exercise instead. Caffeine is more disruptive to the deep restorative sleep we need to get at night than most of us realize. According to a study in *Sleep Medicine Reviews*, any caffeine consumed during the day may reduce total sleep time and worsen perceived sleep quality at night. Deep slow-wave sleep is reduced while wakefulness is increased.[23]
- Get outside late in the afternoon to absorb some red light, which is produced as the sun begins its sweep toward twilight. Red light signals your body to start winding down.

~⊗~

Brain Food—If you struggle with insomnia, are you on a low-carb diet? Our body needs carbohydrates to produce serotonin, and our brains need serotonin to fall asleep and stay asleep. Eat a protein-rich lunch to stay awake and alert all afternoon, and add a low-glycemic carb such as baked yams or brown rice to your dinner to ensure a good night's sleep.

~⊗~

Evening Sleep Hacks

- Take a "media fast." Instead of watching the news after dinner, go for a walk. Too often, the news is designed to upset you. "When it bleeds, it leads," as the newsroom saying goes.
- Wear blue-light-blocking glasses when on your computer at night, and schedule your phones and screens to turn on night mode. Blue light from these devices suppresses melatonin, and low melatonin makes it tough to fall asleep at night. Don't block blue light on your computers and devices during the day, however. Blue light helps keep you alert.
- Turn off phone notifications three hours before bedtime. Any e-mails or texts arriving at that point can wait until the next day.
- Drink a soothing cup of herbal tea. Several herbal teas have sedative properties that help you fall asleep and stay asleep, including chamomile, lavender, and passionflower.
- Keep your bedroom completely dark, or wear an eye mask. Your pineal gland needs complete darkness to signal it to produce melatonin. Any light seeping into your bedroom will slow down the body's natural progression into sleep.

༺ဆ༻

Mental Break—Alcohol helps you fall asleep but makes it more difficult to *stay* asleep. The neurochemical adenosine, which induces sleep, increases while you are drinking, making you drowsy. But once you fall asleep and the alcohol is metabolized by your body, your adenosine level quickly falls. This drop can wake you up and make it tough to fall asleep again.

༺ဆ༻

THE DREAMLAND BANDWAGON

I am thrilled to report that some brain-friendly workplaces are allowing employees to set schedules in line with their circadian rhythms. Others are introducing sleep pods and napping rooms. Companies getting on the dreamland bandwagon include:

- **Google**—The tech behemoth has installed sleep pods for staff naps. The high-tech pods include a built-in sound system for those who like to drift off to relaxing music.
- **Nike**—At headquarters in Portland, Oregon, employees can sleep or meditate in quiet rooms. The company offers flexible schedules to encourage employees to work in line with their circadian rhythms for greater productivity.
- **Procter & Gamble** has installed office lighting systems that dim in the evenings to help employees relax and wind down.
- **Ben & Jerry's** has nap rooms at its headquarters.

All neurosignatures perform better at work when they get plenty of sports, sleep, snacks, and sunshine. High-testosterone/dopamine neurosignatures think they are fine on no exercise and no sleep, because they get so much stimulation from their active dopamine systems. In reality, they are still damaging their ability to learn and perform, and shortening their lives.

If we want greater productivity and neurosignature diversity, we must get rid of workplaces that worship stress and fetishize exhaustion. The best diversity program of all is a brain-friendly workplace that enables employees to enjoy a wonderful quality of life—including a decent night of sleep.

THE BRAIN-FRIENDLY INTERVIEW

Arianna Huffington, CEO, Thrive Global

Two years into founding the *Huffington Post*, Arianna Huffington collapsed from exhaustion, cracking her cheekbone on her desk as she fell. The author of fifteen best sellers realized that she was severely burned out and developed a newfound respect for the power of rest. In 2016, she stepped down from the *Huffington Post* and AOL and founded a new enterprise, Thrive Global, offering "science-based solutions to end stress and burnout." Huffington also wrote *The Sleep Revolution: Transforming Your Life, One Night at a Time*, her book extolling the power of sleep to restore us to our best and most productive selves.

Huffington intends to end the collective delusion that burnout is the price we must pay for success. Thrive helps individuals and organizations improve well-being, performance, and mental resilience with its AI-powered behavior-change technology platform. Thrive's micro-steps—small, science-backed steps to improve health and productivity—have been adopted by employees at more than one hundred organizations in more than forty countries, from frontline and call center workers to executives at multinational companies.

Friederike: How can we convince leaders at the top that productivity and innovation will improve if employees get enough rest and learn to reduce stress?

Arianna: Leaders increasingly realize that sleep impacts our health and performance in practically every way. When I wrote *The Sleep Revolution*, it was rare to see a piece about sleep outside of the lifestyle pages. Now you're as likely to see it in the sports and business sections.

Since I launched Thrive Global, I've found it's less often the case that we have to convince people or business leaders of the importance of sleep. They know how vital sleep is, and they know they don't get enough. The next phase is moving from awareness to action—helping people actually get the amount of sleep they know they should be getting. That's challenging in today's world. And it's also why I founded Thrive Global—to help people create and sustain habits that support their well-being and productivity.

There's been a mindset shift: These leaders now understand that well-being is much more than a benefit. It's an essential strategy for success. Most of the leaders we work with get it, but even the skeptics are won over when they see the science. They see that well-being isn't warm and fuzzy; it's grounded in science and data. Living a sustainable life, and making sure their employees do, too, is the best way for a leader to sustain growth.

Friederike: Women, in particular, are leaving executive positions because so few companies make it possible for them to have families, yet move forward in their careers. As a result, companies lose the thought diversity that women bring to the table. How can companies can better address this problem and gain the benefits of gender diversity?

Arianna: Right now, too many women are being forced to choose between being successful in their jobs or successful in their roles at home. But we can do better. And business leaders can help by supporting working women and recognizing the truth that, yes, we take our whole selves to work, and we perform better when that's not just accepted but encouraged.

Companies can help all employees nurture their mental resilience by creating a workplace where people don't feel like they have to be "on" 24/7, where they're able to say good-bye to their workday and get adequate sleep, and, especially for women and working mothers, where they don't feel like they have to choose between being successful at work and happy at home. That means creating a company culture in which a commitment to well-being isn't just a slogan but is embedded in core company values.

Friederike: What is your favorite micro-step? How has implementing it changed your life for the better?

Arianna: My favorite sleep micro-step is to gently escort my devices out of my bedroom before I go to bed. Phones are amazing tools, but they're also repositories of everything we need to put away to allow us to sleep—our to-do lists, our inboxes, our anxieties. Something as simple as charging our phones outside our bedrooms can make a big difference—by allowing us to sleep better, we'll wake up as recharged as our phones, make better decisions, and be more productive.

Friederike: What are some micro-steps that can be implemented to foster a healthier work/life balance and thereby retain a more diverse workforce?

Arianna: The question I probably get asked the most is about how to maintain work/life balance. But at Thrive, we believe it's not about balance. We start from the idea that work and life, well-being and productivity, are not on opposite sides—so they don't need to be balanced. They're on the same side and rise in tandem.

It's more about work/life *integration*, which means creating workplaces and a way of living that augment our humanity. It's about realizing that we don't have to choose between meeting our life goals and meeting our career goals. The things we value most outside of work aren't obstacles to success that need to be hidden or apologized for, or checked at the door when we arrive at the office. The truth is, burnout is not the price we have to pay for success. With work/life integration, well-being is what fuels our success.

Here are four micro-steps—small, science-backed steps to help build healthy habits—that can be incorporated into our daily lives to boost our physical and mental well-being.

1. Declare an end to the day, even if you haven't completed your to-do list. Effectively prioritizing means being comfortable with incompletions and taking the time to recharge, so you'll return to work the next day ready to seize opportunities.
2. Before you go to sleep, take sixty seconds to write down a list of three things you need to do tomorrow. Research shows that writing down your key priorities can help you fall asleep faster than reflecting on completed activities or things that already happened. Refer back to your list in the morning and dive in.
3. Set aside five minutes each day to meditate. Focusing on the rising and falling of your breath allows you to feel less tense and more present in your life. From this foundation, you'll be less reactive and more resilient—one step closer to being the best version of yourself.
4. Set time on your calendar to focus on your passions each week—even just a few minutes. You wouldn't miss an important meeting or doctor's appointment, so treat this time with the same respect. You'll begin to build the muscle of prioritizing the things that bring you joy.

6

Good Stress

Indolence is a delightful but distressing state; we must be doing something to be happy.

—Mahatma Gandhi

As you discovered in chapter 5, stress isn't all bad. "Good stress" is the "fear" in "fun, fear, and focus" that helps us slide into the super-productive and enjoyable flow state.

Good stress is stress that makes you feel energized and thrilled to be alive. This amount is different for everyone. It depends on your neurosignature and whether you're a "sensation seeker" or a "deep thinker."

Regardless, I cannot "stress" this enough: if you want robust mental health and to bounce out of bed in the morning, read on to learn how to make stress work for you, not against you.

SHORT STRESS VERSUS LONG STRESS

Short bursts of stress actually improve your energy, performance, and health. During the first thirty minutes that you feel stressed, your immune system ramps up strongly. Short-term stress provides a blast of norepinephrine and dopamine that will help you feel happy and focused when you buckle down to work.

Fun ways to create short-term stress include taking a cold shower or fifteen minutes of high-intensity interval training. Even a quick, spicy spat with your significant other can do the trick, as long as you can make peace within a half hour.

If you're still under stress after thirty minutes, though, your immune response starts to drop. After about one hour of stress, your immune system falls to its normal baseline.

If you're under stress for more than an hour, your immune system becomes suppressed. This is one of many reasons why chronic, long-term stress damages mental and physical health. Strive to keep a high-stress experience to under an hour. Remember: short stress = good, long stress = bad.

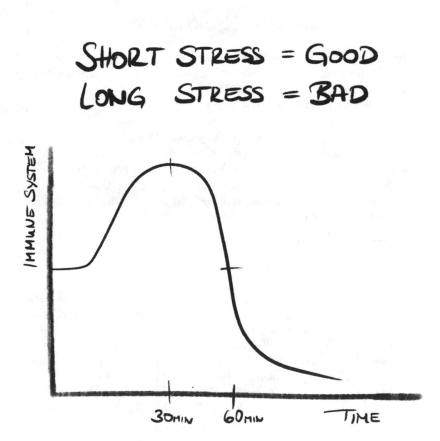

Brain Boost—I take a cold shower or ice bath every day. It makes me feel great. Cold prompts our adrenals to release norepinephrine, activating the brain's energizing dopamine system. One study found a 530 percent increase in norepinephrine and a 250 percent increase in dopamine in subjects who got into fifty-eight-degree water up to their necks for just a few minutes.[1] Cold showers and ice baths reduce anxiety, boost energy and immunity, improve mood, and foster longevity.

Try finishing your shower with a quick blast of cool water. Or drop some ice bags into your bath. You can slowly increase your exposure to the cold in small steps every day. You're looking to induce exhilaration, not frostbite.

⁓☙⁓

STRESSED . . . AND BORED?

Eighty percent of American workers feel stressed, half to the point of exhaustion and misery, according to the 2020 Attitudes in the American Workplace survey.[2] Many reported struggling with insomnia due to job stress. Twenty-five percent said they often feel like screaming.

Meanwhile, the Gallup Institute reports that roughly two-thirds of working people also feel bored and disengaged at work.[3] Clearly, a lot of employees are stressed out *and* bored. That is one miserable way to go through life. It's pointless to say, "Reduce job stress at all costs." We don't need to pump gentle new-age music into our executive suites and make sure everybody tucks in for a nap after lunch. We need a more sophisticated understanding of both stress and boredom. Let's dig into it.

BRAIN SHRINKAGE

Excessive stress literally shrinks our brains. High levels of cortisol—the hormone that spikes when we're under too much stress—are associated with lower brain volumes and impaired memory, according to a 2018 study that reported that "the association is especially evident in women."[4]

During extreme stress, your prefrontal cortex shuts down, making it tough for you to think straight and make intelligent decisions. The basal ganglia, embedded deep in the brain's center, take over. The basal ganglia are the seat of expertise and habits accumulated during your lifetime. The expression "it's just like riding a bike" refers to the fact that once you learn how to ride a bike,

LONG STRESS SHRINKS YOUR BRAIN

that expertise is stored in your basal ganglia for good. Soldiers, firefighters, airplane pilots—any professionals who face extreme threats—train intensively so that when the basal ganglia take over, their automatic reactions save lives.

WHY SOME BRAINS ARE MORE STRESS-RESISTANT

Men and women with high-testosterone neurosignatures appear to be able to handle more stress than the rest of us. One possible explanation is that testosterone has a neuroprotective effect. It raises your threshold for stress.[5] As a result, due to testosterone's blunting effect, this person may be able to absorb more stress.[6] Of course, it's still bad for their performance, but they may be slower to experience fear or anxiety and take longer to go into burnout.

Conversely, less activity in the brain's testosterone system may make someone more sensitive to anxiety and fear. In one fascinating study, a dose of testosterone reduced "the startle response"—our reflexive reaction to being surprised by a loud noise, for example, and a good indicator for how easily someone is stressed—in female subjects.[7] Both men and women have testosterone, but on average, men have ten times more circulating testosterone than women. On the other hand, women seem to be more sensitive to the effects of testosterone.[8] Scientists are still exploring this intricate relationship between stress and testosterone.

Let me be clear: This does *not* mean that men and women with high-estrogen neurosignatures are unable to perform as well as men and women who have high-testosterone brains. It simply means that high-estrogen folks require less stress to achieve peak performance—but also less stress to hit burnout. If you want to temporarily boost your stress resistance, lift weights and enjoy the boost of confidence from the testosterone surge. I lift weights three times a week, and it makes me feel like superwoman—at least for a couple of hours.

⚜

Mind Bender—Forty-two percent of working women say they "often" or "almost always" feel burned out—seven percentage points higher than their male peers—according to the 2021 Women in the Workplace report.[9]

⚜

WHO STAYS STRESSED-OUT LONGER?

On average, the stress response lasts longer in women, with men returning to baseline more quickly, according to Robert Sapolsky, a leading expert on the physiology of stress. During a lecture to Stanford University students that has racked up more than one million views on YouTube, Professor Sapolsky noted that after a fight with a significant other, you'll probably still feel mad even after your partner apologizes. The question is, who stays mad longer, men or women?

Sapolsky added, "There is a pronounced gender difference in how long it takes after strong sympathetic arousal for things to go back to baseline."[10] He then asked the students for a show of hands—who stays mad longer, men or women? The students laughed and agreed that yes, women take longer to cool off.

We've been afraid to talk about these differences between how men and women experience stress, because they could be used as an excuse to block women from leadership positions. I'd like to propose a new way to talk about them: Women are every bit as intelligent, creative, and high-performing as men. They just reach peak performance, on average, at a lower optimal stress point.

FEMALE STRESS RESPONSE: TEND AND BEFRIEND

In addition, women have one stress response, in particular, that may actually be more valuable in today's workplace. When stressed, men are flooded with hormones and chemicals that prep them to fight. Women, in contrast, release the bonding hormone oxytocin. Women under stress will actually get friendlier, whereas men start bristling.

Because it's no longer acceptable to cut off your rival's head with your sword, the female stress response may be more valuable today. It builds compromise and reduces conflict. Because it is not as familiar in the business world, though, it can be erroneously dismissed as "weak" or "placating."

This bonding female stress response was first described in 2000 by distinguished psychology professor Shelley Taylor at UCLA. Taylor reported, "We propose that, behaviorally, females' responses [to stress] are marked by a pattern of 'tend-and-befriend.'"[11] Taylor argued that "fight or flight" became accepted, due to research bias against women, as the "human" response to stress, when in fact it's the "male" response to stress.

Taylor pointed out that, historically, scientific research was conducted on male subjects—from rats to humans. This choice was made, in part, because female bodies are more hormonally complex due to their reproductive systems. It was simply easier to study male subjects. It wasn't until 2017 that the National Institutes of Health began requiring NIH-funded studies to include women and minorities in medical research.

WHAT ABOUT BOREDOM?

My high-powered CEO client was bored—but he didn't realize this was why he felt restless and cranky. Once I explained that he was not experiencing enough exciting good stress, he made two decisions: first, to avoid meetings and people who bored him; and, second, to seek out some big new challenges. He merged his company with several other firms and is now leading a bigger company than ever. He's under more stress—and loads happier.

In 2012, psychologist John Eastwood from Toronto's York University set out to develop a good working definition of boredom. He and his team interviewed hundreds of people about what it feels like to be bored. Eastwood concluded that boredom is "the unfulfilled desire for satisfying activity."[12]

As a neuroscientist, I would add that bored people crave dopamine. When we don't get the excitement that we need to kick-start our dopamine system, we experience the slow-drip torture of boredom.

"When people are bored," Eastwood added, "they're more likely to become internally focused in a negative, ruminative cycle." Eastwood also found that bored employees make more performance errors and are less productive.

"That's a big deal if you're an air-traffic controller or you monitor a nuclear plant," Eastwood noted.[13]

CAN BOREDOM KILL YOU?

Researchers have found correlations between boredom and drug abuse, gambling, overeating—even dying young. The British Whitehall II Study compared civil servants' responses to questions about their lives to their death records more than two decades later. The researchers discovered that those who had reported experiencing a great deal of boredom were more likely to die young.[14]

Boredom can drive us to seek purpose in our lives—or it can drive us to extremes. Social psychologist Wijnand Van Tilburg discovered that after inducing boredom in his research subjects, they were more attracted to extreme political views. "Boredom makes people attempt to re-establish a sense of meaningfulness, and adherence to left- versus right-wing beliefs can serve as a source of meaning," he concluded.[15]

❧

Mind Bender—Researchers at the University of Virginia left subjects alone in an empty room with nothing to do except push a button that would deliver an electric shock to their ankles. Nearly half the people in the study zapped themselves.

"It was like a severe static shock, not a huge jolt, but a little painful," social psychology professor Timothy Wilson told the BBC *Naked Science* program. "They seemed to want to shock themselves out of boredom, so to speak." One subject shocked himself 190 times in fifteen minutes. "I'm not sure what was up with him," Wilson said.[16]

❧

TOM AND OPRAH

If your dopamine system is very active, you'll have a high tolerance for stress and a low tolerance for boredom. You're a sensation seeker who craves stimulation. Skydiving? Yes, please. With a more active serotonin system, you'll have lower tolerance for stress, but can handle more boredom. You're what I call a "deep thinker." Relaxing bubble bath? Yes, please.

If you've never seen Oprah Winfrey's iconic 2005 interview with Tom Cruise bounding all over her couch to express his newfound love for Katie Holmes, watch it on YouTube right now. I can't think of a better example of a deep thinker (Winfrey) and sensation seeker (Cruise) having a fabulous time together.

Winfrey is viewed as a patient, supportive listener. She enjoys finding—and sharing with her followers—the most comfortable pajamas and the plushest towels. Cruise is a hyperintense movie star who performs his own daredevil stunts—from hanging off the side of a plane 25,000 feet in the air to scaling the 2,700-foot Burj Khalifa tower in Dubai. Their pairing on Winfrey's talk show was quite the entertaining spectacle.

~≋~

Sensation seeking is a heritable personality trait linked to the brain's dopamine system. Sensation seekers crave novel, intense experiences and are willing to take risks for them. Sensation seeking runs in families and is correlated with a higher risk of substance abuse.

~≋~

SENSATION SEEKING AT WORK

How sensation seeking manifests is shaped by whether the hormonal side of a person's neurosignature is high estrogen or high testosterone. Sensation seekers with the high-testosterone/dopamine neurosignature crave extreme challenges. Sophie Radcliffe quit her job at a tech startup because she was bored. She chose a new mantra: "one life: live it!" Sophie completed an adventure race through the jungle of Borneo, then cycled from London to Paris in twenty-four hours. In 2014, she became the first person to cycle the Swiss Alps *and* climb the highest mountains in all eight alpine countries.[17]

I'm a sensation seeker, too, but I have a high-estrogen/dopamine neurosignature, so you won't catch me cliff diving. Instead, I freaked out my deep-thinker mom by leaving home to attend universities in different countries. I earned degrees in five countries, becoming fluent in Italian, Spanish, and Swedish, in addition to German, English, and French. I still love to travel and speak foreign languages.

At work, sensation seekers need deadlines, job rotations, and ever-bigger challenges to stay engaged. They bring tons of drive and energy to a project but can be disorganized and willing to take excessive risks. Pair them with deep thinkers, who will keep everybody organized and on track.

Deep thinkers make great bosses because they are approachable and create a positive, trust-based environment. They shine in human resource roles, because they know how to put other people center stage, and care about meeting their needs.

After I explained this during a keynote speech to a Fortune 500 company, the CEO and CFO buttonholed me in the hallway. "I finally understand why it's been so hard for us to work together," the CEO exclaimed, pointing at his CFO. "She wants to plan everything in advance, and I like to be spontaneous. Now I realize it's because the advance planning bores me to tears."

The CFO chimed in, "Right! Now we can understand each other—instead of getting frustrated with each other."

THREE WAYS TO MANAGE STRESS/BOREDOM

In the next few pages, we'll explore three approaches to managing stress and boredom in healthy ways. I recommend applying them in this order:

1. **Change the situation**—Learn the power of boundaries, saying no, and establish autonomy.
2. **Use your body**—Restore your neurobalance with sunlight and circadian rhythms.
3. **Use your brain**—Meditation, gratitude, and emotional labeling are effective, but take time to learn. That can be overwhelming when you're already stressed out, so I recommend trying situation-changing and body-based techniques first.

I always tell my clients, "I'm giving you a bouquet of options. The goal is not to perform or master all of them. Explore the techniques that resonate with you. Choose one or two that you enjoy and can see yourself using on a regular basis." Find what works for you.

CHANGE THE SITUATION, NOT YOURSELF

First, throw out self-help books that try to get *you* to change. I often say, "Don't change the people; change the workplace." To this, I now add my number one antistress/boredom hack: "Don't change yourself; change your situation."

So, sit down with a pen and paper. Don't use your computer for this exercise. Writing by hand is a calming sensory experience that helps your brain process information. First, make a list of things you do at work regularly, such as meeting with clients, composing e-mails, or traveling. Next, make a simple drawing of the fun, fear, and focus curve from chapter 4—or use the free template I provide on my website, fabulous-brain.com.

Map each work activity from your list onto the fun, fear, and focus curve. You'll be able to see clearly which activities bore you, which stress you out, and which put you into flow. Now you can brainstorm how to change or get rid of activities that interfere with your performance.

Here's an example: My new client loved to call me after nine p.m. to chat about his latest brilliant idea. I took those calls at first, but I greatly resented them. They stressed me out just as I was trying to wind down and get ready to go to sleep. I decided to set a boundary and stop taking any client calls after 6 p.m. I responded to my night-owl's voice mails the following morning. He got the hint. The evening calls stopped.

This leads into our first stress-busting tactic: setting boundaries.

LEARN TO SAY NO

I am often waylaid by executives at post-keynote dinners who confide in me, "Friederike, I've tried everything: Meditation, running, yoga . . . nothing works! I'm constantly overwhelmed. My mind is racing. I can't sleep. I feel like I'm losing it. What do you recommend?"

I always tell them the same thing: "You need to learn to say no."

No energy-management technique is more powerful than the word no. Yet, most of us maintain codependent relationships with our jobs. We take on too much, then we behave like martyrs. We feel guilty when we skip networking events to get some rest. We worry that people won't think we're "motivated" or "a team player." This is especially challenging for high-estrogen neurosignatures, who tend to focus on the needs of others while neglecting their own.

If your job is consuming your life, use my book as an excuse to chat with your boss about brain-friendly boundaries you want to establish in order to perform at your best. Explain the concepts of "optimal stress" and "flow." Reassure your supervisor that you want to set boundaries—around communication, meetings, social events, and so forth—in order to become more productive. Set goals, but request autonomy and flexibility in how you achieve them.

No energy-management technique is more powerful than the word no.

⁓≋⁓

If you're a leader, encourage your employees to come to you when they need help managing stress. Create a brain-friendly workplace that empowers all employees to operate at their personal best. Focus on outcomes, not outmoded hustle culture.

⁓≋⁓

Brain Food—Did you know that your gut produces more serotonin than your brain? Add fermented foods such as sauerkraut, kefir, kimchi, miso, or beet kvass to your diet. These are teeming with healthy bacteria that help us feel enlivened and uplifted. At my house, we love homemade ginger beer.

⁓≋⁓

YES-NO-YES

William Ury is the author of *The Power of a Positive No: How to Say No and Still Get to Yes*. In his YouTube interview "Power of a Positive No," Ury relates that Warren Buffett told him, "My job is saying no. I sit at my desk in Omaha and see one investment deal after another. I say no a thousand times until I see exactly what I want, and then I say yes. All I have to do is say yes four or five times in my life, and I'm a billionaire!"[18]

Ury defines a "positive no" as having a three-part yes-no-yes structure:

1. Say yes to a top priority in your life.
2. Deliver a respectful, clear no.
3. Say yes to how you could meet the other person's need.

Imagine that your boss asks you to work this weekend, for example. Start with yes: "I have an important family commitment this weekend."

Then say no: "so I can't work this weekend."

Conclude with a yes that meets your boss's needs—on your terms: "I'd be happy to work late Wednesday and Thursday to get the project done by Friday."

THE TRANSFORMATIVE POWER OF AUTONOMY

Setting boundaries and learning to say no create autonomy in your life. Autonomy is the feeling that you are in control of your life and destiny. Martin Seligman, founder of the "positive psychology" movement, lists autonomy as one of three critical psychological needs:[19]

1. autonomy—the need for a sense of free will;
2. competence—the desire to control one's environment effectively; and
3. belonging—the desire to connect with, relate to, and care for other people.

How much stress you feel is directly tied to your autonomy. One "shocking" animal study illustrates this strongly. First, mice were exposed to random mild electrical shocks. Next, they were divided into two groups. One group of mice were provided with a button they could press with their noses to turn off the shocks. The other group did not get a button.

Mice in the latter group either died or failed to escape when given the opportunity. It was not the mild jolts of electricity that damaged those mice. They were suffering from what the researchers termed "inescapable stress." The mice were so stressed out by fear and their inability to control the shocks that they couldn't cope. They exhibited a depression-like behavior called "learned helplessness."[20]

Similar results have been demonstrated with human subjects. In addition, bosses who work long hours exhibit lower cortisol levels and report feeling less stressed than their employees.[21] Autonomy is a key buffer against stress.

Some brain-friendly companies are increasing employees' autonomy by letting them set their own schedules. Sound bizarre? Not to Dr. Janin Schwartau, global head of learning and transformation at thyssenkrupp. "My team members create their own schedule. Some work nine to five. Others like to work at night and start later in the day," Schwartau told me. She reports that her employees are happier and more productive.

Now that so many people have had a taste of working from home, it's time for companies to embrace the power of autonomy. If companies don't offer greater flexibility, full-time employees will quit rather than return to the office. Companies will have to rely on remote freelancers. This will be corrosive to team building. Instead, why not try flexible schedules, opt-outs for meetings, and a focus on outcomes?

LET THE SUNSHINE IN

In chapter 4, you learned lots of body-based ways to increase well-being. Here's one more: soak in some sunlight. Throw open the drapes and, if at all possible, go outside. Squeeze in a brisk outdoor walk if you can.

Sunlight stimulates feel-good endorphins. It prompts our bodies to produce nitric oxide, which signals our blood vessels to widen so that freshly oxygenated blood can flow into our brains. Insufficient levels of nitric oxide are linked to heart disease, diabetes, and erectile dysfunction, so get that sunshine.

～⚮～

Mental Break—*The 4-Hour Workweek* author and entrepreneur Tim Ferriss jumps rope outside for three to five minutes every morning. "This has a tremendous mood-elevating effect on me," Ferriss said while interviewing neurobiologist Andrew Huberman on the *Tim Ferriss Show* podcast.

"It's definitely not a placebo effect," Huberman responded. "That morning light exposure triggers activation of dopamine—the molecule of motivation and positive anticipation."[22]

～⚮～

Exposure to morning sunlight prompts your body to produce cortisol. Cortisol has been erroneously demonized as "the stress hormone." TV commercials hawk dubious supplements to "curb cortisol and reduce belly fat." In actuality, cortisol is your natural alarm system. You want to use sunlight to wake it up. Healthy levels of cortisol:

- manage how your body uses carbohydrates, fats, and proteins;
- reduce inflammation;
- regulate blood pressure and blood sugar;
- control your sleep/wake cycle;
- boost energy; and
- restore neurobalance after short-term stress.

Excess cortisol builds up in our bodies, though, when we are under "long stress." Persistent elevated cortisol levels are linked to high blood pressure, heart disease, type 2 diabetes, osteoporosis, and other chronic diseases. Too much cortisol signals your body to store fat—a primal reaction to long-term stress. The solution is not pills hawked on TV. The solution is to get plenty of sunlight and manage your stress.

When you trigger your cortisol system in the morning, you'll feel alert and productive throughout the day. Morning sunlight also sends a signal to your melatonin system that your day has begun. It recognizes that it should start producing melatonin in around twelve hours to help you fall asleep that evening.

❦

Brain Boost—A 2021 longitudinal study of more than four hundred thousand people proves that getting outdoor light is critically important. More daylight predicted better outcomes across a range of mood and sleep measures.[23]

❦

BLUE LIGHT/RED LIGHT

Sunlight provides blue light, the kind of light you want to experience in the morning to help you feel awake and alert. Televisions, computers, and smartphones also emit blue light, but, as mentioned in chapter 5, blue-light-blocking glasses are unnecessary during the day. Use them at night, when you want to avoid energizing blue light. Even better, avoid television, computers, and smartphones for three to four hours before bed in order to get a good night's sleep.

As the sun lowers in the sky, it provides a healthy dose of red light. Red light naturally relaxes us and prompts our bodies to start to wind down and prepare for sleep. Walk or bike home from work in that red light if you can, and you'll feel relaxed by the time you get to your door.

Use these simple principles to work with your body's natural circadian rhythms. Human beings used to spend a lot more time outdoors experiencing these natural shifts in light. Today, we spend roughly 87 percent of our lives indoors. We miss the important signals that sunlight and darkness provide for our bodies. Our cortisol levels get thrown off, and our health suffers.

THE MAGICAL IMPACT OF AWE

Marin Pazzani has climbed the Matterhorn five times. When he was sixty-three and still an active climber, he was asked why he climbed mountains. Pazzani replied, "I want to experience awe."[24]

Scientists have discovered that experiencing wonder and awe reduces inflammation and stress—and even lengthens our telomeres. Telomeres protect the ends of our chromosomes from fraying and sticking to each other—rather like plastic tips on shoelaces. Over time, our telomeres shorten, making our chromosomes more vulnerable to damage, aging and, ultimately, death. So, three cheers for awe!

Brain-friendly companies actively create opportunities to experience wonder at work. At BCG, my client Sophia Davies invited digital artist Rafik Anadol to be artist-in-residence for Poptech 2.0, where I was speaking. Anadol created undulating digital sculptures based on brain waves that had attendees gasping with awe.

Another global firm, UBS, tapped WeWork to transform its gigantic cubicle farm at UBS Wealth Management headquarters in Weehawken, New Jersey, into a far more inviting environment. The new campus features green plants, warm wood accents, multipurpose common areas, "dedicated wellness rooms," and huge windows that let in plenty of natural sunlight.

"By partnering with WeWork to create this modern, community-focused workspace, we aim to increase employee productivity and attract the next generation of talent," Marc Montanaro, UBS head of human resources, global wealth management, and Americas region, told *RealEstate NJ*.[25]

UBS also encourages employees to explore the firm's magnificent art collection. In 2020, the company copresented "digital gardener" Jakob Kudsk Steensen. His "catharsis" is a single, continuous shot transporting audiences from the underground roots of a primordial forest to its leafy canopy, accompanied by sounds recorded in North American forests. Awe-inducing, indeed.

I'd like to see brain-friendly companies add art rooms, music studios, and libraries to their offices. Imagine the stress/boredom-relieving potential of painting on your lunch break or jamming with some colleagues.

EMOTIONAL LABELING

Many mind-based techniques designed to relieve stress and imbue your life with greater meaning and joy are worth exploring. My personal favorite is "emotional labeling." This simple practice of "putting feelings into words" has been studied extensively and proven to help people regulate their emotions.[26]

When you feel overwhelmed by a strong negative emotion such as anger, it can be difficult to think clearly, right? That's because your body is being flooded with stress hormones, kicked off by a distress signal from the amygdala to the hypothalamus and adrenal glands. Emotions that trigger this physical reaction include fear, anger, anxiety, and aggression.

Emotional labeling shifts your processing of a stressful emotion from the amygdala to the prefrontal cortex, your brain's seat of reason and mood regulation. This rapidly calms your body's reaction. Brain imaging studies reveal that simply naming your emotions immediately makes sadness, anger, and pain less intense.[27]

Start by saying, "I feel ____." Get very specific about this emotion. Is it anger, or resentment? Sadness, or disappointment? Loneliness? Grief?

Notice how labeling the emotion brings your reaction under control. Your heart rate comes back down, and you're able to take a few deep, calming breaths. Next, if possible, share your emotions with a friend. Notice how even texting "I'm so bored!" during a boring meeting can make you smile. Next time an upset friend calls you for support, now you know how to help—by encouraging your friend to "name that emotion."

The more you practice emotional labeling, the better you'll get at it. Human beings need to label, express, and share our emotions. But in the business world, it's considered unprofessional to show any emotion. Unfortunately, the more we bottle up our feelings, the more likely we are to explode. I have advised many leaders that when they have to let people go, it's very important to allow them to express their emotions verbally—before moving on to offering services such as counseling or job placement.

MORE MIND-BASED STRESS BUSTERS

Other mind-based techniques that work great for stress management include:

- *Mindfulness-Based Stress Reduction (MBSR)*—The most scientifically researched form of mindfulness training, MBSR strengthens the prefrontal cortex, boosts the immune system, improves intuition, and strengthens social networks in the brain. All these positive changes can occur in just eight weeks of daily practice.
- *Gratitude Practice*—People who consciously appreciate the things they're thankful for experience more positive emotions, sleep better, and have stronger immune systems. Gratitude activates brain areas associated with moral cognition and connecting with one's values. It boosts the feel-good neurochemicals dopamine, serotonin, and oxytocin. To practice gratitude, focus daily on what's good in your life.

- *Hypnosis*—Hypnosis has been shown to encourage focused attention, a lack of self-consciousness, and greater control over our emotions. A team of researchers led by Stanford's Dr. David Spiegel found that it leads to increased connectivity between the brain's executive network—for greater focus—and a region called the insula, where bodily sensations are processed. At the same time, the brain's salience and default mode networks become less active, which helps you to be more focused and less distracted.

SEEK EMOTIONAL SUPPORT

Many studies confirm the value of social support in helping us cope with stress and relieve boredom. Why haven't we explored the importance of relationships with friends and colleagues in this chapter? Because we'll delve into this fully in chapter 7, Wired to Be Tribal.

THE BRAIN-FRIENDLY INTERVIEW

Dr. Hubertus Meinecke, managing director and senior partner; chairman, Western Europe, South America, and Africa, BCG

Dr. Meinecke is the chairman of Boston Consulting Group's Western Europe, South America, and Africa region, and serves on the firm's executive committee. He also serves on the BCG Henderson Institute board of directors and represents BCG at the World Economic Forum in Davos.

I met "Hubi" through the Yunus Foundation, which we both actively support. I can attest that he is a true "sensation seeker," out climbing mountains and running ultra-marathons when he's not globe-trotting for BCG.

Friederike: I always enjoy hearing about your adventures hiking up Mount Blanc and trail-running ultra-marathons. If you had an easygoing job that didn't require much from you, you would probably go insane. You thrive under pressure and are energized by it. Does that sound accurate?

Hubertus: Yes, and I think of five pillars that really matter to me: job, adventures, family, nutrition, art. I love to play piano, for example. Definitely the adventures and my running counterbalance the stress of my job. I love to reinvent myself and do new things all the time. Kilian Jornet, the greatest ultra-runner of the past fifteen years, is my role model. He always develops himself further.

I was always into art, and at an art gallery in Berlin three years ago, I began a friendship with two artists. My interest in art deepened and became a new source of energy for me.

Friederike: So, these intense physical challenges and your love of art counterbalance the stress of your job?

Hubertus: Yes. They help me stay healthy and happy on the highest level so I can perform at my best. Another source of joy are my four kids. Three of them play the violin and one the cello. They started at age four and by age six it was very nice to hear. Playing music with them is just wonderful.

Friederike: The pandemic cut into your global travel drastically. Are you eager to get back on the road, or do you think things will be different now?

Hubertus: I don't think people will fly like crazy all the time the way we used to do. I think we pushed too much. I could see my travel going to about 60 percent of what it was pre-pandemic.

Friederike: This is the perfect time to change the old idea that an executive leader must be a jet-lag-resistant person. That outdated paradigm has caused companies to miss out on people with brains that may not thrive under extreme stress—but who have great insights and ideas. Hiring and promoting "deep thinkers" may provide more innovative and thought-diverse leadership.

Hubertus: That's a fantastic point. If you have, for example, one type of CEO who is always pressed for time and never wants to go into detail, then, of course, you have to present that person with three quick points. But often, I find we lose what we could have gained from a less linear approach to our communication. I often feel frustrated when I can only communicate those three points; it's not really enough.

Friederike: Yes, and you are someone who has to serve many different kinds of CEOS, so I imagine you have to adapt your communication style to what they each can "hear" best.

Hubertus: Truthfully, I wanted to study philosophy and ancient Greek in college, but my parents were not going to pay for that, so I studied mechanical engineering. But when I came to work at BCG, I was so drawn to the company's humanistic attributes. That is very important to me.

Friederike: What is something you do to cope when you do feel stressed out or tired?

Hubertus: I breathe in for four beats and breathe out for eight. If you do that for three or four minutes, it has an amazing effect. It's great to practice in a traffic jam, or if you're facing a crisis. I do it in meetings—people don't even notice.

Friederike: That is a wonderful technique for turning off the extreme stress response before it gets too overwhelming.

Hubertus: Yes, it really works when you're stuck in a situation. If you're not stuck, then running for ninety minutes is, to me, the sweet spot. If I can get out and run for ninety minutes, then everything is all right with the world.

Friederike: That will give you lots of good-feeling endorphins and dopamine.

Hubertus: You don't need to run fast, either, for it to work. Walking is also great. We have lost sight of the value of walking. All the great thinkers and philosophers were big walkers: Gandhi, Heidegger, Socrates.

Friederike: I always suggest walk-and-talk meetings to my clients. Whenever you experience "forward ambulation," it activates "optical flow," meaning that scenery is flowing past you. Your amygdala gets deactivated, and that lowers anxiety and stress.

Hubertus: That makes so much sense, because I've noticed that if you pace in a circle, you don't get the same positive effect as you do from going on a walk. I'm meeting later today with a fellow partner who needs inspiration. Instead of taking him to a nice restaurant, as he might expect, I invited him to my home. I'll make us fresh squeezed juice, and then we're going for a walk.

Friederike: Perfect! You get vitamins *and* you get to move.

Hubertus: It also provides him with a different experience than he was expecting.

Friederike: You're hijacking him with a brain hack.

Hubertus: Exactly! I think it's great what you're doing, Friederike. Your approach and insights will benefit a lot of leaders and, hopefully, will create a happier workplace for everybody.

7

Wired to Be Tribal

Call it a clan, call it a network, call it a tribe, call it a family. Whatever you call it, whoever you are, you need one.

—Jane Howard

What do you think is the single most important change you could make to improve your health? Should you quit smoking? Stop drinking? Exercise more?

Actually, the best thing you could do is improve the quality of your relationships. People who have great relationships live on average eight years longer, according to a *PLoS Medicine* study on "Social Relationships and Mortality Risk."[1] Whether you smoke two packs of cigarettes a day, or whether you have bad relationships or feel isolated, the damage to your overall health and well-being is roughly the same.

During the global COVID-19 crisis, Iceland's government asked quarantined citizens who were feeling lonely to go outside and hug some trees. Sounds bonkers. But hugging a pet, a person, and, yes, even a living organism such as a tree, signals the pituitary—a bean-shaped gland at the base of your brain—to release the "love hormone" oxytocin.

Oxytocin is very calming. It helps reduce blood pressure and cortisol levels. Oxytocin also helps us regulate our emotions and bond with others. It promotes sleep and a positive feeling of well-being. Our brains release massive amounts of oxytocin and dopamine during orgasm, which is why having sex can create such powerful bonds. And when a woman gives birth, her body is flooded with oxytocin, helping her to bond deeply with her newborn.

The feel-good bonding effect of oxytocin is also valuable to a brain-friendly workplace—and there are ways to reap its benefits without having sex, giving birth, or even bear-hugging your colleagues. In this chapter, I share "Ten Commandments of Great Work Relationships." These will help you safely generate oxytocin at work, improving bonding and raising trust—and profitability.

Brain Food—Boost your oxytocin levels with foods high in vitamin D, magnesium, and dietary fats. These include avocados, salmon, mushrooms, peppers, tomatoes, and spinach.

MASLOW WAS WRONG

You're probably familiar with Maslow's hierarchy of needs, proposed by American psychologist Abraham Maslow in 1943. Maslow placed "physical needs," such as thirst and hunger, at the base of a pyramid diagram. He argued that humans seek to meet their survival needs for food and water first. Next, they seek safety from predators and enemies. Only after basic needs are met and safety is established will a human being seek out friends and start a family. Maslow believed that only after those social needs have been met would a person advance toward self-actualization—the pyramid's peak.

Maslow's pyramid is still featured in management books and leadership training around the world. But it's wrong. Social needs should be at the base of the pyramid. A baby doesn't survive by going to the forest and picking berries. It survives because it has parents and relatives who take care of it. It survives because it lives within a social network.

For millennia, human beings lived in small tribes of about 150 people who helped each other survive. Although animal predators have always shifted humans into threat mode, from an evolutionary perspective our most threatening enemies have long been other people. You would only survive as a member of your tribe, and only if the other members of your tribe truly had your back. Being banished from the tribe was tantamount to a death sentence. We needed to bond with other people in order to survive. We are wired to be tribal.

MASLOW WAS WRONG

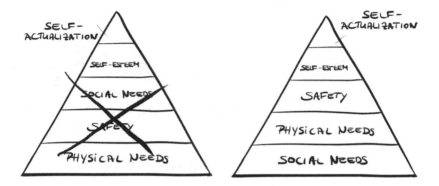

Mind Bender—Banishment is still considered the ultimate punishment among Native American tribes. The modern version involves ordering trouble-makers off the reservation. It can also involve stripping them of their tribal membership, including their portion of any casino profits that the tribe shares with members.

WHY WE REACT BADLY TO "OTHERS"

Then, just as now, not everyone on the same team got along all the time. If someone in your tribe took a strong dislike to you, your predicament could become life-threatening. The next time your tribe is attacked by an enemy tribe, you might find yourself in combat next to your nemesis. Is your tribal bond strong enough that he will fight by your side? Or will he bolt to save his own life, leaving you at the mercy of the enemy?

Modern conflicts at the office may be less deadly, but we've retained the primitive wiring that makes us extra sensitive to potential threats from other people. We're wired to respond much more intensely to negative interactions than to positive ones. This is why we can have strong threat reactions to seemingly benign interactions at work. These emotional reactions are hard to control because they are instinctual. But being aware of this ancient wiring can help us get a grip, especially when combined with a new awareness of the benefits of inclusion and diversity.

Surprisingly, oxytocin also has a dark side. It can lead to bias, discrimination, and racism. When you feel strongly bonded to the group you identify with most, you may feel compelled to exclude "outsiders." Every politician knows this. The worst exploit it.

⤳

We're wired to respond much more intensely to negative interactions than to positive ones.

⤳

THE BRAIN'S SOCIAL NETWORK

Next time you're waiting for the bus or train, notice what you're thinking about. I'll bet it is a relationship—with a friend, a colleague, your significant other . . . or your cat. Warning: Once you're aware of this, you'll notice it all the time.

Our brains run on what's called a default mode network (DMN) whenever we aren't focused on a specific task. Researchers have discovered that the DMN thinks about social relationships most of the time. In his book *Social: Why Our Brains Are Wired to Connect*, UCLA neuroscientist Matthew Lieberman says that by age seven, we've already put in at least ten thousand hours musing about our relationships.[2] You'd think that would make us masters of good relationships—but the truth is, we can always learn how to connect better with the important people in our lives. Good relationships are crucial to both our emotional and financial health.

THE NEUROCHEMICAL OF TRUST

I like to call oxytocin "the neurochemical of trust." As neuro-economist Paul Zak notes, "Oxytocin reduces the fear of trusting a stranger."[3] Although oxytocin increases empathy, extreme stress is a potent oxytocin inhibitor. That's why when we're stressed out, we don't play nicely with others.

"Employers who don't understand how oxytocin works try to bond employees through activities—like karaoke nights or weekend retreats," Zak explains.

"While such efforts might boost workplace happiness in the short term, they fail to have any lasting effect on talent retention or performance."[4]

What works instead, Zak argues, is building a culture of trust. "Employees in high-trust organizations are more productive, have more energy at work, collaborate better with their colleagues, and stay with their employers longer than people working at low-trust companies," Zak says. "They also suffer less chronic stress and are happier with their lives, and these factors fuel stronger performance."[5]

I believe this works because feelings of trust and connection generate oxytocin, which is a powerful catalyst for other neurochemicals that make your brain feel great. Oxytocin triggers the release of dopamine, which provides bursts of energy and feelings of joy. Oxytocin also jump-starts serotonin, the neurotransmitter that helps us achieve emotional stability and reduces anxiety. Whenever you release oxytocin at work, you're also activating this potent combination of neurochemicals.

⌘

Brain Boost—When humans are in trouble, we're triggered by our neurochemicals to help each other—unless we have limited *emotional empathy*, which is our ability to share the feelings of another person.

Psychopaths lack emotional empathy, but they do have *cognitive empathy*, the ability to view a situation from another person's perspective. In fact, some psychopaths are extremely high in cognitive empathy and use it to "read" and manipulate others. They understand how you're feeling. They just don't care.

⌘

MORE TRUST EQUALS MORE PROFIT

Trust may even make companies more profitable. Zak studied three hundred large companies in the United States. He found that companies where employees report strong bonds and high levels of trust between colleagues generated on average $10,000 more revenue per employee per year.[6] Correlation is not causation, but Zak estimated that for a company with five thousand employees, raising the trust level could potentially bring in an additional $5 million in revenue.

The return on investing in improving relationships between employees looks quite promising but can be overlooked by high-testosterone/dopamine leaders, who tend to promote competitive employees over collaborators. In his book *The Moral Molecule: How Trust Works*, Zak reported that women tend to be more collaborative at work, whereas men tend to be more competitive.[7] The brain-friendly workplace values both approaches. As *Brain Rules* author John Medina told me, "The more women there are on the team, the higher the C-factor. C stands for 'collective,' and groups with a high C-factor just solve problems like a son of a gun."

COUNTRIES WITH MORE TRUST ARE MORE PROSPEROUS

Countries in which people trust each other tend to be more prosperous than countries coping with a lot of distrust. This correlation is true even when you remove such factors as education. In the 2016 World Value Survey, more than 60 percent of respondents from Sweden, Norway, Finland, and Denmark reported that they "think people can be trusted." This was correlated with their stable, prosperous economies.[8] In contrast, fewer than 10 percent of respondents in Colombia, Brazil, Ecuador, and Peru agreed that "people can be trusted." These countries are dealing with business-strangling corruption, more red tape, and lower economic growth.[9]

⸺

Mind Bender—Compared with people at low-trust companies, people at high-trust companies report[10]

- 74 percent less stress;
- 106 percent more energy at work;
- 50 percent higher productivity;
- 13 percent fewer sick days;
- 76 percent more engagement; and
- 40 percent less burnout.

⸺

BEING REJECTED HURTS . . . REALLY

Why does trust have such a strong impact on profitability? Because humans genuinely suffer when we experience social pain.

One of the most fascinating neuroscience experiments ever done with functional MRI brain scanning involved a simple game of catch between three participants.[11] As he lay by himself in a scanner, one of the participants—let's call him Joe—played electronic catch with the two other participants, both of whom presumably were lying in scanners of their own.

When I viewed Joe's scan, I was shocked. This was a brain in pain. Activity was clearly visible in the anterior cingulate cortex, processing pain in the medial prefrontal cortex. It looked as if Joe had been tortured in the brain scanner. His brain was coping with a lot of agony.

Did one of the researchers hit Joe's thumb with a hammer, or hold a lighter to the soles of his feet? Actually, we neuroscientists are not allowed to do that stuff anymore. Here's what really happened.

During the experiment, Joe and the other two subjects tossed an electronic ball back and forth while Joe was in the brain scanner. Joe was enjoying himself. His fMRI scan showed a brain that was happy and relaxed.

But after a few minutes, the other two players abruptly started tossing the ball between themselves, deliberately leaving out Joe. The truth was that the two other "participants" were actually computer simulations that had been programmed to exclude Joe after ten minutes of three-way play. The effect of being left out was dramatic. Joe's second fMRI captured his brain as it struggled to cope with the emotional pain that he was feeling due to his social exclusion.

You know the saying "sticks and stones may break my bones, but words will never hurt me"? From a neuroscience perspective this is definitely not true. Social pain, like rejection, is processed much like physical pain in our brains. In fact, you can take Tylenol when you're feeling rejected, and it will make you feel better, just as it would if you had a headache or other physical pain. You can even take Tylenol to ease a broken heart.[12]

⌒⧓⌒

Mind Bender—According to the Center for Creative Leadership, unmanaged employee conflicts cause at least 65 percent of all performance issues at work.

⌒⧓⌒

Feeling rejected or experiencing intractable conflicts at work can be just as painful. Luckily, you can do simple things to create trusting, enjoyable relationships at work, based on what we know about oxytocin and how our brains process our interactions. These are my "Ten Commandments for Great Work Relationships."

Commandment 1: IRL Matters
Connecting with someone IRL (in real life) at the start of your working relationship is a wonderful opportunity to generate oxytocin and trust. No, I'm
not asking you to cuddle. But do meet in person and shake hands.

The moment you shake hands, oxytocin will be released in both your
brains. It really does help you bond when you can meet in person and share
this safe, consensual touch. This sets a positive base of trust and good-feeling
neurochemicals for interactions to come, even if much of your work together
will be virtual. Physical touch matters, and physical presence makes a difference. Meeting in person is not always possible, of course. Just know that meeting IRL has a stronger positive impact than meeting only virtually.

If you are shy, be aware of your tendency to use conference calls and Zoom
meetings to avoid meeting colleagues or clients in person, and try to overcome
it. Have coffee with a client. Go out to dinner with a team member. Don't
worry: The oxytocin that is released when we connect in person will also help
you overcome social anxiety. IRL matters!

Commandment 2: Get It Right in the Beginning
When my husband met me, he was living in his dream post-divorce bachelor
pad. This place was flawless: color-coordinated, beautifully designed; his
sanctuary.

The first thing I did when I moved in was hang my cheesy paintings of
pink hearts on his carefully curated walls. I wasn't going to be an unobtrusive
guest in his perfect life. I wanted to be his partner. You want me? Deal with
my terrible taste in art.

He didn't speak to me for two days. I toughed it out, because I knew that
the impression you make in the beginning of a relationship sets the tone for
the future. You can also get away with a lot in the beginning of a relationship.
That's when the oxytocin is flowing. Luckily, my gamble worked. Five kids
and ten years of marriage later, we laugh really hard about my experiment—in
our messy but full-of-love home.

When we first meet someone, we feel a warm surge of oxytocin. This softens
us up a bit and makes us more flexible and open. Use that moment wisely. By
the second meeting, we are already establishing habits—that's how the brain
saves energy. Make sure these are the habits you *want* to establish.

Do you want to have long, boring team meetings? Hold one the first day,
and that habit will take root. Are your associates always late? Nip that in the
bud, or expect to deal with it forever. People slip into habits very easily, so
beware. Today's unsanctioned behavior is tomorrow's standard. Get it right in
the beginning.

Commandment 3: The Magic Ratio Is 20:1

Researcher John Gottman is able to predict divorce rates with 94 percent accuracy, simply by observing couples for ten minutes. Gottman invites couples into his Love Lab and asks them to argue about something. During their spat, he measures their heart rates and other stress indicators. Gottman has discovered that couples who can maintain a 5:1 ratio of positive versus negative interactions during fights are likely to stay together. In addition, Gottman's research shows that when a couple is not fighting, this ratio needs to be closer to 20:1 to keep them together long-term.[13]

So, if you want good work relationships, strive to make sure positive interactions outweigh negative interactions by 20:1 during good times, and at least 5:1 during rough moments. Yes, sometimes you must deliver negative feedback or turn down a deal. Be sure to follow up with positive interactions, though, to restore that magic ratio. Share your appreciation. Speak your colleague or client's name warmly during your conversations. Simple positive interactions like these add up quickly, getting you to the magic ratio of 20:1.

Commandment 4: Manage Your Stress

Stress is contagious. Entire organizations can develop an unhealthy stressful atmosphere when leaders fail to manage their own stress. Let me give you an example.

Early in my career, I worked for a boss who was fueled by fear and espresso. She nagged me morning, noon, and night before every client presentation: "Do you have the sales data? Did you bring the presentation? Did you mess it up?" She was so nervous that it drove me crazy. She passed out on the floor from anxiety three times while I worked there.

Worse, she put me in charge of a gigantic Excel spreadsheet with more pages than a dictionary. Back then, Excel was new to me. I was terrified of making a mistake—and I was terrified of her.

Sure enough, I made a mistake—and we couldn't find it. My boss went bananas: "Did you find it yet? If you don't find it, we're going to fire you." My cortisol levels shot through the roof. My hands were shaking. I could barely think straight, let alone calm down enough to comb through the spreadsheet to find the error.

When people are stressed out, oxytocin levels drop. Employees lose the ability to empathize and connect with each other. Trust declines, and so does productivity. Use what you learned in chapter 6 and manage your stress. Everyone around you will thank you.

Mind Bender—A 2013 study found that memories of traumatic experiences in mice seemed to be passed down as genetic imprints on future generations as fearful responses to specific triggers.[14] A small study of Holocaust survivors and their children also suggests that traumatic events may imprint on the genes of future generations.[15]

Commandment 5: Spice It Up

I gave a keynote recently at a firm where the partners seemed to genuinely love each other. They hung out together often, laughing, joking, and having a great time. Their spouses seemed to know each other really well, too. What was the secret to their strong connection, I asked?

Turns out that a few years before, the partners and spouses had attended a weekend sailing retreat. During a sudden storm, their boat was swamped by a huge wave. They had to scramble to stay afloat and make it back to shore. Their scary adventure created a powerful bond. But why?

A life-threatening experience triggers your adrenal glands to release norepinephrine—the "fear" in fun, fear, and focus, remember? Norepinephrine coursing through your system prompts a cascade of dopamine. Dopamine triggers oxytocin, which heightens empathy and bonding. So, take your colleague or client on an adventure. Instead of a dull steak dinner, go for spicy Ethiopian food. Try bungee jumping. Experiencing a rush of dopamine and oxytocin together will create a marvelous foundation for a happy, long-term work relationship.

Commandment 6: Thou Shalt Not Lie

Ever seen video of President Bill Clinton declaring, "I did not have sexual relations with that woman," regarding his affair with twenty-two-year-old intern Monica Lewinsky? That lie not only got him impeached, but it damaged his reputation forever. You can build trust for years and destroy it with one lie.

My advice is simple: Never lie at work, even if you have to deliver bad news. People can handle the truth, but they will never forgive you for lying to them. Keep in mind how key trust is to profitability, productivity, and good relationships.

I gave this advice to the leaders of a struggling multinational pharmaceutical company that was about to let tens of thousands of employees go. "Don't sugarcoat this situation," I told the leadership. "That will only enrage your employees and destroy your credibility. When the police come to your door to tell you that a relative has died, they don't chitchat about the weather first.

SPICE IT UP

That would be monumentally insulting. When you have bad news, deliver it quickly and honestly."

~❧~

Mental Break—Back in 1998, psychologist Paul Ekman saw Bill Clinton deny his affair with Monica Lewinsky on television and instantly knew that the president was lying. Ekman, aka "the lie detective," is an expert in deception detection. He trains FBI and CIA agents to detect barely perceptible facial micro-expressions that indicate when someone is lying. Ekman says humans across cultures are highly sensitive to any indication that someone is lying. That's how important trust has been to our evolution.[16]

~❧~

Commandment 7: Make Rituals Habitual

I asked a firm's high-powered CEO whether he performed any rituals with his clients. He raised an eyebrow and answered, "Not really."

"What do you do for your key clients?" I pressed him. "Is it always just business, or do you see them outside of work as well?"

As it turns out, he has many rituals in place. He goes running every Saturday morning with one client. He and his family celebrate Oktoberfest with another client's family every year. He meets his second-in-command every weekday morning at Starbucks, and they walk to the office together. He had never thought of these routines as rituals, but they are.

Rituals, such as special gestures, ceremonies, and celebrations, raise our oxytocin levels. Paul Zak took blood samples at weddings and found that after the vows are spoken, oxytocin levels among the wedding party skyrocket.[17] People just love that moment.

Leverage the power of ritual at work to raise oxytocin and increase trust and bonding. Send your clients handwritten thank-you notes. Create in-person kickoff meetings. Take your team out for dinner to celebrate meeting a deadline. Make rituals habitual.

Brain Boost—My client, Accenture, created a system that employees working in hybrid teams can use to send each other appreciative eCards—in recognition of a job well done, for example. People love finding these in their inboxes and getting a little hit of oxytocin.

Commandment 8: Quit Trying to Be Perfect

When you meet a new colleague or client, do you make an extra effort to be perfect? If you show some vulnerability and are honest about your weaknesses, people will connect with you more easily, so quit trying to be perfect. Remember, humans are wired to help each other. Go ahead: ask for help with a project, a reference, or a connection.

When you admit that you're not perfect, you show that you're capable of trusting someone else with seeing your flaws. This advice works especially well for leaders, as showing a bit of humility and vulnerability is humanizing. This might not work so well when you are interviewing for your first job, however. Use the power of imperfection wisely.

Mental Break—One of my clients, the tech company trivago, holds monthly F**k Up Fridays. Everyone gathers over drinks to share their biggest failures of the month and what they learned from them. Trivago actively encourages "failure culture," embracing imperfection and mistakes as necessary by-products of innovation. As a former trivago employee noted in *Medium*, "Everybody is actually encouraged to fail—fail often, fail fast, fail cheaply."[18] This relaxed attitude toward failure can increase trust and reduce stress.

⤳

Commandment 9: Find Common Ground

If you've ever gone camping, I'm sure you've been warned to be extra careful should you accidentally intrude upon a mother bear with her cubs. Mother animals can be quite aggressive. That's because oxytocin interacts with the hormone vasopressin to create the "guard and defend" response.

The guard-and-defend response can be activated at work, too. Sometimes, the more we bond with "our" team, the more guarded we feel toward newcomers we perceive as "different." This can crush diversity efforts at a company. The antidote is to find common ground.

Jeff Furman, a board member at Ben & Jerry's for more than forty years, tells me that the company's activism played a valuable role in creating common ground throughout the company. "This whole world of business is simply about relationships," Furman explains. "We would put all the employees and managers together on one bus. We traveled together to all sorts of climate marches. We'd march together and stay together."

Finding common ground by supporting a cause has an additional benefit. Humans love to help, and when they help together, this generates oxytocin and encourages bonding.

Commandment 10: Maximize Fairness

Economists tell us that people seek to maximize profit during their interactions. Actually, they may seek to maximize fairness. In 2002, game-theory psychologist Daniel Kahneman received the Nobel Prize in Economic Sciences for using "the ultimatum game" to prove that most people will turn down an unfair deal, even if they would profit from it.

I've tried the experiment myself, with fascinating results. At a keynote, I'll ask two volunteers to come on stage. Let's call them Sophie and Jason. I hand Sophie ten dollars in singles, and say, "Please share these with Jason. Here are the rules: If you offer him a certain amount and he accepts your offer, you each get to keep your share. If Jason refuses the split that you're offering, neither of you gets any of the money."

Let's say Sophie offers a 50/50 split and Jason accepts. They each get five dollars.

Next, I ask Jason, "If you had been offered just one dollar would you have accepted the deal?"

Jason replies, "No."

To which I respond, "But it's free money!"

"It wasn't a fair deal," Jason invariably responds.

See? It's not about the money. It's about perceived fairness. I've run this experiment many times, in different countries and at different companies. I've found that whenever "Jason" is offered three dollars or less, he refuses the offer, and I get to keep my money.

People are even willing to lose money to punish an unfair player. In men, in particular, the pleasure networks in their brains light up when they get to punish someone they perceive as an unfair player.[19] Divorce lawyers take full advantage of this fact.

VaynerX chairman Gary Vaynerchuk takes fairness a step further. His motto is "Give more than you take." Vaynerchuck has used this approach to grow his company to a net worth of $200 million in 2022.[20] In his article "Giving Without Expectation," Vaynerchuk notes that "fostering relationships is paramount to guiding the ways our lives unfold."[21] I hope my "Ten Commandments of Great Work Relationships" will help you foster wonderful relationships in your work life—and your personal life.

THE BRAIN-FRIENDLY INTERVIEW

Dr. John Medina, Brain Rules *author and molecular biologist*

Medina's *New York Times* best seller, *Brain Rules,* was published in 2008. It was the first book that I felt related to what I was trying to do—and what Medina was doing so skillfully—apply neuroscience to business.

Medina is a warm teddy bear of a guy who is also a scientific heavy hitter of wide-ranging brilliance. He's a developmental molecular biologist who studies genes involved in human brain development and the genetics of psychiatric disorders. Medina is an affiliate professor of bioengineering at the University of Washington School of Medicine and former founding director of the Talaris Research Institute in Seattle. In 2004, he was appointed an affiliate scholar at the National Academy of Engineering. His many books include the *Brain Rules* series and *Attack of the Teenage Brain.* He also writes the "Molecules of the Mind" column for the *Psychiatric Times.*

Friederike: What surprised you most while researching your new book, *Brain Rules for Work*?

John: The inspiration for the book was a lecture called the Five Fingered Glove that I gave to a business school. The first question I posed to the students was really simple: Why do we have five-fingered gloves? Because we have five fingers.

I made the case that when a brain enters the workplace, it operates in certain ways—but we fail to create a cognitive five-finger glove for the brain at work, even though we should. Surprisingly, when I sought to identify ten things from the literature about how the brain processes information, a common theme emerged: If you really want to have a brain-friendly workplace, one of the most important things is to not be self-centered. This is key, due to what power does to the human brain. There are five known things that power does. Most of them are pretty ugly.

Friederike: What are those five effects of power on the brain?

John: The definition of power is simple: It's the ability to control resources and exercise control over interpersonal relationships. If you become a business executive, you have the power to fire somebody and ruin their life, or reward somebody and create that person's career.

First, when the brain gets power, a lot of empirical research suggests that you lose the ability to decode accurately the emotional information coming from somebody's face. Second, you become less empathetic to specific cues that used to trigger empathy in you.

Friederike: How was that proven?

John: The heartbreaking experiment is to show pictures of kids in cancer wards to someone whose brain is being scanned with an fMRI. These pictures elicit an empathic response that you will see in the brain—except when you get power. The more powerful you become, the less reactive you are to emotional information—like pictures of sick kids—that used to create a fair amount of empathy in you. You become more detached.

Third, you begin to untether yourself from your ability to understand the consequences of your own actions. You begin to think that the rules that apply to everybody else don't apply to you anymore, and because they don't apply to you anymore, you can do what you darn well please.

Fourth, you stop caring about the consequences of your own actions, you just want to get your way. See where that's going with self-centeredness?

Friederike: Amazing; yes.

John: Fifth, as you obtain power you begin to over-sexualize your environment, and your self-perceived "mating value" rises. Basically, when you have been exercising the wheels of power for a while, you begin to think you're sexually hot, even if you're not. Add that to your inability to read facial cues and lowered empathy, and you begin to develop a sense of impunity and believe that you have mating rights. This is how we get powerful sexual harassers at work who get themselves into deep trouble.

My point is that the self-centeredness that people can bring to the workplace is just as important to address as fashioning the workplace itself.

Friederike: This is so spot-on and in line with my book. Do the five power problems you describe apply to females as well?

John: Yes, as we know, women who get into top positions can exhibit this power behavior as well.

Friederike: What do you suggest to mitigate the negative side effects of power in the workplace?

John: One option is called "prophylactic education." This was researched at Johns Hopkins University and also with a group of folks in the Naval Academy. The researchers simply taught men, in this particular case, what was likely to happen to them when they acquired power.

They were warned, for instance, that they were likely to start oversexualizing work interactions and to be on guard against that. In fact, the researchers studied that most intimate work relationship—a cis hetero male mentoring a cis hetero female. Could you reduce sexual interaction between them?

The answer is yes, by educating the men about the pitfalls of power. You just tell them, "This is likely to happen to you." If they understand that, they can be alert to it and start knocking off the tendencies.

Friederike: Fascinating! Is there another approach that works, too?

John: A second approach is to discourage the "shift response." A group of researchers in the Midwest asked the question, "When we're in a conversation, how often do we shift the conversation so that we can talk about ourselves?" That's the shift response.

Sixty percent of the conversations the researchers sampled involved the shift response. The shift response is very tempting because you give yourself a dopamine lollipop when you talk about yourself. Your brain just lights up.

Let's say my coworker comes up to me and says, "You know, Diana really made me mad; I need to talk about this." If I respond, "Yeah, Diana makes me mad, too. Let me tell you what she did to me today," I've just shifted the conversation to be about me.

What you want to develop instead is the "support response" to decrease self-centeredness at work. The support response to your coworker would be, "Wow, you look really upset. What in the world happened between you and Diana? Tell me what's going on."

This is such a small thing to offer someone, but it makes a huge difference.

Friederike: That would change the atmosphere of a workplace profoundly. What is your take on the future of work at this point?

John: What do I think of the future of work? Get back to person-to-person as soon as you possibly can and stay there. We weren't built for Zoom. We were built to be together.

As you know, the brain is capable of detecting micro-expression changes between people as they're talking. We receive a tremendous number of cues when we interact in person that we are not able to perceive on a Zoom call, for example. The instant you clip that off so that you can no longer get the social cues, you get impoverished communication. That impoverished communication cuts people off.

You cut people off long enough and any genetic susceptibility they may already have, say, to clinical depression or generalized anxiety disorder—which they may never have gotten if they had been in a normal social equilibrium—just comes right to the front because now they're isolated.

Friederike: In this chapter, I share "Ten Commandments of Great Work Relationships" to encourage people to connect and share simple things such as a handshake to promote the flow of oxytocin and enhance trust and bonding.

John: Yes! The first great idea of the social brain hypothesis is that it was cooperativity that allowed us to double our biomass by not waiting twenty-five million years to create a larger body column like the elephants did. Instead, you just change a few very important regions in the brain, and all of a sudden you have a cooperativity that essentially doubles your biomass by making an ally, or at least getting the concept of ally out there. We lived not because of our dominance, but because of our restraint. We created friends. How about that? A great idea!

8

The Social Neurogap

There's zero correlation between being the best talker and having the best ideas.

—Susan Cain

I kicked off this book with exciting new data about a corporate "neurogap"—a "stress gap" that favors people with high-testosterone/dopamine neurosignatures. We explored how this has drained talent—particularly female talent—and made thought diversity difficult to achieve. We discovered that people with other neurosignatures were leaving workplaces that failed to respect their gifts or meet their needs.

This phenomenon accelerated dramatically during the Great Resignation of 2021. A record 4.4 million Americans quit their jobs in September 2021 alone, seeking greater flexibility and joy. By October 2021, people-analytics firm Visler estimated that nearly one in four workers had quit their jobs, unwilling to return to traditional workplaces.[1] Visler Vice President Ian Cook explains, "People are rethinking their careers, their work/life balance and how they engage in work. And that's what employers need to be engaged in if they want to keep their employees."[2]

Companies have an unprecedented opportunity right now to shift to a brain-friendly paradigm for the future of work that will help them retain and attract top talent. To that end, I'd like to share another neurogap I've uncovered: between extroverts and introverts. According to additional unpublished data that NeuroColor has shared with me, corporate leadership appears to favor extroverts over introverts. I call this neurogap between introverts and extroverts at work a "social gap" because it relates to our social behavior. In this chapter, we'll explore the surprising strengths that introverts bring to work and how brain-friendly companies can benefit from the quiet power of introversion.

⤜⤚

An **extrovert** feels recharged and energized from engaging with other people. People high in extroversion are action oriented and tend to seek out attention, social stimulation, and opportunities to engage with others. They thrive working in teams. Extroverts may find it challenging or uncomfortable to spend time alone.

⤜⤚

PARTY ON, WAYNE

Whether you're an introvert or extrovert comes down to how you answer one simple question: Do you feel energized by socializing, or do you prefer to replenish your energy by spending time alone? Are you *Wayne's World's* Garth Algar exclaiming, "Party on, Wayne!"? Or reclusive actress Greta Garbo, who avoided her own movie premieres, and was famous for intoning, "I vant to be alone"?

If the party's winding down and you're exhausted and eager to crawl into bed, you're probably introverted. If you're shouting, "Hey, that was awesome! What else is going on tonight?" you're extroverted. Introverts feel depleted after hectic social interactions. Extroverts feel energized by them.[3]

Introverts feel more energized by spending time alone. An introvert will seek to replenish energy by doing something like reading a book or going for a walk in the woods.

⤜⤚

An **introvert** feels recharged from solitude and can feel drained after socializing. People high in introversion tend to be calm, self-aware, deliberate, and independent. They thrive on working alone and prefer to observe and analyze before they act.

⤜⤚

POWERSTATION

INTROVERTED   EXTROVERTED

EXTROVERTS ARE NOT BETTER LEADERS

Like all personality traits, introversion and extroversion exist on a spectrum. Most of us are a mix of both traits. New NeuroColor data indicates, however, that executive suites are skewed toward people who are "highly extroverted." In a data set of fourteen thousand executive leaders, NeuroColor found that highly extroverted people were disproportionately represented. Male executive leaders showed a seventeen percentage-point increase in being highly extroverted, compared to the general population. Female executive leaders exhibited a ten percentage-point increase in being highly extroverted, compared to the general population. In this data sample, women tended to be more introverted than men, which may explain the lower percentage of highly extroverted female executive leaders.

Here's the rub: Extroverts are *not* better leaders than introverts. Introverts and extroverts are equally effective leaders, according to research by organizational psychologist Adam Grant. When people are unmotivated and unengaged, Grant notes, an extroverted leader can be more effective at pushing them to get their work done. But when people are motivated and engaged, Grant found that introverted leaders consistently perform better.[3]

THE SOCIAL GLASS CEILING

Most companies are not aware of this social neurogap at work between introverts and extroverts. Think of companies that insist, for example, that executive leaders attend lots of social events. Extroverted leaders feel energized by parties and dinners. Introverts, in contrast, find this kind of socializing draining. Talented introverted leaders who are pushed to "network" at after-work social events will escape to brain-friendly workplaces that understand introversion and don't pressure them to be social butterflies.

As author Susan Cain points out in *Quiet: The Power of Introverts in a World That Can't Stop Talking*, "We make room for a remarkably narrow range of personality styles. We're told that to be great is to be bold, to be happy is to be sociable. We see ourselves as a nation of extroverts—which means that we've lost sight of who we really are. One-third to one-half of Americans are introverts—in other words, one out of every two people you know."[4]

As I mentioned, on average, women are more introverted than men. The social neurogap between introverts and extroverts in executive leadership is a second unaddressed neurogap that disproportionately affects women and makes gender parity difficult to achieve. This "social glass ceiling" may block talented introverted women from ascending to top leadership positions in workplace cultures that excessively value extroverted leaders.

THE BABBLE HYPOTHESIS

Why should you care if extroverts dominate executive leadership? Because, to quote Susan Cain again, "There is zero correlation between being the best talker and having the best ideas."[5]

How did this social neurogap take hold then? A combination of bias and self-selection is likely at play. In 2016, psychologists studying extroversion determined that a central feature of extroversion is "tending to behave in ways that attract social attention."[6] Extroverts love being in the spotlight, so it's only natural that they gravitate toward leadership positions that demand lots of social interaction. An introvert, in contrast, may decide that a leadership position within a highly extroverted workplace is not a good fit.

A study commissioned by the U.S. Army on the "babble hypothesis" uncovered a fascinating bias: People who talk the most in a group tend to emerge as the group's leaders, *regardless of their intelligence.*[7] People who talk the most are also perceived as more competent.[8] Executive leaders who are not aware of these biases may inadvertently promote those who talk the most, not necessarily those with the best ideas.

Finally, because highly extroverted executives are more widely represented in leadership positions, they may be unconsciously more likely to promote other extroverts—unless they've read this chapter. When they do, they'll understand that introverts bring to work remarkable competitive strengths that businesses should not overlook.

SUCCESSFUL INTROVERT LEADERS

I have a client who is a very successful CEO—and an introvert. "How do you work as a CEO while being an introvert?" I asked him. "Don't you find all the social obligations exhausting?"

"Oh, I skip all those tiresome networking dinners," he replied. "I arrive at the office every morning refreshed and ready to go. My colleagues appreciate that I'm focused on our work, not out marketing myself the night before."

"How else does your introversion affect your leadership?" I asked.

"You know," he mused, "power plays never interested me. I think they are a huge waste of time and energy. So, when I took over, I sent out a very clear communication to everyone that I would tolerate no politics or backstabbing. I want us to focus on our work and enjoy positive relationships with each other. People have shared with me how much they appreciate this. It keeps our workplace drama-free, productive, and enjoyable."

"Also," he added, "since I don't go to all those after-work functions, I have time to exercise. I have time for my family. I enjoy my free time. That recharges me far more than going out at night would. So, I do think it's possible to be a good leader and an introvert."

∽⇌⌐

Mind Bender—Super-accomplished introverts in history include:

- Albert Einstein
- Eleanor Roosevelt
- Al Gore
- Abraham Lincoln

- J. K. Rowling
- Meryl Streep
- Michael Jordan

⤬

SPA SECRETS

Given that my career involves striding confidently onstage and giving keynote speeches to thousands of people, you'd probably bet that I'm an extrovert. Let's see if you're right.

Recently, I gave a keynote during a conference at a luxury hotel. I eagerly checked the schedule to see when I might be able to sneak off for a spa break. It looked like most everyone would be at the plenary session the next morning, so when I woke up, I put on my bathrobe and stepped into the hall. The coast was clear. On my way to the spa, I spotted the executive lunch buffet table, loaded with fancy snacks and drinks. I tiptoed in to grab a few treats.

Suddenly, I was spotted by one of my clients. He gave me a huge smile and waved me over to a table at the nearby cafe, where he was grabbing a coffee. Although I was inwardly groaning—and embarrassed at being in my robe—it would have been very impolite to ignore him. So, instead of spending my break blissfully inhaling steam alone in the spa sauna, I sat down with him and ordered an espresso. We chatted cordially for about forty-five minutes before I excused myself to run back to my room and change into my suit for the rest of the day's activities.

Extroverts live for this kind of impromptu mingling at conferences. They find it wonderfully invigorating. I find it exhausting. In case you haven't guessed by now, I'm an introvert. I need alone time to recharge.

THE OUTGOING INTROVERT AND OTHER MYSTERIES

People often confuse being outgoing with being extroverted and being reserved with introversion. Actually, whether you are introverted or extroverted is only about one thing: Do you replenish your energy by being alone, or by being around other people? Whether you are outgoing or reserved is a completely separate issue. According to NeuroColor's framework, the outgoing-reserved spectrum gauges show how you behave when interacting with other people.

Outgoing people find it easy to share their emotions and opinions, as I did when I sat down for an espresso with my client. I'm introverted, but I'm also outgoing. Reserved people are slower to reveal their emotions and opinions. We all fall somewhere within the four quadrants represented on this chart.

I'm in the upper left quadrant. I'm an I/O, or Introverted/Outgoing. You can be an outgoing person—like me—and still be introverted.

You can also be reserved and still be an extrovert. My friend Sarah is slow to warm up to people and share her innermost thoughts. She tends to speak only when she has something meaningful to add to a conversation. Sarah is reserved. But when she wants to replenish her energy, Sarah loves to go out dancing with friends. She feels energized from hanging out with other people—as long as they don't pry into her personal life too much. Sarah is E/R—Extroverted/Reserved.

Additional previously unpublished data from NeuroColor found an eighteen percentage-point increase in being "highly outgoing" among male executive leaders compared to the general population. NeuroColor identified a twenty-two percentage-point hike in being "highly outgoing" in female executives compared to the general population. NeuroColor also identified a

INTROVERSION AND EXTROVERSION

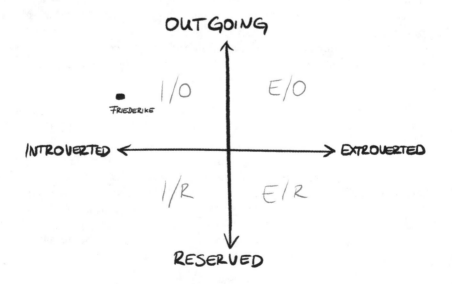

six percentage-point gap in being "highly outgoing" between male and female executives. Again, it's helpful to be aware of these neurogaps and how they affect a company's leadership and the quality of its thought diversity.

~⊗~

Mind Bender—Pianist Vladimir Horowitz was a dazzling performer and a famous introvert. He once quipped that his fee was $100,000—$5,000 to play the piano and $95,000 to attend the reception.

~⊗~

INTROVERTS HAVE MORE "INTRINSIC MOTIVATION"

Now, let's explore the introvert superpowers I mentioned earlier in this chapter. Don't get me wrong: I adore the extroverts in my life. Both extroverts and introverts bring wonderful qualities to work. I'm just trying to level the playing field a bit by raising awareness of the gifts that introverts have to offer, so we can close the social neurogap in our workplaces.

But first, let me tell you about my adorable five-year-old, Henry. He drove his kindergarten teacher up the wall. Why? Because Henry didn't like to participate in group activities. She called me constantly, worried about Henry and begging me to tell him that he must "participate more."

Was he finishing his work and keeping up with the other children? I asked. Yes, she replied, adding that he was a very smart little boy. That's when I knew it was the teacher who had to go.

You see, at home, Henry plays with his Lego set for hours in his room. Often, when I call him for dinner, he's so lost in concentration that he doesn't hear me. I'll yell, "Henryyy!" again, and he'll shout down, "I just gotta finish this, Mom!"

This invariably piques my curiosity, so I trot up to his room. The other day I found that he had built a very skillfully constructed Lego roundabout.

"This is amazing, Henry!" I exclaimed. "How did you come up with this?"

"It was in my head, so I built it," he replied calmly.

Introverts like my son exhibit more "intrinsic motivation" than extroverts.[9] Like Henry, they find inherent satisfaction in their work. And they aren't wild about group activities, preferring to work in peace on their own. Extroverts, in contrast, are more motivated by "extrinsic motivation" such as attention, praise—and bonuses.[10]

I found Henry a more brain-friendly school with teachers who understand concepts such as introversion and extroversion. Henry's new teacher doesn't pressure him to join in group activities. As long as he's learning, she's happy, and so am I.

The moral of the story is: let your introverts work alone in peace, if that's their preference. They require less supervision than your extroverted employees because they have more intrinsic motivation—and that's a good thing.

⤳

Intrinsic motivation involves feeling motivated to do something because the activity is inherently satisfying. When intrinsically motivated, a person is moved to act by enjoyment, rather than by external pressure or reward.

⤳

INTROVERTS PUT IN THE HOURS

When Albert Einstein was a child, his teachers thought he was a bit dim. Einstein was a quiet loner who seemed a million miles away, lost in his thoughts. When he was sixteen, Einstein failed his entry exam for Zurich Polytechnic and entered a Swiss trade school instead. He persevered, however, and got into Zurich Polytechnic at seventeen. At only twenty-seven, Einstein published his mind-bending papers on quantum theory, Brownian motion, and the special theory of relativity.

Einstein said, "It's not that I'm so smart. It's that I stay with problems longer."[11] This ability to focus intensely and deeply is a key characteristic of introverts, who tend to have more extended focus than extroverts. They are capable of examining a problem from many angles and enjoy detailed research and examination.[12]

Because they enjoy spending time alone, introverts tend to be more willing than extroverts to put in the hours alone necessary to master a skill. At the moment, the world champion in chess is Magnus Carlsen from Norway, who became the world's youngest grandmaster at age thirteen. When asked to explain his success, Carlsen told CNN, "First of all, I put in the hours."[13]

⤳

Brain Food—If having to socialize at a party raises your blood pressure, try a shot of beet juice when you get home. You can also mix red beet power in water, or dump some into your favorite smoothie. The nitric oxide in beets lowers blood pressure and helps relax and widen blood vessels. Researchers found that people who drank 250 milliliters (or about 8.4 ounces) of beet juice daily lowered both systolic and diastolic blood pressure.[14]

❧

INTROVERTS THINK MORE

Researchers have discovered that introverts have thicker gray matter in the prefrontal cortex of their brains than do extroverts. In people who are strongly extroverted, scientists have found that the gray matter is consistently thinner. Introverts also show more activity in the frontal lobes, where analysis and rational thought take place.[15]

One study scanned brains of both introverts and extroverts and found that, even in repose, the introverted brain was more active, with more blood flow. Even when they are chilling out, introverts seem to be thinking more than extroverts.[16]

Introverts and extroverts both have brains that crave rewarding surges of dopamine—we all do. The difference lies in how we get those rewards. A Cornell University study found that extroverts derive pleasurable feelings from interacting with their immediate environment. Introverts derive pleasurable feelings from their inner thoughts instead. Perhaps this is why introverts need a little more downtime to daydream.[17]

❧

Mental Break—"Most inventors and engineers I've met are shy and they live in their heads," says Apple cofounder Steve Wozniak. "In fact, the very best of them are artists. And artists work best alone where they can control an invention's design without a lot of other people designing it for marketing or some other committee. I don't believe anything really revolutionary has been invented by committee . . . I'm going to give you some advice that might be hard to take. That advice is: Work alone. You're going to be best able to design revolutionary products and features if you're working on your own. Not on a committee. Not on a team."[18]

❧

70 PERCENT OF GIFTED PEOPLE ARE INTROVERTS

On average, introverts and extroverts are the same in terms of intelligence. But statistics do show that around 70 percent of gifted people are introverts.[19] People are considered "gifted" when they exhibit above-average intelligence or a superior talent for something, such as music, art, or math.

If your workplace is dominated by extroverts who criticize those who prefer to work alone—or skip after-work cocktails—as "not team players," it may inadvertently alienate gifted people. Building an introvert-friendly workplace, on the other hand, is likely to attract gifted, focused, and intrinsically self-motivated employees. Later in this chapter, I'll provide you with a seven-step plan to do just that.

⁓≥⁓

Mind Bender—Scientists studied five thousand gifted children for forty-five years and found that most of them were extremely successful. "Whether we like it or not, these people really do control our society," Jonathan Wai, psychologist at the Duke University Talent Identification Program, told *Nature*. "The kids who test in the top one percent tend to become our eminent scientists and academics, our Fortune 500 CEOs and federal judges, senators and billionaires."[20] And around 70 percent of them are likely to be introverts.

⁓≥⁓

INTROVERTS DO THE RIGHT THING

On December 1, 1955, a white bus driver in Montgomery, Alabama, demanded that an African American seamstress named Rosa Parks surrender her seat to a white passenger. Parks looked calmly at the driver and said, "No."[21]

The bus driver threatened to have her arrested.

"You may do that," Parks replied softly.

Parks was arrested and convicted of violating racial segregation laws. Her quiet strength in the face of blatant racism came to symbolize the nonviolent civil rights movement of the 1960s. Parks also famously said, "You must never be fearful about what you are doing when it is right."[22]

A 2013 study on social conformity found that extroverts are more willing to go along with the opinion of the majority, even when it's wrong. The researchers found that extroverts were more likely than introverts to succumb to social pressure. The researchers concluded, "The higher the pressure, a larger number of conforming responses are given by extroverts," and noted that, in contrast, "there is no difference in conforming responses given to high- and low-pressure levels by introverts."[23]

Introverts tend to be less swayed by external events and more by their inner moral compass. Adding introverts to your workforce can provide a hedge against scandal. Introverts will feel less pressure to cover up for a corrupt colleague or conform to an unprofessional work environment.

I don't mean to imply that introverts are saints—or that extroverts fall short on moral fortitude. You only have to look at the Bill Gates sexual misconduct scandal that exploded in 2021. America's most prominent introvert was accused of having made unwanted sexual advances toward Microsoft employees for decades, and his twenty-seven-year marriage fell apart.

Nonetheless, statistics show that extroverts commit more crimes, get arrested more often, cheat on their partners more, and face higher divorce rates than introverts, on average.[24] Extroverts are also more likely to be injured or killed in accidents. Spring break in Florida? Extrovert heaven.

Now that we've explored the benefits of hiring and promoting introverts, let's look at my seven-step plan for creating a more introvert-friendly workplace.

Step 1: Learn about Introversion
Step 1 is to hand your colleagues this book and have them read this chapter so they recognize and appreciate introversion—in themselves and others.

The millions of fans who've watched his television show, read his books, or listened to his podcasts might never guess that Phillip Calvin McGraw, better known as Dr. Phil, is an introvert. Yet on an episode of *The Skinny Confidential* podcast, he admitted as much to the audience, adding, "If I go to hell, it will be a cocktail party."[25]

The fact is, introverts are all around us. When I tell my clients—many of whom are highly extroverted leaders—that I'm an introvert, for example, they laugh or roll their eyes. They don't get it at first because they think an introvert is some shy, nerdy wallflower. Sometimes we are, but more often, we are simply people who find socializing tiring and are less likely to be out and about promoting ourselves. Introverts can be overlooked, as a result, in a workplace where the leadership is dominated by extroversion.

Step 2: Provide Privacy
I was eager to see my client's expensively redesigned new headquarters. I'd heard that his designer had replaced all the office walls with see-through glass barriers.

As the CEO ushered me onto the floor, my jaw dropped.

"Voilà," he announced, sardonically.

I stood there, shocked, as my client explained that his extroverted em-ployees loved the new design—loved it! The introverts considered it a living nightmare. They had reacted by barricading themselves behind bookshelves, file cabinets, piles of cardboard boxes, and coat racks festooned with parkas, scarves, and jackets. The office resembled a series of living-room forts built by children.

My client's award-winning designer had overlooked one thing: Extroverts may love to see everybody all the time, but introverts need privacy. The solu-tion is a flexible work environment that provides silence and private space for introverts and lively, interactive open space for extroverts.

Pixar Animation Studios, in Emeryville, California, is a wonderful example. The sixteen-acre campus is centered around a huge atrium that contains the cafeteria and mailboxes. This encourages impromptu encounters between em-ployees to foster new creative collaborations. Pixar also provides lots of private office space that employees can decorate however they want. There are even egg-shaped soundproof pods employees can hide in when they need complete privacy and silence in order to dive deep into flow.[26]

Microsoft's headquarters in Redmond, Washington, is also a highly flexible environment. Most employees have private offices, but these are equipped with sliding doors and movable walls. Employees can choose when they want to collaborate with others and when they need to squirrel away.[27]

When I posted on LinkedIn about how open-space offices damage produc-tivity, the post went viral. Hundreds of people commented that they hated not having privacy and silence at the office and were far more effective working from home. Businesses must start listening to employees if they expect to woo them back into the office.

Step 3: Respect Boundaries

The brain-friendly workplace also respects personal preferences regarding boundaries and working styles. Some people are comfortable with open-door policy; others find it intrusive and disruptive. Did you know that when you are fully focused and you are interrupted, it takes up to twenty minutes for you to regain full focus again? For heaven's sake, allow people to shut their office doors whenever they want.

Performance will only improve when people can shut their doors and work uninterrupted for significant portions of their day. If you're concerned about what they're doing in there, remember to focus on outcomes, not hustle cul-

CREATING AN INTROVERT-FRIENDLY WORKPLACE

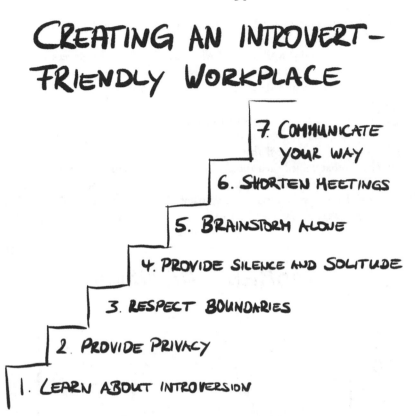

7. COMMUNICATE YOUR WAY

6. SHORTEN MEETINGS

5. BRAINSTORM ALONE

4. PROVIDE SILENCE AND SOLITUDE

3. RESPECT BOUNDARIES

2. PROVIDE PRIVACY

1. LEARN ABOUT INTROVERSION

ture. Set goals, make sure they're met, but don't worry so much about how and when your employees are meeting their goals.

Added bonus: Your introverts will love you, and your company will attract more of them—including perhaps some who are gifted.

Step 4: Provide Silence and Solitude

During my keynotes, I always ask, "Where do you get your best ideas?"

"In the shower," people call out.

"While walking my dog."

"When I'm doing the dishes."

Nobody ever replies, "At the office" or "in a meeting."

I'm not surprised. As a neuroscientist, I know that in order for you to experience an "aha" moment of insight, your brain must go through a specific series of stages. This amazing experience is very unlikely to happen in a noisy, distracting office.

The brain-friendly workplace provides places where employees can find silence when they want to concentrate. This is especially appreciated by introverts, but silence is also necessary for extroverts to experience aha moments of insight.

Here's how insight works whether you're introverted or extroverted. In 2015, researchers applied stimulation directly to the brain to try to promote insight. The researchers discovered that they could trigger a surge in creativity using stimulation that helped their subjects' brains produce alpha waves.[28]

Alpha waves arise when the brain is conscious, yet relaxed. While experiencing alpha waves, you may find yourself closing your eyes. This sinks you deeper into a state that may lead to insight; in fact, this is called the "alpha insight effect."

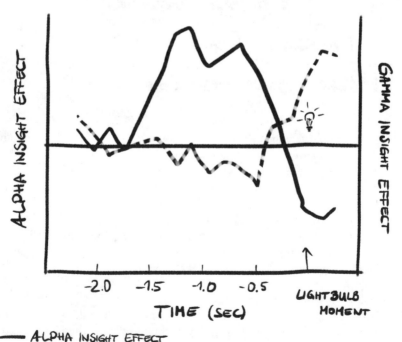

In response, your brain may start producing subtle, rapid oscillations called gamma waves. Brain areas that rarely communicate start interacting and connecting. In this state, aha insights are most likely to happen—unless you're interrupted by noise.

A buzzing open office kills innovation and creativity, because it's impossible to get into deep brain states while our concentration is continuously interrupted and disrupted. So, go ahead: Provide opportunities for silence and solitude. This will lead to more innovation and creativity from everyone, including your extroverts.

~⊗~

Brain Boost—Novelist Jonathan Franzen uses sensory deprivation to boost his creativity. When he sits down to write in his soundproof office, Franzen inserts earplugs, then places ear muffs over his ears and a blindfold over his eyes. Franzen says he discarded "thousands of pages" before he tried this method and found that it helped him sink deeply into his writing while working on his acclaimed 2001 novel, *The Corrections*.

~⊗~

Step 5: Brainstorm Alone
Love to hold free-for-all brainstorming sessions? Think they're key to your team's creativity? You might be surprised by what University of California, Santa Barbara psychology professor Jonathan Schooler uncovered.

Schooler divided people into two groups and tasked them with solving the same problem. One group was encouraged to brainstorm a solution together. The other group was told to develop solutions on their own and then share them with the group.

Schooler discovered that group brainstorming "stifled" innovation and insight. In contrast, when people brainstormed as individuals, they came up with more innovative and effective solutions.[29]

Putting people in a room and letting them shout ideas at each other sounds like fun. But the research shows that if you want to maximize innovation and creativity, let employees generate ideas by themselves before sharing them in a group. Bonus: Your introverts will be far more comfortable sharing their ideas this way.

Step 6: Shorten Meetings
Introverts, as you can probably guess, are not fans of meetings. Brain-friendly companies are radically shortening meetings—and shrinking the number of people invited to attend them.

"Underlying bad meetings is deep insecurity in people," VaynerMedia Chief Heart Officer Claude Silver tells me. "They feel they have to be in the meeting because they don't want to be left out." Silver encourages everyone to keep meetings under fifteen minutes and to let go of the idea that the entire office has to be invited to every meeting so that no one feels left out. "People should feel comfortable being left out of meetings," Silver says. "Once you change the culture in this way, meetings get much better."

Other companies are instituting "no meetings" days. Facebook, for example, has no meetings company-wide on Wednesdays. Citi, the third-largest bank in the United States, has "no-Zoom Fridays," during which Zoom meetings are banned. Increasingly, brain-friendly companies are realizing that meetings can be damaging to productivity and to flow. Too many meetings will also prompt introverts to start looking for work elsewhere.

Step 7: Communicate Your Way

I prefer e-mails to phone calls. Most introverts do. In contrast, more extroverts enjoy handling business on the phone.[30] Encourage employees to choose the method of communication that they prefer—even if it differs from yours.

During the lockdowns, many of my clients begged me to do keynotes to convince people to turn their cameras on during Zoom calls. Human resources folks, in particular, were really after me about this—they were convinced that people were not "connecting" if they couldn't see each other on video.

Frankly, when bosses insist on video, it's because they want to see what people are doing and make sure they're paying attention. If you shorten meetings and improve their quality, then you don't have to worry about whether attendees have their cameras on or off.

The solution is twofold: Give people a choice of whether to turn their cameras on or off, and create shorter, better meetings. Then you won't have to worry about whether they're scrolling Twitter during a boring Zoom call.

❧

Mind Bender—People experience more "empathetic accuracy" during a voice-only call when compared to a video call, according to a 2017 study by social psychologist Michael Kraus from the Yale School of Management. Empathic accuracy is the ability to infer another person's inner states. Kraus concluded that most people will be more focused on a voice-only call.[31]

❧

LET MY PEOPLE . . . REST

As NeuroColor cofounder Dave Labno tells me, "Introverts are often exhausted in their current workplace—because many of their colleagues do not understand their introversion. This is a big aha moment!"

I remember when the highly extroverted leader of a company I was working for took all of us employees on a three-day bonding extravaganza. On just the first day, we zipped from a morning workshop to a group hike, followed by an afternoon art exhibition. Then, we hopped on a boat that ferried us to a beautiful restaurant on the water. After dinner, when I was secretly praying that we were headed back to our luxury hotel for some blissful alone time, we were chauffeured to a jam-packed beer garden. The extroverts were having the time of their lives; the introverts were losing it. So, if you'd like to attract more introverted talent to your business, my last piece of advice is, "Let my people rest."

I hope you enjoyed this peek into the world of introversion and the strengths that introverts bring to work. The future of work is all about more choice and autonomy. Both will retain and attract wonderful, diverse talent while closing the social neurogap between extroverts and introverts at work.

THE BRAIN-FRIENDLY INTERVIEW

Claude Silver, chief heart officer, VaynerMedia

Coaching. Team building. Performance maximization. These are just a few of the skills Claude Silver honed over three decades of leadership positions at major ad agencies, plus a track record of nurturing exceptional talent inside large-scale global teams. Today, Silver leverages her skills and experience in her unique position as VaynerMedia's first chief heart officer, working closely with founder Gary Vaynerchuk.

Friederike: How did you come to become chief heart officer?

Claude: My passion has always been coaching, facilitating, mentoring—really leaving people better than I find them. During my first year at VaynerMedia, Gary asked, "What do you want to do?" I said, "I only care about the heartbeat of this place; I only care about the people." Gary wanted someone he could trust to scale him and our culture, so we created the "Chief Heart Officer" role.

Friederike: You encourage people to be emotionally optimistic. What does that mean?

Claude: Emotional optimism is the opposite of toxic positivity. It's understanding that we all have emotions and lives before we come on-screen, or go to the office. We've taken the dog out, we've gone to the gym, maybe we got in a fight with our spouse. We have emotions that we then bring into the office.

I want people to have the liberty to feel their emotions, and I want people to also feel like they can regulate their emotions. And that's something we have to teach. You learn to use your emotions as data—to say, for example, "OK, I'm feeling triggered because I just had this fight with my spouse," and find a way to feel those feelings, and then be in control as much as you possibly can regarding how you want to go forward.

Friederike: Can you tell me more about "kind candor"?

Claude: We are a kind company. Gary and I want to cultivate a kind culture where people care about each other and want to do right by each other. They want to turn each other into champions and try to be the bigger person in every situation. We can assume that we're going into every conversation with this intention, and then we can give someone our honest observations.

I might say something like, "Hey, I think you could have given that presentation in a clearer way, and then the clients might have been more engaged, instead of looking down at their phones"—sharing my observation, rather than speaking as if I'm the judge and jury.

Friederike: I like that you used "could" instead of "should."

Claude: Yes! I want the person to understand that, as your manager, I only want the best for you. I only want you to grow. We are working together to get you to where you want to go. And I want my manager to get me wherever I want to go. That requires an enormous amount of trust.

Friederike: How are you handling getting people to return to the office?

Claude: All of our offices are open. It's not a requirement to be there. People in different geographies are responding differently. In London, everyone seems to go in on Mondays and Thursdays. In LA, the office is only open Tuesday, Wednesday, Thursday. In New York, it's open all the time. I'll go in tomorrow. I need to be in New York City, and I can get a lot done there.

We're open for hybrid and remote work. We trust that you will know what to do with your time and how to manage your time and your energy. If you don't, then hopefully, you will say something, and we'll help you. The idea is not "do whatever you want." It's "do whatever you want as long as you're productive."

Friederike: That is exactly my message for the brain-friendly workplace.

Claude: I worked in creative advertising agencies for years. I didn't think that you could be productive and do exceptional creative work at home. I was proved wrong within two weeks of us going home, which was fantastic and incredibly humbling.

Friederike: How do you handle onboarding, though? Doesn't that require learning from your more experienced colleagues?

Claude: We have a three-day orientation that every single new hire goes through, no matter where you're located and no matter your role. For those three days, new hires have hour-long sessions with subject-matter experts and with me. They're learning who we are, how we think about creative, media, and more.

We strongly encourage connectivity, as well. I will introduce new hires to other people all over the company, such as, "This is Jennifer. She loves archery and riding horses on the weekend and worked on the M account at Chase. Can you find fifteen minutes to chat with her over the next two weeks?"

As a new hire, you might meet thirty people in thirty days for fifteen-minute chats. You get to ask them, "How can I succeed at VaynerMedia? What should I do in my first ninety days?" Everyone from interns to C-suite employees does this. Interconnections develop, and a great deal of osmosis learning takes place.

Friederike: How would you describe your collaboration with Gary?

Claude: We have a very friendly, warm, and respectful relationship, and I think we're two sides of the same coin. We both come from a place of great belief and trust in people. We trust first. I've never met someone before I met Gary who does that. And we want the best for people; we take care of people. The bottom line for us is kindness. We expect people to be kind. My job is to help them express that kindness toward themselves and others in the organization.

9

What about the Children?

There is no greater insight into the future than recognizing . . . when we
save our children, we save ourselves.

—Margaret Mead

My friend Wendy was the most career-obsessed millennial I'd ever met. She
was a highly paid executive at a biomedical company who worked fourteen-
hour days and jetted around the world on iced coffee, jelly doughnuts, and no
sleep. When we met and became friends, we were both pregnant with our first
child. I couldn't wait to go on maternity leave; Wendy was planning to work
right up to her due date. She had already scheduled an overseas business trip
for three months after delivery.

A year after her baby was born, Wendy quit her beloved job. I was stunned.
She told me that her company's human resources department had been unwilling to make *any* allowances for the fact that she had a newborn. No flex-time,
no backup child care, nonstop international travel, and so on. In short, Wendy
had experienced the corporate head-in-the-sand approach to parenthood that
forces talented, ambitious women onto the mommy track—or out of their jobs.

Wendy's manager didn't believe employees were working hard enough if
they weren't stressed to the gills. Wendy was exhausted, running constantly
from meeting to meeting with no time to exercise or eat properly. Worse, she
felt guilt-ridden about the lack of time she was spending with her baby and
husband.

"Enough was enough," she told me. "I was miserable. The money and prestige simply weren't worth the toll my job was taking on my health and my family."

Wendy quit, but she didn't stop working. She founded a "sustainable bridal fashion" business that has become very successful. Wendy's not any less ambitious, and she doesn't necessarily work less. But she is her own boss and sets her own schedule, one that works for her family. Like many mothers I know, including myself, Wendy left corporate life and created her own brain-friendly workplace, focused on autonomy and outcome.

"I'm so much happier," she reports today. "I love connecting with my customers and being able to set my own hours. I'm every bit as productive, but now I can take far better care of myself and my family."

❧

Mental Break—The United States currently requires companies with fifty or more employees to offer twelve weeks of unpaid maternity leave. In contrast, Canadians receive 55 percent of their pay for seventeen weeks of maternity leave, and either parent can take an additional thirty-five weeks unpaid. Swedish parents get sixty weeks at 80 percent of their pay.[1]

❧

HOW THE CHILD-FREE WORKPLACE HAS FAILED

I know many Wendys, and I bet you do, too. The workplace that provides little to no parental leave and zero flexibility is a failed experiment that forces parents to choose between their careers and their children. If we genuinely want to increase gender and thought diversity in the workplace, we have to stop denying this reality. If companies want to attract and retain top talent, then our workplaces must become part of the village we need to raise our children.

I believe the child-free workplace also has a negative impact on neurosignature diversity. Men and women with high-estrogen neurosignatures are more relationship oriented. They're more likely to drop out of workplaces that fail to provide family leave, flex-time options, and other benefits that support their home lives.

Frankly, we all deserve to have both careers and fulfilling personal lives, whether or not we're raising children. Some people have children. Others have pets that are their children. Some care for older relatives. Others need to help a partner who is experiencing a serious illness. All of us deserve to work, yet still enjoy our lives. In this chapter, we'll explore how the brain-friendly workplace can better support our home lives in exchange for happier, more productive employees and greater talent retention and diversity.

∼❧∼

The workplace that provides little to no parental leave and zero flexibility is a failed experiment that forces parents to choose between their careers and their children.

∼❧∼

THE PINK ELEPHANT IN THE ROOM

Currently, companies are losing the drive, innovation, and entrepreneurial spirit that women like Wendy have in spades. The impact on women's mental health of juggling work and family is also clear. Women in developed countries

are 75 percent more likely than men to suffer from depression and 60 percent more likely to suffer from anxiety.[2] Women in developed countries report experiencing more neuroticism—feelings of anxiety, worry, and guilt—than women in less-developed countries.[3]

I think of the female attorney for an investment bank who told me, "I work twelve-hour days and get home around 10 p.m. All I have the energy to do is pack my daughter's lunch for the next day. Yes, we can afford private schools and family vacations in Tuscany, but I feel guilty all the time about how much of my kids' lives I'm missing."

Guilt is something all working mothers experience—but we don't talk about it. It's the pink elephant in the room. So, let's talk about it. Chronic guilt has serious mental and physical health consequences. It can cause insomnia, loss of appetite, and even depression. Guilt may also weaken the immune system. Researchers found lower levels of the illness-fighting blood protein IgA in subjects who were experiencing guilt.[4]

～❦～

Mind Bender—Boys and girls receive strong signals about gender-specific expectations that, when not fulfilled, can provoke guilt. "Women build self-esteem through relationships," says Mary Ann Bauman, MD, author of *Fight Fatigue: Six Simple Steps to Maximize Your Energy*. "As women, we have to make sure no one thinks we're being selfish," Bauman explains. "It causes us to absolutely overextend ourselves." Men, in contrast, Bauman notes, "learn to build self-esteem through their accomplishments."[5]

～❦～

ROLE MODELS?

Women are bombarded with wildly unrealistic female "role models." Maybe you heard on the news about French justice minister Rachida Dati, who returned to work five days after delivering her baby.[6] Or BeautyBio founder Jamie O'Banion, who expounded on *The Skinny Confidential* podcast about being a CEO mom. O'Banion described rising at 5 a.m. to get her children ready for school, followed by carpooling. She said she attends her first meeting at 8:30 a.m., works until 4 p.m., and then picks up her children. Once the children are in bed, O'Banion tackles her e-mails, from 8 p.m. until 1 a.m.[7]

While I was listening, I was doing math in my head. Wait, this woman sleeps four hours per night? Is she superhuman? If O'Banion has a high-dopamine/testosterone neurosignature, then she can handle an extreme-stress schedule better than the rest of us, but this lack of sleep is still terrible for her health and performance. Are working parents really supposed to aspire to this lifestyle?

⌁

Mind Bender—The American College of Obstetricians and Gynecologists (ACOG) recommends that women take at least six weeks off work following childbirth. According to the advocacy group Paid Leave US (PL+US), one in four women in the United States returns to work just two weeks after giving birth.[8]

⌁

THE KIDS ARE (NOT) ALL RIGHT

What about the children? When corporations demand long hours and extensive travel from employees, has anyone checked on what that means for their children? In 2020, UNICEF released a study on "life satisfaction" among children in thirty-eight developed countries. Children in the United States ranked thirty-sixth, third from bottom. Here are some disturbing quotes from this UNICEF report:[9]

> In 12 of 41 developed countries, less than 75 percent of children aged 15 have high life satisfaction.
> Across the set of rich countries . . . suicide is one of the most common causes of death for adolescents aged 15 to 19.
> In 10 countries, more than one in three children is overweight or obese. The number of obese children (aged 5–19) worldwide is expected to grow from 158 million to 250 million by 2030.

Clearly, the kids are not all right. The UNICEF report posited that the primary reason is "no good quality of relationships."[10] Children in developed nations, where most parents work outside the home, reported feeling lonely, isolated, and unhappy. If we do not begin to integrate family life and work, we will continue to raise miserable children.

⌁

Mental Break—In 2020, ByteDance—the company behind TikTok—began selling the Dali Smart Lamp. It uses AI to help kids do their homework and includes a 5G camera that enables parents to supervise remotely. The lamp is pulling in $1.5 million per month in revenue, fueled by sales to China's time-starved working parents. This has kicked off a billion-dollar product war dubbed the "War of a Thousand Lamps," as other companies dive into the new "edutech" category.[11]

⤙⤚

YOUR CHILD'S FAVORITE DRUG

Tech companies know that exhausted working parents find it hard to resist using smartphones and tablets to entertain their children. Drug use among teenagers has declined in the United States—but phone use has risen dramatically. American teenagers average nine hours per day on the internet.[12] The phone is your child's favorite drug, and it's very bad for a developing brain.

A new fMRI study on adolescents found that teenagers who spend lots of time online show altered brain functions—their brains are literally addicted. The study's authors add that "increases in depressive and suicide-related symptoms among United States adolescents have been recently linked to increased use of smartphones."[13]

Nonetheless, Facebook was eagerly developing Instagram Kids, targeted at children under thirteen, when whistleblower Frances Haugen testified before the U.S. Congress in October 2021. Haugen provided reams of documents showing that Facebook knows its products are harmful to the mental health of teens and preteens.

⤙⤚

Brain Boost—Children raised in countries that guarantee more maternity leave have better health outcomes. Every extra week in guaranteed maternity leave correlates with a 2 to 3 percent decline in infant deaths.[14]

⤙⤚

SOCIAL NETWORKS ADDICTION

BIG TECH KNOWS ITS PRODUCTS ARE ADDICTIVE

In 2018, Apple CEO Tim Cook said to a college audience, "I don't have a kid, but I have a nephew that I put some boundaries on. I don't want him on a social network."[15] Let that sink in for a moment.

Cook knows that we get an addictive dopamine rush every time we open our social media and see those red notifications. Your brain's dopamine system reacts strongly to two things: novelty and intermittent reinforcement. A 2021 study in *Nature* analyzed more than one million posts from four thousand plus individuals on multiple social platforms. The researchers found that it's the intermittent nature of reactions to your post that compels you to check and recheck your notifications.[16]

This is because your dopamine system is triggered by *anticipation* of reward. If you *get* the reward, you feel a surge of pleasure, followed by a feeling of emptiness that motivates your brain to seek out that dopamine trigger again. The same cycle of anticipation and reward that drives a drug addict to seek a fix is triggering you to compulsively check your social media.

In 2017, founding Facebook president Sean Parker, who left the company in 2005, unloaded on the social media giant with unprecedented honesty. Parker told *Axios*, "It was all about: 'how do we consume as much of your time and conscious attention as possible?' That means we need to give you a little dopamine hit every once in a while, because someone liked or commented on a photo or a post. That's going to get you to contribute more content. It's a social-validation feedback loop . . . exactly the kind of thing a hacker like myself would come up with, because you're exploiting a vulnerability in human psychology."

Parker summed things up ominously when he said, "God only knows what it's doing to our children's brains."[17]

THE VIDEO GAME HIJACK

I don't let my children play video games. Here's why: Video games hijack your brain's dopamine system. They are deliberately designed to be as addictive as any drug that provides your brain with a rush of dopamine.

Yes, there are many smart, well-adjusted gamers, and video games may even improve certain brain functions. But the frontal lobes of children and teens are still developing, meaning that they lack judgment and restraint. Worse, once a child is regularly triggering dopamine blasts with an exciting, unpredictable experience such as gaming, the real world can seem blah. This can lead to feelings of depression.

I won't expose my children to the intense rush that video games provide any more than I would expose them to heroin or cocaine. I want them to enjoy playing outdoors with their friends in the real world, not get hooked on a dopamine-triggering addiction.

Sometimes after I give a keynote, a parent will confide in me privately about a child's depression or anxiety. The first question I always ask is, "How does he spend his free time?" Usually, the child is cranking away on video games and social media.

I always suggest cutting his gaming and phone time to zero and getting him outdoors every day for a hike or game. Invariably, the parent will tell me later that—after some screaming fights—the child is feeling much better.

My friend Angelica Renhuvud is a member of the Sami indigenous people of northern Scandinavia. The Sami herd reindeer, and Angelica grew up close to nature. "My children thrive being outdoors," she says. "I can see clearly on the days we don't get outside how they get wired up and start picking more fights and don't sleep as well. When they get to run around outdoors, they are much calmer, happier, and more content."

THE PROBLEM WITH MONOPARENTING

"It takes a village to raise a child," the proverb says. Yet, in Western culture, a misunderstanding of attachment parenting has taken hold that I call "monoparenting."

In the 1930s, British psychologist John Bowlby developed his theory that a secure attachment to one empathetic caregiver is essential for a child's well-being. I agree fully with Bowlby's extensive studies that secure attachment is key to a child's healthy development. Somehow, though, it's been forgotten that Bowlby also emphasized the importance of social networks and multiple caregivers in raising children. Western mothers who believe in attachment parenting, but aren't aware of this, can feel very guilty about leaving their children with other caregivers.

Monoparenting is a misguided view of child rearing, in my opinion, and it's rough on working parents. It makes them feel bad about accepting support outside the nuclear family, or having any expectations that the workplace should be part of their "village."

MONOPARENTING

INTENSIVE PARENTING INTENSIFIES THE PROBLEM

Recently, an even more demanding form of parenting called "intensive parenting" has taken hold in the United States. Intensive parenting involves scheduling children for multiple extracurricular activities and relentlessly advocating for them with schools and other institutions.

"I would describe it as the dominant cultural model of parenting in the US right now." Sociology professor Patrick Ishizuka told the BBC in 2020. He added that intensive parenting is sweeping European nations as well.[18]

As Canadian-American psychologist Steven Pinker has observed, "In contemporary middle-class American culture, parenting is seen as an awesome responsibility, an unforgiving vigil to keep the helpless infant from falling behind in the great race of life. And that race goes to the smartest, the most competitive, the most independent."[19] Sadly, we are raising our children to compete in the extreme-stress workplaces that we have experienced. I would argue, instead, that we need to demand that the workplace changes for the better.

ALLOPARENTING AROUND THE WORLD

In most indigenous cultures, children are raised by many people. This is called alloparenting, from the Greek word *allo*, which means "other." Alloparenting is child care provided by parents, friends, and relatives. It is a universal human behavior that has shaped our evolutionary history and is still important in many cultures today.

Remember, child-free workplaces are a relatively recent development in human history. They didn't become dominant until the early 1900s. For around 99.99 percent of human history, we worked far fewer hours, and work and family life were well integrated. We shared parenting duties with other members of our villages, clans, or tribes.

In *Our Babies, Ourselves: How Biology and Culture Shape the Way We Parent*, Meredith Small relates that in the Efé pygmy society, an infant spends around 50 percent of its first four months being cared for by adults other than its mother. A baby typically is nursed by several women who are lactating. This multifaceted bond produces a tight network of social relationships.[20]

Canadian anthropologist Richard B. Lee studied the !Kung San people of Botswana, one of the last remaining hunter-gatherer tribes. In *Kalahari Hunter-Gatherers: Studies of the !Kung San and Their Neighbors*, Lee describes a society in which children grow up loved by their parents and multiple caregivers. As children get older, they move into mixed age groups. Older siblings and relatives serve as their teachers. By the age of four, the transition to this multiage group is complete.[21]

I previously mentioned Angelica Renhuvud, a Sami raised in Sweden. She tells me that the Sami people practice alloparenting and use multiage groups to take care of children. "Everybody helps out," Renhuvud says. "You get a lot of responsibilities early on. I was twelve years old the first summer I took care of my two-year-old cousin. Everybody is needed, and I love how we were raised. It made us see how important we are for the community to work, even when you're just a child."

I'd love to see Western culture move away from the isolation and stress of monoparenting toward "modern alloparenting." And let's include the brain-friendly workplace as part of the village we use to raise our children.

ALLOPARENTING

WHAT ABOUT THE DADS?

Working from home has made some dads less willing to return to sacrificing fatherhood on the altar of the extreme-stress workplace. In December 2021, actor Ryan Reynolds told *People* that he was taking a break from acting. "I don't want to miss this time with my kids," Reynolds said. He explained that shooting a movie requires "incredibly long hours" away from his family. Of life during lockdown with wife Blake Lively and their three daughters, Reynolds said, "I certainly don't miss Zoom school, but it was lovely to have that insight and visibility into my kids' real daily lives." Now, Reynolds adds, "I really enjoy being a present dad."[22]

Only 5 percent of American dads take at least two weeks of parental leave, according to research by Ball State sociology professor Richard Petts. "Workplaces need to become more supportive of men taking leave," Petts argues, "as evidence suggests that offering and using paid leave increases worker productivity and loyalty."[23]

The average paternity leave in the United States is one week. In comparison, paternity leave in the European Union averages 6.3 weeks. In Germany, where I live, more men are taking parental leave than ever before.[24] Yet, President Joe Biden's transportation secretary Pete Buttigieg was pilloried by some media outlets for taking four weeks of paid parental leave upon the birth of his twins.

✥

Brain Boost—In March 2021, McKinsey published research it had conducted across ten countries regarding paternity leave. Dads who took parental leave reported stronger bonds with their children and improved relationships with their partners. Household finances improved because maternal income rose approximately 7 percent for each month that a child's father spent at home on paternity leave. McKinsey now recommends that companies provide the same leave benefits to men as to women.[25]

✥

ESG RATINGS DON'T INCLUDE FAMILY-FRIENDLY PROGRAMS

I wish I could share with you myriad thrilling examples of corporations developing wonderful programs to support all neurosignatures in our quest to have great careers *and* happy home lives. Although some companies are getting on board, the concept of the workplace as part of our "village" is not yet institutionalized in a meaningful way.

Nearly every major company has a women diversity initiative, a racial justice initiative, sustainability programs, and LGBTQ+ programs. These companies participate in annual environmental, social, governance (ESG) ratings to measure their progress. This motivates companies to continue to invest in these programs in order to improve their ratings. Unfortunately, initiatives that support working families aren't included in these ratings, so there's little incentive to pour resources into them.

Some countries are leading the way, though. Sweden, Norway, and Denmark, for example, have established policies aimed at reconciling work with family life and increasing the well-being of children. These policies include guaranteed parental leave, free universal preschool, and a monthly allowance for children that parents may use to offset child-care costs. This incentivizes companies in these countries to provide paid parental leave and adopt family-friendly practices such as shorter workdays and flexible work options.

⚜

Brain Food—I asked Boston Consulting Group (BCG) Chief Recruiting/Talent Officer Amber Grewal how she maintains her glowing health, despite her demanding schedule.

"I focus on gut health," Grewal replied, "as the gut is the second brain. I like to get probiotics first thing in the morning by eating natural Greek yogurt." She also drinks plenty of water, noting, "My goal is to drink thirty-three ounces of water before 8 a.m. and ninety ounces total for the day."

⚜

SIX WAYS THE BRAIN-FRIENDLY WORKPLACE CAN SUPPORT HOME LIFE

Here are six ways brain-friendly workplaces can help us enjoy our home lives with less guilt and fatigue. In turn, companies will benefit from greater talent retention, gender and neurosignature diversity, and productivity.

Provide Paid Parental Leave

Pregnancy, childbirth, and breast-feeding are physically demanding, and it takes about six months after giving birth for a woman's hormones to return to pre-pregnancy levels. The effects of pregnancy on the brain have largely gone unstudied (surprise), but in 2016 researchers produced the first evidence that pregnancy causes substantial brain changes, including a gray-matter reduction that lasted for at least two years—the length of the study.[26] Further research needs to be done on how long-lasting these changes actually are. In addition, separating children from their mothers soon after birth can saddle kids with neurobiological vulnerabilities that last into adulthood.[27]

Despite the clear science about these impacts, when I was pregnant with my first child, my boss tried to pressure me into skipping the paid maternity leave to which my family was entitled. Most working moms in Germany take around one year of the fourteen months of paid parental leave guaranteed to families by law.

"I don't know any women who actually do that," my boss snapped. Naturally, he had a stay-at-home wife taking care of his children.

The brain-friendly workplace must acknowledge the undeniable facts about pregnancy and childbirth and provide significant paid leave for working parents. In Sweden, for example, parents are entitled to 480 days of paid parental leave when a child is born or adopted. Each parent is entitled to 240 of those days, and single parents get 480 days.

Focus on Outcomes

As Stephan Aarstol of Tower Paddle Boards explained in chapter 3, he was motivated to try the five-hour workday at his company so he could spend more time with his son. Brain-friendly companies can support our home lives by shortening the hours we spend at work. Companies should focus on setting goals and measuring outcomes, rather than counting how many hours people spend at work.

The Netherlands is one of the world's most productive nations and has the world's shortest workweek, averaging twenty-nine hours per week. Denmark consistently ranks in the top five or the world's most productive nations, with a full-time workweek of thirty-seven hours.[28]

Recently the Danish town of Odsherred instituted a four-day workweek for the city's three-hundred-person staff. In December 2021, the UAE announced that it will transition all federal employees to a 4.5-day workweek. The government described the shortened week as an effort to "boost productivity and improve work-life balance."[29]

Be Flexible

The lockdowns that forced so many people to work from home had one silver lining: Employees could finally prove to their employers that they did not need to be at the office under constant supervision to be highly productive. Many are refusing to return to "the way things were." The hybrid work world in which we now find ourselves lends itself beautifully to being able to commute less as well. This gift of hours no longer spent in transit is a boon to our home lives. Let's not be too quick to return it.

The brain-friendly workplace provides flexible work hours and more autonomy regarding when and where employees work. Companies such as Patagonia and SAP are already on board, encouraging employees to set their own schedules and work at home several days a week. A diverse and rapidly growing number of companies, including ADP, Airbnb, Raytheon, American Express, and BCG, are following suit. Remote and flexible work options are the future, benefiting both employees and businesses.

Offer Child Care Assistance

As the *Harvard Business Review* noted in 2021, "Childcare Is a Business Issue." The *HBR* reported, "One third of the U.S. workforce, an estimated 50 million workers, has a child under 14 in their household." Yet, "data shows that the United States' gross domestic product could be 5 percent higher if women participated in the workforce at the same rate as men. Given these economic realities, the question we pose is: Why is childcare still an employee issue and not a business issue?"[30]

Goldman Sachs opened its first on-site "backup" child-care center in its New York City headquarters in 1993. It has since expanded this service to Goldman Sachs offices around the world and provides day care at some offices. More companies need to provide on-site day care, not merely backup care for parents to use when child-care arrangements fall through.

Imagine being able to visit your child during your lunch break. How much saner would it be to have child care at work, instead of having to drive all over town dropping off your children at different day-care centers?

Provide Concierge Services

When working full-time, it can be difficult to find time for chores such as picking up dry cleaning or hiring a dog walker. Increasingly, companies such as Accenture, American Express, EY (Ernst & Young), and Capital One

Finance are providing concierge services that help employees take care of these personal tasks.[31]

Concierge services at work may help female employees in particular to cope with the "mental load" that falls disproportionately on women in their families. Mental load refers to the invisible, unpaid overseeing of the mundane details of family life, such as deciding when it's time to shop for groceries or organizing doctor appointments for the children.

Even as men take on more household responsibilities, psychologist Lucia Ciciolla notes, "Women are recognizing that they still hold the mental burden of the household even if others share in the physical work, and that mental burden takes a toll."[32] Companies that want to retain female talent should provide employees with useful concierge services they need to run their lives—before they, like Wendy, leave to start their own companies.

Supply Co-Working Spaces Near Homes

After working from home, there's a new demand among employees for shorter commutes. "It would take a couple more zeroes on my paycheck to get me back to commuting," health-care salesman Paul Doran told the *New York Times* for "Why Co-Working Spaces Are Betting on the Suburbs." Doran needed somewhere to meet with clients, however, so his employer enabled him to join the co-working space Daybase near his home.[33]

Co-working spaces are proliferating to meet this demand, and their emergence in residential neighborhoods is a trend I applaud mightily. Anything that saves employees hours of commuting improves their ability to get adequate rest, exercise, and time with their children. As companies start to accept that hybrid work is here to stay, placing co-working hubs closer to our homes will play a key role in a more brain-friendly future for work.

THE BRAIN-FRIENDLY INTERVIEW

Amber Grewal, managing director and partner, chief recruiting/talent officer, Boston Consulting Group (BCG)

I met Amber after I delivered a keynote at BCG Poptech 2.0. I was struck by her radiant energy and obvious enthusiasm for exploring the future of work, including creative new ways to help BCG employees reach their full potential.

Grewal is responsible for redefining, augmenting, and future-proofing BCG's human capital strategy. She joined BCG in January 2020, bringing twenty years of experience in the art and science of attracting, developing, and advancing talent. Amber was formerly chief talent officer at Intel and held senior leadership roles at IBM, GE, Microsoft, and KPMG. She serves as a board member for the IoT Consortium, the NOVA Workforce Board, and Eightfold A.I.

Friederike: What are some BCG programs that help employees develop a healthy work/life balance?

Amber: In 2014, BCG formalized our approach to flexible working with multiple programs.

My personal favorites include FlexiTime and FlexiLeave.

FlexiTime offers flexibility in day-to-day working arrangements so people can spend time with family/loved ones. Some employees use FlexiTime to take a full day off each week; others take two half-days. Still others take reduced hours each workday.

Critically, employees who opt for FlexiTime don't lose ground in terms of their career track. For our consultants, for example, promotion is linked to tenure in their roles, and a consultant who works at 80 percent capacity still receives 90 percent credit toward BCG tenure.

The FlexiLeave program allows our consulting teams to take up to two months' leave of absence—for any reason—while retaining their positions and benefits. I have a few people on my team who have taken advantage of both these programs. They loved having the option to flex their work schedules.

BCG was at the forefront of this, and the company continues to develop more offerings to support our employees with flexibility. We are constantly looking for what could make our employees thrive and feel supported. We engage employees at all levels—and across business units, functions, and regions—to set a collective vision for how our policies should function.

Friederike: Does BCG have any initiatives that encourage employees take better care of their physical and mental health?

Amber: Yes, built upon our 5Rs: reinforcing, recognizing, reconnecting, recharging our teams, and reimagining the future. The majority of our ninety-plus office locations have access to a variety of amazing experiences, such as free subscriptions to apps and services for eating, mediation, exercise, and more. Headspace, for example, is a mindfulness app providing personalized skills and access to world-class experts.

Friederike: What is your secret to being such a likable, yet effective leader?

Amber: I strive to be relatable and demonstrate that I am genuinely interested by listening. But what matters most as a leader is that you're exceptional at what you do, and you empower your team to be the best version of themselves. Success depends on your ability to help other people unlock their potential. No matter how high you climb in your career, you cannot succeed alone. In fact, the higher you climb, the more your success depends on the ability to make other people successful.

The best leaders are decisive, proactive, knowledgable, fair, and willing to make decisions that favor long-term goals over short-term popularity. Ultimately, having a vision and the courage to take risks is far more important than being likable.

Friederike: You have a very demanding career, including lots of global travel. Are there any "life hacks" you use to stay healthy and energized?

Amber: Rest, recovery, and reflection play a critical part of my overall well-being. My day starts early in the morning, so I commit to going to bed early. I put my phone on "do not disturb." Then, as part of my nightly routine of reflection, I ask myself five questions:

1. What have I accomplished today?
2. What do I want to let go of before I go to sleep?
3. What do I want to accomplish tomorrow?
4. How do I want to feel tomorrow?
5. How will I start my day on the right track?

This helps me let go of any lingering concerns and set the right intentions for the following day.

I start my morning with gratitude and yoga. I have a yoga mat right by my bed, and even if I'm only able to practice for a few minutes, I find it helps me feel energized. Before turning to my phone or checking e-mail, I meditate for ten to fifteen minutes. This allows me to get centered and mentally ready to start a new day with a focused mind.

10

Group Flow

The Antidote to Groupthink

We have met the enemy and he is us.

—Walt Kelly

Not long ago, I attended a meeting where the executives were discussing how badly they needed to add a female or black executive to their white, all-male team.

"Yes!" a member cried. "Let's find a black woman. Let's just make sure she thinks like us."

That's not how you build thought-diverse leadership, people. It's how you populate your company with folks who think alike. Conflicts may be minimized, but so will inspiration, innovation, creativity, and growth. Teams will become mired in groupthink quicksand.

Groupthink takes over when a group of people prioritizes harmony and conformity over critical thinking and alternate viewpoints. Groupthink squelches innovation. It results in irrational and dysfunctional decision making. The pervasive groupthink that infected the Nazi regime during World War II and enabled the Holocaust is one of history's most extreme and horrific examples.

In the workplace, groupthink leads to mediocrity, as people who want to fit in become hesitant to share any "outside-the-box" ideas with their teams. Creativity is strangled by the group's drive toward social conformity.

Groupthink is a phenomenon that occurs when the desire for group consensus overrides the members' willingness to present alternative ideas, critique each other's ideas, or express contrarian opinions.

⌘

I wanted to conclude with this chapter for one simple reason: You can put all the thought diversity in the world in place at your workplace. It will be useless unless your team leaders understand how to spot and defuse groupthink. Here's the good news: Once you understand the underlying mechanisms of groupthink, you'll see it clearly, in many situations. In this chapter, we'll explore the pitfalls of groupthink and how to avoid it. You'll also discover how brain-friendly workplaces are promoting group flow instead.

GROUP FLOW IS GROOVY

Remember the flow state from chapter 4, "Fun, Fear, and Focus"? Now, think about a time when you were working with a group and you were all sparking ideas off each other. Didn't that feel exciting and wonderful? That's group flow—the magical moment when group members feel "in the zone" and are experiencing flow together.

When I need inspiration to remind me what group flow feels like, I think of a concert by a great rock band. The band members transcend their individual selves while in performance, reaching new creative heights collectively and inspiring ecstasy in their listeners. But is this just an illusion, or could we actually see group flow in action in the brain?

In 2021, researchers used EEGs to measure the brain activity of ten teams while they played music video games together. For the first time, researchers could clearly see when a team was experiencing group flow by looking at the members' brain waves. The scientists discovered that brain waves synced up strongly across team members when a team was experiencing flow. Team members also showed increased beta and gamma waves in their middle temporal cortices when the team was in flow. This creates a highly pleasurable brain state—even better than what we experience as individuals during solo flow.[1]

⌘

Mental Break—At Pixar Animation Studios, directors and producers show their work daily, with a guarantee of no repercussions from any "negative" feedback. Everyone, including crew members, is encouraged to offer candid feedback. Dissenting opinions and alternative viewpoints are welcome—the goal is to spark more creative ideas. Daily back-and-forth discussions like these help team members get comfortable being honest with each other and sharing even their zaniest ideas. This creative free-for-all environment leads naturally to group flow.

GROUPTHINK IS NATURAL . . . AND CAN BE DEADLY

Groupthink, on the other hand, stems from our strong human desire to belong and conform. The problem is that groupthink overwhelms critical thinking and good judgment. When a team is mired in groupthink, people

- hesitate to share new ideas,
- feel anxious about sharing candid feedback, and
- look to the group leader for signals regarding how to think and behave.

The 1941 bombing of the Pearl Harbor naval base in Honolulu by Japanese warplanes is considered a classic example of groupthink. Although intelligence officers in Washington, D.C., had intercepted Japanese messages concerning a possible attack on American forces in the Pacific Ocean, U.S. Navy command in Hawaii did not take these intelligence warnings seriously. Admiral Husband E. Kimmel, commander in chief of the Pacific Fleet, scoffed at the prospect of a Japanese attack. His team strongly believed that Japan would never dare attack the United States.

Instead of preparing for attack, Kimmel and his team rationalized why it was a ridiculous thing to even consider. Even when 353 Japanese warplanes appeared overhead on December 7, 1941, American servicemen at the base initially refused to believe that they were under attack. According to eyewitnesses, when told that the Japanese were attacking, one soldier retorted sarcastically, "So are the Germans."[2] The groupthink at Pearl Harbor had deadly consequences—2,403 Americans and 129 Japanese were killed in the biggest air battle the United States has ever seen.[3]

Groupthink may not have such dire consequences at your job, but it can still be a significant drag on performance. Imagine that four mutual fund managers at an investment firm meet weekly to discuss investing strategies and share their top picks for the funds they each manage. These managers have become pals, often meeting for cocktails and dinners with their spouses.

During one meeting, Jerry announces that he plans to buy a large chunk of shares of a company with strong fundamentals that he thinks is undervalued. "This one's a winner," he declares.

Naturally, Jerry's buddies feel a strong urge to be supportive of his decision. "Sounds great," Dave chimes in.

"Tell me more," Karen cries.

Nobody genuinely challenges Jerry's stock pick. Instead, together, the managers conduct a superficial analysis of the company. They all decide to make significant investments in it for their funds. A month later, the company's stock tanks. The fund managers were victims of groupthink, and so were their investors.

YOU MAY THINK YOU'RE IMMUNE TO THE STUFF

You may think you're immune to groupthink, but a fascinating 2021 neuroscience experiment reported in *Nature* illustrates just how vulnerable human beings are to this phenomenon.[4]

Imagine that you're invited to score the trustworthiness of strangers by looking at their faces. After you turn in your scores, the researcher shows you how other people participating in this experiment assessed the trustworthiness of these same strangers. You are then given the opportunity to change your scores. Will you do it?

In 50 percent of the trials, the people who participated in this experiment at HSE University changed their opinion. They revised their scores to bring them more in line with what the other subjects believed about the trustworthiness of the strangers.

Here's where things really get weird. This experiment was the first time that researchers used magnetoencephalographic (MEG) source imaging to observe long-term neural correlates of social conformity occurring in real time in the brain. They saw astounding evidence of why we're so vulnerable to groupthink. Whenever subjects adjusted their scores to bring them in line with how other participants assessed the strangers, the subjects' brain pleasure centers lit up like pinball machines.

"Our study shows the dramatic influence of others' opinion on how we perceive information," HSE professor Vasily Klucharev explained. "We live in social groups and automatically adjust our opinions to that of the majority, and the opinion of our peers can change the way our brain processes information for a relatively long time."[5]

Human beings love feeling part of a group. When you agree with the majority of people around you, your brain lights up in pleasure. But when you disagree? Your brain gets an "error" signal. You feel uncomfortable. You feel internal pressure to "fix" this "mistake." This is why people subconsciously adapt their opinions to fit in with a group. We are wired to fear conflict and want to resolve it to reduce this discomfort.

⤚⤙

Mind Bender—During the HSE University study, the scientists noticed that the subjects didn't realize that they were changing their minds to align more closely with a group consensus. Instead, the subjects convinced themselves that they fully believed their revised opinion about the trustworthiness of a stranger's face. The researchers noticed activity in the superior parietal cortex, where we store long-term memories. This indicates that when we change our opinions to fit in with a group, those changes are likely to stick.[6]

⤚⤙

NEUROSIGNATURE DIVERSITY AND GROUPTHINK

The question is, how do we combat the dangers of groupthink at work? I know what you're thinking: *Here's where Friederike extols the virtues of neurosignature diversity yet again.* Well, you're right . . . and you're wrong.

Adding just one person with a high-estrogen neurosignature to a team of ten people with high-testosterone neurosignatures won't make a dent in the team's groupthink. When you balance your teams with multiple neurosignatures, now you have a shot. The entire culture of the group may begin to shift toward being open to fresh ideas.

Even so, the human desire for social conformity will still exert subconscious pressure . . . unless you know how to recognize and combat it. Neurosignature diversity is a very important first step, but it alone is not enough to combat groupthink. Let's dig deeper into how to recognize and short-circuit groupthink.

BUCKLE UP FOR A THOUGHT-DIVERSE RIDE

Neurosignature diversity is a smart first step toward combating groupthink. If you do create or join a thought-diverse team, though, buckle your seat belt.

A team of people with different neurosignatures will be lively and inspiring—
and potentially more combative than a team of people who all think the same.
At times this will be a bumpy ride.

One easy way to reduce conflict on a neurosignature-diverse team is to teach
team members about the benefits of thought diversity. If team members learn
about the benefits of both linear and lateral thinking, for example, they will be
less likely to become frustrated with each other. Similarly, if everybody learns
about introversion and extroversion, this will help the introverts and extroverts
on a team to appreciate each other's strengths.

STATUS-SEEKING AND LOYALTY CAUSE GROUPTHINK

When assembling a team, beware of your natural human tendency to seek out
people you believe will be loyal to you and your point of view. Keep an eye out
for status seekers, as well. Both loyalty and status-seeking lead to groupthink.

I'm currently experiencing dreadful groupthink as a member of a think
tank composed of experts from many different fields. A variety of high-status
business people, government officials, artists, scientists, and environmentalists
participate in this group.

You would expect this diverse team to be productive and innovative, but I have rarely experienced a team so narrow-minded and homogenous in its thinking. Our meetings make me cringe. The leaders seem to be intoxicated by their power and grandeur. Whenever I attempt to share an alternate viewpoint, they stare at me like I'm an alien. Anyone who raises an objection or a difference of opinion is shut down aggressively by members seeking to demonstrate their loyalty to the leaders and align with them to bolster their status. Dissent is nipped in the bud.

On paper we look like a thought-diverse team. In truth, we were assembled because the organizers wanted to attain specific predetermined goals. Consulting our think tank makes it *look* as if there has been diverse discussion. Sadly, this often happens when government officials or corporate bigwigs create advisory boards. They appoint "experts" they believe are both loyal and status-seeking. That's how the organizers get their programs rubber-stamped.

HOW TO RECOGNIZE GROUPTHINK

How can you tell whether a team is finding genuine agreement and harmony or is mired in groupthink? The term originally was coined by Yale professor Irving Janis in his 1982 book *Groupthink*. Below, I have paraphrased Janis's eight "symptoms of groupthink."[7] See if you can spot the mistakes made by the admirals who failed to defend Pearl Harbor, our four mutual fund managers, or the think tank I described. Do any of these resonate with your experience?

1. **Invulnerability**—An illusion of invulnerability encourages the group to be excessively optimistic and take abnormal risks.
2. **Rationale**—Members rationalize away negative information that could cause the group to reconsider its assumptions.
3. **Morality**—Members believe unquestioningly in the morality of the group.
4. **Stereotypes**—Members share and amplify negative stereotyping of their "enemies."
5. **Pressure**—Members pressure any individual who voices concern or doubt about the group's shared views.
6. **Self-Censorship**—Members censor themselves, keeping doubts or concerns to themselves.
7. **Illusion of Unanimity**—Because members self-censor, an illusion develops that the majority view the group expressed is unanimous.

8. **Mind Guards**—Members protect the group and its leader from information that may contradict the group's views.

Groupthink Quick Test

Want a quicker way to spot groupthink? Just look for these two factors:

1. **Hubris**—This high level of arrogance is a common by-product of power and status. As *Brain Rules* author John Medina tells me about power, "We're no longer living on the slopes of the Ngorongoro Crater, yet our brain still thinks we are. So, the instant you get power, you begin to feel a sense of self-impunity."
2. **Dissent Intolerance**—The more eagerly members of a group attack dissenters, the more likely it is that groupthink has taken hold. Shutting down dissenting opinions is a sure sign that a group has lost the ability to entertain alternate points of view.

DISSENTERS CREATE CHANGE

Why should you care about groupthink? Isn't it better if we all just get along?

Well, historically dissenters change the world for the better. Astronomer and physicist Galileo Galilei, in the face of enormous pressure, stubbornly maintained his conviction that the earth circled around the sun. For his "heresy," Galileo was sentenced by the Roman Catholic Church to life imprisonment at his home in 1633. It took another hundred years for Galileo's breakthrough to be widely accepted and 359 years for the Catholic Church to admit he was right.

Sigmund Freud was derided when he started developing his theories about personality development, yet became the founding father of psychotherapy. Suffragette Elizabeth Cady Stanton demanded a women's right to vote in 1848, when even many suffragettes thought that was too radical a concept. Civil rights leader Martin Luther King Jr. is revered today; yet, in 1968, when King was assassinated, 75 percent of Americans polled disapproved of King's nonviolent protests against racism, the Vietnam War, and economic inequality.[8]

DISSENT SPARKS INNOVATION

When businesses are disrupted by shifts in technology, companies stuck in groupthink have a tough time coping. Eastman Kodak invented the first digital camera back in 1975, yet held back from investing in digital photography for fear of hurting Kodak's lucrative film business. Kodak did capture 90 percent of the photographic film market in the United States, but by January 2012, the company had to file for Chapter 11 bankruptcy protection. Analysts have blamed Kodak's stodgy, inflexible managers and their aversion to change for the company's failure to adapt and innovate.[9] Sounds like groupthink to me.

Kodak's primary competitor, Fujifilm, faced the same nightmare. But Fujifilm's management team proved more willing to get creative. Fujifilm elected a new CEO, Shigetaka Komori, who went into crisis mode. Komori details how the company dramatically retooled in his book *Innovating Out of Crisis: How Fujifilm Survived (and Thrived) as Its Core Business Was Vanishing.* "The lives of more than seventy thousand employees worldwide, and their families, were on the line," Komori wrote. [10]

Komori focused on finding new uses for the technology Fujifilm owned. He encouraged the company's scientists to think outside the box and consider no idea too wild or crazy. Fujifilm wound up using its photo labs to create Astalift, a new line of antiaging skin care based on anti-color-fading technologies originally applied to film conservation. The company also applied its film technology to unexpected medical applications, including mammography and digital X-rays. By the time Kodak was filing for bankruptcy, Fujifilm was earning $3.4 billion annually from its new products and only 1 percent of its revenue from film sales.[11]

REPLACE GROUPTHINK WITH CREATIVE CONFLICT

Companies such as Fujifilm and Pixar figured out how to replace groupthink with creative conflict. Pixar, for instance, established its Creative Brain Trust. This is a committee of creative leaders in the company that directors and producers can access to help solve problems. Unlike traditional studio development executives, however, the advisers of this committee have no authority. This cuts out the loyalty/status incentive to conform. Instead, the trust is tasked solely with offering creative input and advice.

Pixar cofounder Ed Catmull explains: "When a director and producer feel in need of assistance, they convene the Creative Brain Trust (and anyone else they think would be valuable) and show the current version of the work in progress. This is followed by a lively two-hour give-and-take discussion, which is all about making the movie better. There's no ego. Nobody pulls any punches to be polite. This works because all the participants have come to trust and respect one another. They know it's far better to learn about problems from colleagues when there's still time to fix them than from the audience after it's too late. The problem-solving powers of this group are immense and inspirational to watch."[12]

At Pixar, creatives are encouraged to be open to daily input from all and to call upon the Creative Brain Trust when stumped. These methods discourage groupthink from taking hold. Lots of sharing throughout the production process allows for errors in storyline, dialogue, or visual effects to be caught early—before a movie is too far along for these problems to be fixed.[13]

THE DARK TRIAD LOVES GROUPTHINK

Unfortunately, some leaders prefer to encourage groupthink to take hold of their teams. The dark triad leader, in particular, loves it. The term "dark triad" was coined by researchers Delroy L. Paulhus and Kevin M. Williams in 2002. It refers to three negative personality traits—narcissism, Machiavellianism, and psychopathy—that share common malevolent features.

Dark triad leaders are focused on their own power and status. They can be selfish, exploitative, and manipulative. They focus on strengthening their own positions while implementing a climate of fear. They don't want to empower members of their team or promote group flow; they want their visions executed, no questions asked.

When a dark triad leader calls in external experts to speak to the team, it's usually a ploy to push for groupthink. Watch out for phrases such as "the data makes clear" or "as the expert has shared." Don't underestimate the power a leader wields by choosing experts or data that "prove" that his vision is the one the group must get behind.

Sometimes dark triad leaders are so successful that their dangerous behavior is overlooked. Film producer Harvey Weinstein got away with screaming tirades and sexually assaulting women for three decades, thanks to producing Oscar winners such as *Shakespeare in Love*. It wasn't until he was convicted of rape in 2020 that Weinstein finally fell from grace. Miramax, the company he cofounded with his brother, was bombarded with lawsuits and had to file for bankruptcy protection. The Weinstein Company was liquidated to pay Harvey Weinstein's sexual-misconduct victims $17 million in court-awarded damages.

THE DARK TRIAD NEUROGAP

"Not all psychopaths are in prison—some are in the boardroom," forensic psychiatrist Robert Hare famously noted during his lecture "The Predators Among Us."[14] In the workplace, the dark triad has been linked by researchers to increased fraud, workplace bullying, sexual harassment, low morale, scandal, and reduced individual and team performance.[15]

The base rate for psychopathy alone is three times higher in corporate boards, according to research published in the *Harvard Business Review*. The fifteen-year longitudinal study found that "individuals with psychopathic and narcissistic characteristics gravitate toward the top of organizational hierarchies and have higher levels of financial attainment."[16] This dark triad is a third neurogap that I call an "empathy gap." It is overrepresented in top leadership, like the two other neurogaps I've identified in this book: the prevalence of the testosterone/dopamine neurosignature and of extroversion among executives.

In a brain-friendly workplace, it is critical to close this empathy gap. Currently, few companies screen for the dark triad, but that is starting to change. Psychometric assessments are emerging, such as the Dark Triad of Personality at Work (TOP) questionnaire released in the United Kingdom in 2019. I hope we'll see the development of more HR tools to help organizations spot people with dark triad traits before hiring or promoting them.

SIX HACKS FOR CHANGING GROUPTHINK INTO GROUP FLOW

The key difference between groupthink and group flow is that with group flow leaders seek no preconceived outcome. People spark off each other's ideas, and when somebody floats a new idea, everyone is open to hearing it. The outcome of a group in flow is fluid, not dictated by leadership. The group members are free to focus on the task at hand, rather than on guarding their own power and status within the group.

As Amber Grewal, chief recruiting/talent officer at Boston Consulting Group (BCG), tells me, "When people feel free to communicate and express their ideas—and when they trust their employers and leaders—they are more likely to innovate and come up with new solutions."

Here are six brain-friendly principles to help teams and organizations replace groupthink with healthy dissent, creative conflict, and delicious group flow.

1. DISSENT IS VALUABLE . . . EVEN WHEN IT'S WRONG

University of California, Berkeley psychology professor Charlan Jeanne Nemeth is a leading researcher into the power of dissent. Her studies prove that
when people discuss their ideas with someone who has a different opinion,
they process information more deeply and are pushed to think better.[17] Dissent stimulates *everybody's* thinking, so encourage it, even when you think the
dissenter is dead wrong.

That Nemeth reported in her book *No!: The Power of Disagreement in a
World that Wants to Get Along,* "We found the same pattern of results over
and over. Consensus narrows, while dissent opens the mind. Both affect the
quality of our decisions. The take-home message . . . is that there are perils in
consensus and there is value in dissent."[18]

On occasion, dissenters on your team may get on your nerves. You may
even think they're slowing down your team, especially if you have a high-
testosterone neurosignature, which may make you feel a bit impatient during
healthy debate. On the other hand, if you have a high-estrogen neurosignature
and are strongly driven toward harmonious relationships, debate might make
you feel anxious and uncomfortable. Trust me: A healthy level of disagreement
on your team will make it stronger, more innovative, and even happier. You'll
get used to it, if you let it happen. Some dissent will lift everybody to new
heights—and the excitement helps stimulate group flow.

⤳

Brain Boost—One of the most influential dissenters of our time may turn
out to be Edward Snowden, the American CIA consultant who leaked classified documents from the National Security Agency that revealed massive
unconstitutional surveillance of citizens by the U.S. government. Snowden's
controversial act of dissent shed light on the danger that digital surveillance
poses to our personal privacy. Like any worthwhile dissenter, he has stimulated
new thinking on this topic—even if you disagree with his methods.

⤳

2. DISSENT MUST BE AUTHENTIC

You can't fake dissent, although people try all the time. Phony dissent is encouraged by team leaders who are really just looking for the team to rubber-
stamp their agenda.

I spoke recently with a well-known expert on group processes who recommends placing a "devil's advocate" on teams. "I have some great advice for your book!" she exclaimed. "Assign one person in the group to play devil's advocate and challenge everybody's opinions."

"I hate to break it to you," I replied, "but that method has been scientifically debunked. Charlan Nemeth proved that people's brains are only stimulated by dissent when it's true and authentic dissent."

Nemeth's studies found that installing a devil's advocate prompts people to become even more polarized and staunchly entrenched in their positions. "Results indicated that the authentic minority was superior to all three forms of 'devil's advocate,'" Nemeth wrote, "underscoring the value and importance of authenticity and the difficulty in cloning such authenticity by role-playing techniques."[19]

If you know someone is disagreeing with you just to be disagreeable, it's pretty irrelevant, right? Dissent must be genuine to spur creative conflict and group flow.

3. LEADERS SHOULD AMPLIFY OTHER VOICES

If the leader lays out a meeting's agenda right off the bat, the rest of the group will feel strongly compelled to fall in line. Instead, rotate who speaks first throughout the group. Encourage team leaders to amplify other voices, and take a back seat. Instead of "leaders," call them "facilitators" and reorient them toward facilitating both discussion and dissent.

⌁

Brain Boost—When you amplify the voices of others, your own status increases as well. According to a study in the journal *Academy of Management*, "employees can help peers get a status boost, while also raising their own status, by introducing the concept of *amplification*—public endorsement of another person's contribution, with attribution to that person."[20]

⌁

4. WRITE DOWN IDEAS BEFORE SHARING THEM

In one classic study, people were given a "magic pad" they could use to write down their ideas. The pad was erasable—and boy did people use that function.

As soon as members realized that their ideas were not fitting in with the group's dominant direction, they were surreptitiously erasing their ideas.[21]

If you want to encourage creative input, encourage team members to write down their ideas and submit them *before* engaging in a group discussion, so they can't erase or modify them. This simple hack short-circuits that subconscious desire we all have to "go along to get along."

5. ALWAYS VOTE ANONYMOUSLY

If you ask people in a group to vote by raising their hands—virtually or in person—most will look around to see how the high-status people in the group are voting. So, if you vote, vote anonymously. Studies have found that people are not as honest during public voting as they are during anonymous voting.[22]

And please, for the love of God, don't lie to your employees and tell them they're voting anonymously when they really aren't. Sadly, I have witnessed leaders swearing to employees that polling tools, 360-degree assessments, "team mood tools," and so on were anonymous when, in fact, the leaders had full access to all data, including identities.

Backstage at a conference, for example, I overheard a business leader tell the tech team to set up a smartphone polling tool so that it *looked* anonymous but he could still see how every person in his company was responding. It's natural to want to be surrounded by people who share your values and convictions, but I hope this chapter has convinced you how much that impulse undermines creativity and innovation.

6. ENCOURAGE KINDNESS AND COMPASSION

Research shows that people who practice kindness or compassion meditation become less judgmental and more open-minded. This is great for group flow.

In one study, for example, people tested as less racist after a short kindness meditation.[23] In another, a six-week practice of brief daily loving kindness meditation (LKM) changed subjects' attitudes toward homeless people from negative to more compassionate.[24]

LKM at work is an underleveraged resource. It's easy to learn and inexpensive to implement. It doesn't take much time and has a powerful positive impact on our brains and our ability to be more open to other people and their ideas.

Brain Food—Our brains are nearly 60 percent fat, so we need to consume essential fatty acids to keep them healthy. Not only do walnuts look like mini-brains, but they promote brain health because they are an excellent source of alpha-linolenic acid (ALA), an omega-3 essential fatty acid. A one-ounce serving of walnuts provides 2.5 grams of ALA.

c≈

HOW TO DISSENT WELL

Finally, let's not sugarcoat the fact that dissent can be tricky, especially if you work at a company that values conformity. Be courageous, though, because dissent is contagious. Once you start to offer alternate viewpoints, other people on your team will feel emboldened, too. Groupthink that may be plaguing your team will start to break up. You might be pleasantly surprised by the creative insights that begin to emerge.

Here are some tactics you can use to dissent effectively:

1. Take the high road.

Always convey your dissenting opinion in a respectful and positive way. As Michelle Obama says, "When they go low, we go high." Strive to be composed, thoughtful, and informed.

2. Find an ally.

When you plan to offer a dissenting opinion at a meeting, call up someone on the team privately ahead of time and ask for support. Having an ally in dissent combats a team's natural tendency toward conformity.

We know this works due to the famous conformity experiment that social psychologist Solomon Asch conducted during the 1950s. Asch showed subjects a drawing of several vertical lines of varying heights. The subjects were asked to choose a match for that drawing from among a selection of other drawings with vertical lines. The subjects correctly matched up the drawings—until Asch introduced fake "subjects" who were "in" on the experiment. Asch instructed the fakers to deliberately match up drawings that didn't actually match at all.

SOCIAL CONFORMITY IN ACTION

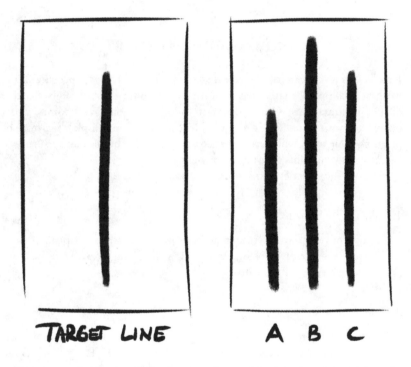

TARGET LINE   A   B   C

You can probably guess what happened next. Nearly 75 percent of the subjects changed their answers to conform with the fakers—even though it was blatantly obvious that the two drawings did not match.

What broke up the groupthink? The introduction of an ally. When Asch introduced one actor into the group who consistently matched the drawings correctly, conformity dropped to 5 percent.[25]

3. Be consistent in your message.

Research shows that if you stick to a consistent, steady message of dissent, you are more likely to win over the people in your group. Charlan Nemeth reported in her studies of conformity, "Those who had faced a dissenter who was consistent—who had shown no compromise—changed their attitudes. The majority had moved in the direction of the dissenter's position."[26]

Consistency is key. If you have to compromise or make a deal to stay in the game, do it at the very end to keep your credibility.

FLOW ON

Groupthink can lead a team to some very dark places. In group flow, however, the members of a team receive a near-magical opportunity to become much more than the sum of their individual talents. Group flow feels great and helps all team members joyfully reach their full human potential. Isn't that what we want to experience at work?

Throughout this book, I've made a case for a brain-friendly workplace and the power of thought diversity. By introducing the concept of different neuro-signatures and raising awareness of neurogaps in the workplace, my hope is to unleash everyone's potential. Group flow is important because if we're going to work in thought-diverse teams, we want them to be both effective and enjoyable.

When a group is in flow, amazing things can happen. When we understand and accept ourselves and others, and our needs are met by a brain-friendly workplace, the future of work shines bright.

Together, we can use what we know about the brain to make the workplace—and the world—a better place. You can reach me at Contact@fabulous-brain.com.

THE BRAIN-FRIENDLY INTERVIEW

Jeff Furman, president, Ben & Jerry's Foundation

Jeff Furman is often referred to as the "&" in Ben & Jerry's Ice Cream. Furman served on the Ben & Jerry's corporate board for nearly forty years, providing in-house legal counsel and top-level management, and fostering many of the company's groundbreaking social and environmental initiatives.

Furman is currently board of directors' emeritus and president of the Ben & Jerry's Foundation. Furman is also president of Social Ventures. He is cofounder of the Community Dispute Resolution Center and a community microfinance program in Ithaca, New York, where he resides. Furman is also an adviser to the Dorothy Cotton Institute, Alliance of Families for Justice, and serves on the board of the Oakland Institute. He speaks around the world on the power of business to impact social change.

Friederike: How did you get involved with Ben & Jerry's?

Jeff: I was just a friend helping out a little at first. Ben and I met at a school for twenty-five students in the mountains. I was the bus driver; he came to teach pottery and arts and crafts. I had a degree in business, so he said, "Hey, could you help us?" And I said, "Sure."

Friederike: How did the company develop such a strong social conscience?

Jeff: I think what made Ben & Jerry's different is that we always operated from our heart, not from a spreadsheet. When we had an idea, we didn't ask, "Is this going to hurt the company?" or "How can we say this in a way that doesn't make anybody mad at us?" We had the blessing when we started the company of not knowing what we were doing. We didn't have any resources, so we had to be creative. We were just a few people who knew each other and were going to start one store, run by Ben and Jerry, and that would be it.

Friederike: As the company grew, how did you maintain that commitment to creative thinking and group flow? How did you build teams that had shared values, yet could talk to each other honestly?

Jeff: If we were going to a protest about an environmental issue in Vermont, for example, we would take the employees with us. We'd all go together in one bus— management, employees, everyone. We would march together and stay together. That kind of broke down any potential barriers between us.

After the killing of Trayvon Martin, who was shot walking home from a grocery store armed with iced tea and Skittles by a vigilante who didn't think Trayvon should be in his neighborhood, we began talking at the company about our role dealing with the racial injustice problem in the United States. We brought in people of color who were experts in the field of racial injustice, and we traveled with employees down south to some historic civil rights sites.

We try to engage as many people in the company as we can with our activism so that it gets into their hearts.

Friederike: How do you avoid groupthink at Ben & Jerry's? How did you, as a leader of the company, find out what people were really thinking?

Jeff: This whole world of business is simply about relationships. It's made my life better, just talking on the bus with somebody who might be working in the factory. As chair of the board, I felt responsible for that person's well-being. I would ask questions like: How can we make sure that you're safe at work? How do we make sure that you're getting enough health insurance and care? Have you had any problem getting your health insurance covered for something that might have happened to your family? We ask, and we let people know that we want to hear the truth.

Friederike: How did you make sure the company became more diverse as it grew?

Jeff: The primary hiring I did was board recruitment. I recruited people from different races; and by the time I left the board, I had ensured that it was run predominantly by women. The chair of the board is a woman of color whom I recruited. I wanted someone from that demographic, who also had strong values and a willingness to stand up to Unilever, in case we had some issues. [Ben & Jerry's became a subsidiary of Unilever in 2000.]

Our board is empowered to protect and defend our integrity as a company. It has to be led by people willing to stand up for what they believe is right. When we decided that all our products should be GMO-free, for example, our number-one best seller was Heath Bar Crunch. We were unable to produce it entirely GMO-free.

What do you do about your number-one flavor when it can't be made to fit a value to which the company is committed? This question came before the board and the debate lasted under a minute—we discontinued the product. Unilever was not happy, but this was the right move for Ben & Jerry's.

Friederike: What happens when the board is not all on the same page? How do you encourage dissenting points of view?

Jeff: We've had hard fights at the board level when people felt differently about certain issues. We encouraged everyone on the board to speak up and to be transparent about their views. It can be challenging to maintain our own organizational structure now that we're inside this giant multinational. It's complicated, and we have definitely had struggles internally. Also, we have to think about the fact that our employees on the ground take the impact when we make a statement around white supremacy, for example, or Palestine.

Friederike: It seems that people are more emotional and easily outraged than ever these days. One key point I make in this chapter is that we need to be able to tolerate dissent and be civil toward people who have different ideas than our own. Otherwise, toxic groupthink can take over.

Jeff: Yes, very, very polarized. We seek to connect to the human element when we get involved with a cause. For example, a friend asked me why we got involved with climate change concerts. What does that have to do with Ben & Jerry's? I sent him pictures of my granddaughter and said, simply, "That's why." We can all relate to wanting to leave our kids a healthy planet. At the same time, we want employees to challenge the company to do more and do better.

Acknowledgments

Alone we can do so little; together we can do so much.

—Helen Keller

First and foremost, I'd like to thank my literary agent, Jeff Herman of the Jeff Herman Agency, for believing in me and helping me share my message. I love books, and you have enabled me now to place my second book on the bookshelves of the world. Here's to many more! Big thanks, as well, to Rowman & Littlefield senior editor Suzanne Staszak-Silva for her perceptive editing, for believing in this book's message and giving it a home. Thanks also to Susan Hershberg, Elaine McGarraugh, Deni Remsberg, and Alyssa Hawkins at Rowman & Littlefield for your support throughout the publication process. Special thanks to Carolin Nischwitz for your charming illustrations, which enrich each chapter with your intelligence and creativity. Thanks to Ross J. Q. Owens for your thoughtful edits to this book and for being there again.

Thank you to Dave Labno, Liisa Labno, and Dr. Helen Fisher at Neuro-Color for sharing your insights with me. Your work connects people across the globe based on a better understanding of how the brain works. I'm grateful for everything I've learned from you.

Thank you, Dr. Scott Barry Kaufman, for your inspiring and thoughtful foreword. Your knowledge of psychology runs so deep that it's no wonder that *The Psychology Podcast* ranks number one.

To Eithne Jones, my wonderful speaking agent at Speaker Ideas, thank you for always, always having my back. You've made so many connections for me, and I know you're always in my camp. A huge shout-out to all my clients, who allow me to share my ideas in keynote speeches on physical and virtual stages. I am so grateful for the opportunities you provide me to reach several hundred thousand executives every year doing what I love most.

I also deeply appreciate the thoughtful interviews given for this book by Dr. Scott Barry Kaufman, Julie Linn Teigland, Stephan Aarstol, Dr. Janin Schwartau, Arianna Huffington, Dr. Hubertus Meinecke, Claude Silver, Dr. John Medina, Amber Grewal, Jeff Furman, Riaz Shah, Dave Labno, Dr. Helen Fisher, Angelica Renhuvud, Ingrid Stolz, Judith Wallenstein, Evelyn Doyle, and Madelene Hjelm.

Thanks also to Martin Lindstrom and Jeff Stonefield for their priceless insights into the inner workings of the publishing industry.

To my parents, Dr. Marianne von Siegfried and Dr. Bernhard Wiedemann, and my siblings, Dr. Juliane Ebert and Konrad Wiedemann, thank you for filling our home with love and books. I wouldn't be where I am today without your unconditional support.

Finally, I'd like to thank my husband, Jochen. I'm so grateful that I met you, as with you I can be myself. Benita, Wolf, Heinrich, Sylvester, and Nike: I am so grateful that I get to be your mom. Thank you for your patience while I worked on this book. I love you all more than words can say.

Notes

INTRODUCTION

1. Lauren Weber, "Forget Going Back to the Office—People Are Just Quitting Instead," *Wall Street Journal*, June 13, 2021, https://www.wsj.com/articles/forget-going-back-to-the-officepeople-are-just-quitting-instead-11623576602.

2. Women in the Workplace 2021 report, McKinsey & Company, LeanIn.org, https://womenintheworkplace.com/.

3. Ginia Bellafante, "How the Pandemic Has Made the Creative Class Feel Free," *New York Times*, April 2, 2021, https://www.nytimes.com/2021/04/02/nyregion/covid-life-families.html.

4. Yoni Blumberg, "Companies with Female Executives Make More Money—Here's Why," *CNBC Make It*, March 2, 2018, https://www.cnbc.com/2018/03/02/why-companies-with-female-managers-make-more-money.html.

CHAPTER 1

1. Yoni Blumberg, "Companies with Female Executives Make More Money—Here's Why," *CNBC Make It*, March 2, 2018, https://www.cnbc.com/2018/03/02/why-companies-with-female-managers-make-more-money.html.

2. Women in the Workplace 2021 report, McKinsey & Company, LeanIn.org, https://womenintheworkplace.com/.

3. Women in the Workplace 2021 report.

4. Joanne Lipman, "How Diversity Training Infuriates Men and Fails Women," *Time*, January 25, 2018, https://time.com/5118035/diversity-training-infuriates-men -fails-women/.

5. Frank Dobbin, Alexandra Kalev, and Erin Kelly, "Diversity Management in Corporate America," *American Sociological Association* 6, no. 4 (Fall 2007): 21–27, https://doi.org/10.1525/ctx.2007.6.4.21.

6. "Diversity Fatigue," editorial, *The Economist*, February 11, 2016, https://www .economist.com/business/2016/02/11/diversity-fatigue.

7. Richard Branson, *Screw It, Let's Do It: Lessons in Life* (London, UK: Virgin Books, 2011).

8. "The Buffett Formula: Going to Bed Smarter Than When You Woke Up," Farnam Street Media, 2021.

9. "Steve Jobs Quotes: The Man in His Own Words," *The Guardian*, October 6, 2011, https://www.theguardian.com/technology/2011/oct/06/steve-jobs-quotes.

10. Cory Stieg, "Steve Wozniak: When Apple Got Big Money, Steve Jobs Changed," *CNBC Make It*, February 6, 2020, https://www.cnbc.com/2020/02/06/steve-wozniak -on-steve-jobs-personality-shift-as-apple-co-founder.html.

11. Stieg, "Steve Wozniak."

12. Sarit Alkalay, Yonathan Mizraki, and Eden Agasi, "Toward a Biological Basis of the FFM Meta-traits: Associations between the Fisher Type Indicator (FTI) Tem- perament Construct and the Hierarchical Five Factor Model (FFM) of Personality," *Personality and Individual Differences* (February 2022), https://doi.org/10.1016/j .paid.2021.111266.

13. Caroline J. Edwards, Rosanna Crombie, and Mark R. Gardner, "Subjective Thirst Moderates Changes in Speed of Responding Associated with Water Consumption," *Frontiers in Human Neuroscience* 16, no. 7 (July 16, 2013), https://doi.org/10.3389 /fnhum.2013.00363.

14. Emily Alford, "The Problem with Shitty Women Bosses Isn't That They're Women. It's That They're Assholes," *Jezebel*, July 1, 2020, https://jezebel.com/the -problem-with-shitty-women-bosses-isnt-that-theyre-w-1844234775.

15. Women in the Workplace 2021 report.

16. Melissa J. Williams and Larissa Z. Tiedens, "The Subtle Suspension of Backlash: A Meta-Analysis of Penalties for Women's Implicit and Explicit Dominance Behavior," *Psychological Bulletin* 142, no. 2 (February 2016): 165-97, https://doi.org/10.1037 /bul0000039.

17. Adam Grant (@AdamMGrant), "When will we stop punishing dominant women for violating outdated gender stereotypes?" *Twitter*, July 24, 2021, https:// twitter.com/AdamMGrant/status/1418920379708489734.

18. Kavita Sahai, "Female Millenials: Why They're Leaving Corporate Life," *Forbes*, July 28, 2017, https://www.forbes.com/sites/forbescoachescouncil/2017/07/28/female -millennials-why-theyre-leaving-corporate-life.

19. Sharon Kimathi, "Goldman Sachs Analysts Reveal Abusive Working Condi- tions in Leaked Survey," *FinTech Futures*, March 19, 2021, https://www.fintechfutures

.com/2021/03/goldman-sachs-analysts-reveal-abusive-working-conditions-in-leaked-survey/.

20. Kimathi, "Goldman Sachs Analysts Reveal Abusive Working Conditions."

21. Jose Maria Barrero, Nick Bloom, and Steven J. Davis, "60 Million Fewer Commuting Hours Per Day: How Americans Use Time Saved by Working from Home," *Becker Friedman Institute for Economics, University of Chicago*, September 8, 2020, https://bfi.uchicago.edu/insight/finding/60-million-fewer-commuting-hours-per-day-how-americans-use-time-saved-by-working-from-home/.

22. "The Female Leadership Crisis: Why Women Are Leaving (and What We Can Do About It)," *Network of Executive Women*, 2016, https://www.nextupisnow.org/.

CHAPTER 2

1. Joseph Stromberg and Estelle Caswell, "Why the Myers-Briggs Test Is Totally Meaningless," *Vox*, October 8, 2015, https://www.vox.com/2014/7/15/5881947/myers-briggs-personality-test-meaningless.

2. Alison Beard, "If You Understand How the Brain Works, You Can Reach Anyone: A Conversation with Biological Anthropologist Helen Fisher," *Harvard Business Review*, March–April 2017, https://hbr.org/2017/03/if-you-understand-how-the-brain-works-you-can-reach-anyone.

3. Beard, "If You Understand How the Brain Works."

4. Beard, "If You Understand How the Brain Works."

5. Lucy L. Brown, Bianca Acevedo, and Helen E. Fisher, "Neural Correlates of Four Broad Temperament Dimensions: Testing Predictions for a Novel Construct of Personality," *PLoS One* 8, no. 11 (November 13, 2013): e78734, https://doi.org/10.1371/journal.pone.0078734.

6. Astrid Nehlig, "The Neuroprotective Effects of Cocoa Flavanol and Its Influence on Cognitive Performance," *British Journal of Clinical Pharmacology* 75, no. 3 (March 2013): 716–27, https://doi.org/10.1111/j.1365-2125.2012.04378.x.

7. Beard, "If You Understand How the Brain Works."

8. Karren Brady, "Kate Middleton Looked Every Inch the Graceful and Stoic Royal at Prince Philip's Funeral," *The Sun*, April 17, 2021, https://www.the-sun.com/news/2722566/kate-middleton-prince-philip-funeral-karren-brady/.

9. Kelly Faircloth, "The Forging of Kate Middleton into a Future Queen," *Jezebel*, April 29, 2021, https://jezebel.com/the-forging-of-kate-middleton-into-a-future-queen-1846767001.

10. Sari M. van Anders, Jeffrey Steiger, and Katherine L. Goldey, "Effects of Gendered Behavior on Testosterone in Women and Men," *PNAS* 112, no. 45 (October 26, 2015): 13805-13810, https://doi.org/10.1073/pnas.1509591112.

11. Paola Sapienza, Luigi Zingales, and Dario Maestripieri, "Gender Differences in Financial Risk Aversion and Career Choices Are Affected by Testosterone," *PNAS* 106, no. 36 (September 8, 2009): 15268–73, https://doi.org/10.1073/pnas.0907352106.

12. "Angelina Gets Candid about Stunts, Firearms at Comic-Con," *Popsugar*, July 22, 2010, https://www.popsugar.com/entertainment/Angelina-Jolie-Talks-About-Salt -Comic-Con-2010-07-22-151806-9233536.

CHAPTER 3

1. Stephan Aarstol, "What Happened When I Moved My Company to a 5-Hour Workday," *Fast Company*, August 30, 2016, https://www.fastcompany.com/3063262 /what-happened-when-i-moved-my-company-to-a-5-hour-workday.

2. Neetish Basnet, "Tower Paddle Boards Surfs to $30M in Sales After 'Shark Tank,'" *Dallas Business Journal*, August 15, 2018, https://www.bizjournals.com/dallas /news/2018/08/15/tower-paddle-boards-surfs-to-30m-in-sales-after.html.

3. Sendhil Mullainathan and Eldar Shafir, *Scarcity: Why Having Too Little Means So Much* (New York: Times Books, 2013).

4. Stephan Aarstol, *The Five-Hour Workday: Live Differently, Unlock Productivity, and Find Happiness* (Carson City, NV: Lioncrest, 2016).

5. Bill Chappell, "4-Day Workweek Boosted Workers' Productivity by 40%, Microsoft Japan Says," *All Things Considered*, November 4, 2019, https://www.npr .org/2019/11/04/776163853/microsoft-japan-says-4-day-workweek-boosted-workers -productivity-by-40.

6. Chappell, "4-Day Workweek Boosted Workers' Productivity."

7. Melanie Curtin, "In an 8-Hour Day, the Average Worker Is Productive for This Many Hours," *Inc.*, July 21, 2016, https://www.inc.com/melanie-curtin/in-an-8-hour -day-the-average-worker-is-productive-for-this-many-hours.html.

8. Curtin, "In an 8-Hour Day."

9. Tim Herrera, "How to Actually, Truly Focus on What You're Doing," *New York Times*, January 13, 2019, https://www.nytimes.com/2019/01/13/smarter-living/how -to-actually-truly-focus-on-what-youre-doing.html.

10. Jessica Stillman, "For 95 Percent of Human History, People Worked 15 Hours a Week. Could We Do It Again?", *Inc.*, September 10, 2020, https://www.inc .com/jessica-stillman/for-95-percent-of-human-history-people-worked-15-hours-a -week-could-we-do-it-again.html.

11. Stillman, "For 95 Percent of Human History."

12. Juliet B. Schor, *The Overworked American: The Unexpected Decline of Leisure* (New York: Basic Books, 1993).

13. "Long Working Hours Increasing Death from Heart Disease and Stroke: WHO, ILO," World Health Organization joint press release, May 17, 2021, https:// www.who.int/news/item/17-05-2021-long-working-hours-increasing-deaths-from -heart-disease-and-stroke-who-ilo.

14. Danielle Pacheco, "Women and Sleep" Sleep Foundation, January 22, 2021, https://www.sleepfoundation.org/women-sleep.

15. "Long Working Hours Increasing Death from Heart Disease and Stroke."

16. "Long Working Hours Increasing Death from Heart Disease and Stroke."

17. Marie Solis, "What's the Point of Non-Essential Work?" *Jezebel*, December 29, 2020, https://jezebel.com/whats-the-point-of-non-essential-work-1845891375.

18. Solis, "What's the Point of Non-Essential Work?"

19. Solis, "What's the Point of Non-Essential Work?"

20. Alex Ledsom, "How France Plays Hard While Being One of the World's Most Productive Countries," *Culture Trip*, August 29, 2017, https://theculturetrip.com /europe/france/articles/how-france-plays-hard-while-being-one-of-the-worlds-most -productive-countries/.

21. "Most Productive Countries 2022," *World Population Review,* https://world populationreview.com/country-rankings/most-productive-countries.

22. "Holiday Allowance," *Business.gov.nl,* https://business.gov.nl/regulation/holiday -allowance/.

23. Sarah Berger, "4 Day Workweek Is a Success, New Zealand Experiment Finds," *CNBC Make It,* July 19, 2018, https://www.cnbc.com/2018/07/19/new-zealand -experiment-finds-4-day-work-week-a-success.html.

24. Nathalie Gaulhiac, "A Digital Agency Trial Led a 5-Hour Working Day to Increase Productivity—and It Worked So Well It's Staying for Good," *Business Insider,* June 27, 2018, https://www.businessinsider.com/how-this-digital-agency-increased -productivity-with-a-25-hour-week-2018-6.

25. Gaulhiac, "A Digital Agency Trial Led a 5-Hour Working Day."

26. Gaulhiac, "A Digital Agency Trial Led a 5-Hour Working Day."

27. "Rheingans Digital Enabler setzt Fünf-Stunden-Tage für alle um," *Chefsache Initiative,* https://initiative-chefsache.de/rheingans-digital-enabler-setzt-5-stunden-tage -fuer-alle-um/.

28. Jack Kelly, "Now that Working from Home Has Proven Successful, Unilever Is Trying a Four-Day Workweek," *Forbes,* December 1, 2020, https://www.forbes .com/sites/jackkelly/2020/12/01/now-that-working-from-home-has-proven-success ful-unilever-is-trying-out-a-four-day-workweek.

29. Selvaraju Subash et al., "Neuroprotective Effects of Berry Fruits on Neuro-degenerative Disorders," *Neural Regeneration Research* 9, no. 16 (August 15, 2014): 1557–66, https://doi.org/10.4103/1673-5374.139483.

30. Steven G. Rogelberg, Cliff W. Scott, and John Kello, "The Science and Fiction of Meetings," *MIT Sloan Management Review,* January 1, 2007, https://sloanreview .mit.edu/article/the-science-and-fiction-of-meetings/.

CHAPTER 4

1. Susie Cranston and Scott Keller, "Increasing the 'Meaning Quotient' of Work," *McKinsey Quarterly,* January 1, 2013, https://www.mckinsey.com/business-functions /people-and-organizational-performance/our-insights/increasing-the-meaning-quo tient-of-work.

2. Cranston and Keller, "Increasing the 'Meaning Quotient' of Work."

3. "When the Impossible Becomes Possible—The Secrets of Flow Revealed with Steven Kotler," *Science of Success Podcast*, July 26, 2018, https://www.successpodcast.com/show-notes/2018/7/25/when-the-impossible-becomes-possible-the-secrets-of-flow-revealed-with-steven-kotler.

4. Jiang Xin, Yaoxue Zhang, et al., "Brain Differences between Men and Women: Evidence from Deep Learning," *Frontiers in Neuroscience* (March 8, 2019), https://doi.org/10.3389/fnins.2019.00185.

5. "What Is a Flow State and What Are Its Benefits?," *Headspace Blog*, n.d., https://www.headspace.com/articles/flow-state.

6. Victoria Woollaston, "How Often Do You Check Your Phone?," *Daily Mail*, October 8, 2013, https://www.dailymail.co.uk/sciencetech/article-2449632/How-check-phone-The-average-person-does-110-times-DAY-6-seconds-evening.html.

7. Kep Kee Loh and Ryota Kanai, "Higher Media Multitasking Activity Is Associated with Smaller Gray-Matter Density in the Anterior Cingulate Cortex," *PLoS One* 9, no. 9 (September 24, 2014): e106698, https://doi.org/10.1371/journal.pone.0106698.

8. Joshua S. Rubenstein, David E. Meyer, and Jeffrey E. Evans, "Executive Control of Cognitive Processes in Task Switching," *Journal of Experimental Psychology* 27, no. 4 (2001): 763–97, https://doi.org/10.1037//0096-1523.27.4.763.

9. Robert Sapolsky, "Dopamine Jackpot! Sapolsky on the Science of Pleasure," *ForaTV*, March 2, 2011, YouTube video, https://youtu.be/axrywDP9Ii0.

10. Ethan S. Bernstein and Stephan Turban, "The Impact of the 'Open' Workspace on Human Collaboration," *Royal Society Publishing*, July 2, 2018, https://doi.org/10.1098/rstb.2017.0239.

CHAPTER 5

1. Jordi P. D. Kleinloog et al., "Aerobic Exercise Training Improves Cerebral Blood Flow and Executive Function: A Randomized, Controlled Cross-Over Trial in Sedentary Older Men," *Frontiers in Aging Neuroscience* (December 4, 2019), https://doi.org/10.3389/fnagi.2019.00333.

2. Zurine De Miguel et al., "Exercise Plasma Boosts Memory and Dampens Brain Inflammation via Clustering," *Nature* 600 (2021): 494–99, https://doi.org/10.1038/s41586-021-04183-x.

3. Catherine N. Rasberry et al., "The Association between School-Based Physical Activity, Including Physical Education, and Academic Performance," *Preventive Medicine* 52, suppl. 1 (June 2011): S10–20, https://doi.org/10.1016/j.ypmed.2011.01.027.

4. Tim Halford, "Richard Thaler: 'If You Want People to Do Something, Make It Easy,'" *Financial Times*, August 2, 2019, https://www.ft.com/content/a317c302-aa2b-11e9-984c-fac8325aaa04.

5. Yvon Chouinard, *Let My People Go Surfing: The Education of a Reluctant Businessman* (New York: Penguin, 2006).

6. Brigid Schulte, "A Company That Profits as It Pampers Workers," *Washington Post*, October 22, 2014, https://www.washingtonpost.com/business/a-company -that-profits-as-it-pampers-workers/2014/10/22/d3321b34-4818-11e4-b72e-d60a 9229cc10_story.html.

7. Schulte, "A Company That Profits as It Pampers Workers."

8. Schulte, "A Company That Profits as It Pampers Workers."

9. Nick Bloom and John Van Reenan, "Management Practices: Work/Life Balance and Productivity," *Oxford Review of Economic Policy* 22, no. 4 (2008): 457–82, https:// doi.org/10.1093/oxrep/grj027.

10. Joe Verghese et al., "Leisure Activities and the Risk of Dementia in the Elderly," *New England Journal of Medicine* 34, no. 25 (June 19, 2003): 2508–16, https://doi .org/10.1056/NEJMoa022252.

11. Corinne Newell, "How Weight Training Changes the Brain," *Curtis Health*, August 7, 2019, https://curtishealth.com/2019/08/how-weight-training-changes-the -brain/.

12. J. A. Blumenthal et al., "Effects of Exercise Training on Older Patients with Major Depression," *Archives of Internal Medicine* 159, no. 19 (October 25, 1999): 2349–56, https://doi.org/10.1001/archinte.159.19.2349.

13. May Wong, "Stanford Study Finds Walking Improves Creativity," *Stanford News*, April 24, 2014, https://news.stanford.edu/2014/04/24/walking-vs-sitting-042414/.

14. Lucas J. Carr et al., "Total Worker Health Intervention Increases Activity of Sedentary Workers," *American Journal of Preventive Medicine* 50, no. 1 (January 2016): 9–17, https://doi.org/10.1016/j.amepre.2015.06.022.

15. Tom Taylor, "How Michael Phelps's Body Has Changed over His Five Olympic Games," *Sports Illustrated*, August 7, 2018, https://www.si.com/olympics/2016/08/07 /michael-phelps-rio-olympics-recovery.

16. John Cline, PhD, "Are We Really Getting Less Sleep than We Did in 1975?" *Psychology Today*, January 18, 2010, https://www.psychologytoday.com/us/blog/sleep less-in-america/201001/are-we-really-getting-less-sleep-we-did-in-1975.

17. Anne Trafton, "In Profile: Matt Wilson," *MIT News*, October 19, 2009, https:// news.mit.edu/2009/profile-wilson.

18. Bjorn Rasch and Jan Born, "About Sleep's Role in Memory," *Physiological Reviews* 93, no. 2 (April 2013): 681–766, https://doi.org/10.1152/physrev.00032.2012.

19. Matthew Walker, *Why We Sleep: Unlocking the Power of Sleep and Dreams* (New York: Scribner, 2017).

20. "Dr. Andrew Huberman, A Neurologist on Optimizing Sleep, Enhancing Performance, Reducing Anxiety, Increasing Testosterone, and Using the Body to Control the Mind," *Tim Ferris Show*, podcast, July 6, 2021, https://tim.blog/2021/07/08 /andrew-huberman-transcript/.

21. Walker, *Why We Sleep*.

22. Mark O'Connell, "Why We Sleep by Matthew Walker Review—How More Sleep Can Save Your Life," *The Guardian*, September 21, 2017, https://www.theguard ian.com/books/2017/sep/21/why-we-sleep-by-matthew-walker-review.

23. Ian Clark and Hans Peter Landolt, "Coffee, Caffeine, and Sleep: A Systematic Review of Epidemiological Studies and Randomized Controlled Trials," *Sleep Medicine Reviews* 31 (February 2017): 70–78, https://doi.org/10.1016/j.smrv.2016.01.006.

CHAPTER 6

1. P. Šrámek et al., "Human Physiological Responses to Immersion into Water of Different Temperatures," *European Journal of Applied Physiology* 81, no. 5 (March 2000): 436–42, https://doi.org/10.1007/s004210050065.

2. "2020 Attitudes in the American Workplace VII," American Institute of Stress, February 9, 2021, https://www.stress.org/workplace-stress.

3. Jim Harter, "U.S. Employee Engagement Rises Following Wild 2020," *Gallup Workplace*, February 26, 2021, https://www.gallup.com/workplace/330017/employee -engagement-rises-following-wild-2020.aspx.

4. Justin B. Echouffo-Tcheugui, Sarah C. Conner, et al., "Circulating Cortisol and Cognitive and Structural Brain Measures," *Neurology* 91, no. 21 (November 20, 2018): e1961–70, https://doi.org/10.1212/WNL.0000000000006549.

5. Jenna McHenry et al., "Sex Differences in Anxiety and Depression: Role of Testosterone," Frontiers in Neuroendocrinology 35, no. 1 (January 2014): 42–57, https://doi.org/10.1016/j.yfrne.2013.09.001.

6. McHenry et al., "Sex Differences in Anxiety and Depression."

7. Erno J. Hermans et al., "A Single Administration of Testosterone Reduces Fear-Potentiated Startle in Humans," *Biological Psychiatry* 59, no. 9 (May 1, 2006): 872–74, https://doi.org/10.1016/j.biopsych.2005.11.015.

8. Jaroslava Durdiakova, Daniela Ostatnikova, and Peter Celec, "Testosterone and Its Metabolites—Modulators of Brain Functions," *Acta neurobiologiae experimentalis* 71, no. 4 (2011): 434–54, https://ane.pl/linkout.php?pii=7147.

9. Women in the Workplace 2021 report, McKinsey & Company, LeanIn.org. https://womenintheworkplace.com/.

10. Dr. Robert Sapolsky, "14. Limbic System," Stanford University, February 1, 2011, YouTube video, 1:28:43, https://youtu.be/CAOnSbDSaOw.

11. Shelley Taylor, "Bio Behavioral Responses to Stress in Females: Tend-and-Befriend, Not Fight-or-Flight," *Psychological Review* 107, no. 3 (July 2000): 411–29, https://doi.org/10.1037/0033-295x.107.3.411.

12. John D. Eastwood et al., "The Unengaged Mind: Defining Boredom in Terms of Attention," *Perspectives on Psychological Science* 7, no. 5 (September 5, 2012): 482–95, https://doi.org/10.1177/1745691612456044.

13. Eastwood et al., "The Unengaged Mind."

14. Annie Britton and Martin J. Shipley, "Bored to Death?," *International Journal of Epidemiology* 39, no. 2 (April 2010): 370–71, https://doi.org/10.1093/ije/dyp404.

15. Wijnand A. P. Van Tilburg and Eric R. Igou, "Going to Political Extremes in Response to Boredom," *European Journal of Social Psychology* 46, no. 6 (October 2016): 687–99, https://doi.org/10.1002/ejsp.2205.

16. Jonathan Webb, "Do People Choose Pain over Boredom?" *BBC News*, July 4, 2014, https://www.bbc.com/news/science-environment-28130690.

17. Kenneth Carter, "Lust for Life," *Psychology Today*, October 15, 2019, https://www.psychologytoday.com/us/articles/201910/lust-life.

18. William Ury, "Power of a Positive No," 50 Lessons, March 4, 2016, YouTube video, 4:03, https://youtu.be/OvrW-jTVCvE.

19. Eranda Jayawickreme, Marie J. C. Forgeard, and Martin E. P. Seligman, "The Engine of Wellbeing," *Review of General Psychology* (December 1, 2012), https://doi.org/10.1037/a0027990.

20. Dominc Landgraft et al., "Dissociation of Learned Helplessness and Fear Conditioning in Mice: A Mouse Model of Depression," *PLoS One* 10, no. 4 (April 30, 2015): e0125892, https://doi.org/10.1371/journal.pone.0125892.

21. Meena Kumari et al., "Measures of Social Position and Cortisol Secretion in an Aging Population: Findings from the Whitehall II Study," *Psychosomatic Medicine* 72, no. 1 (December 7, 2009): 27–34, https://doi.org/10.1097/psy.0b013e3181c85712.

22. "Dr. Andrew Huberman, A Neurologist on Optimizing Sleep, Enhancing Performance, Reducing Anxiety, Increasing Testosterone, and Using the Body to Control the Mind," *Tim Ferris Show*, podcast, July 6, 2021, https://tim.blog/2021/07/08/andrew-huberman-transcript/.

23. Angus C. Burns et al., "Time Spent in Outdoor Light Is Associated with Mood, Sleep, and Circadian Rhythm-Related Outcomes: A Cross-Sectional and Longitudinal Study in over 400,000 UK Biobank Participants," *Journal of Affective Disorders*, 295 (December 1, 2021): 347–52, https://doi.org/10.1016/j.jad.2021.08.056.

24. Carter, "Lust for Life."

25. Joshua Burd, "UBS Taps WeWork to Redesign Weehawken Office," *Real Estate NJ*, August 14, 2018, https://re-nj.com/ubs-taps-wework-to-redesign-weehawken-office/.

26. Jared B. Torre and Mathew D. Lieberman, "Putting Feelings into Words: Affect Labeling as Implicit Emotion Regulation," *Emotion Review* 10, no. 2 (March 20, 2018): 116–24, https://doi.org/10.1177/1754073917742706.

27. "Putting Feelings into Words Produces Therapeutic Effects in the Brain," University of California, *Science Daily*, June 22, 2007, www.sciencedaily.com/releases/2007/06/070622090727.htm.

28. Heidi Jiang et al., "Brain Activity and Functional Connectivity Associated with Hypnosis," *Cerebral Cortex* 27, no. 8 (August 2017): 4083–93, https://doi.org/10.1093/cercor/bhw220.

CHAPTER 7

1. Julianne Holt-Lunstad, Timothy B. Smith, and J. Bradley Layton, "Social Relationships and Mortality Risk—A Meta-Analytic Review," *PLoS Medicine* 7, no. 7 (July 27, 2010): e1000316, https://doi.org/10.1371/journal.pmed.1000316.

2. Matthew D. Lieberman, *Social: Why Our Brains Are Wired to Connect* (New York: Crown, 2013).

3. Paul Zak, "The Neuroscience of Trust," *Harvard Business Review*, January–February 2017, https://hbr.org/2017/01/the-neuroscience-of-trust.

4. Zak, "Neuroscience of Trust."

5. Zak, "Neuroscience of Trust."

6. Zak, "Neuroscience of Trust."

7. Paul Zak, *The Moral Molecule: How Trust Works* (New York: Plume, 2013).

8. Esteban Ortiz-Ospina and Max Roser, "Trust," *Our World in Data*, 2016, https://ourworldindata.org/trust.

9. Ortiz-Ospina and Roser, "Trust."

10. Zak, "Neuroscience of Trust."

11. Naomi Eisenberger and Matthew D. Lieberman, "Does Rejection Hurt? An FMRI Study of Social Exclusion," *Science* 302, no. 5643 (October 10, 2003): 290–92, https://doi.org/10.1126/science.1089134.

12. C. Nathan Dewall et al., "Acetaminophen Reduces Social Pain: Behavioral and Neural Evidence," *Psychological Science* 21, no. 7 (July 2010): 931–37, https://doi.org/10.1177/0956797610374741.

13. Emily Esfahani Smith, "Masters of Love," *The Atlantic*, June 12, 2014, https://www.theatlantic.com/health/archive/2014/06/happily-ever-after/372573/.

14. Ewen Calloway, "Fearful Memories Passed Down to Mouse Descendants," *Nature*, (2013), https://doi.org/10.1038/nature.2013.14272.

15. Martha Henriques, "Can the Legacy of Trauma Be Passed down the Generations?," *BBC Future*, March 26, 2019, https://www.bbc.com/future/article/20190326-what-is-epigenetics.

16. Julian Guthrie, "The Lie Detective: S. F. Psychologist Has Made a Science of Reading Facial Expressions," *San Francisco Chronicle*, September 16, 2002, https://www.sfgate.com/news/article/The-lie-detective-S-F-psychologist-has-made-a-2768998.php.

17. Linda Geddes, "My Big, Fat Geek Wedding: Tears, Joy, and Oxytocin," *New Scientist*, February 10, 2010, https://www.newscientist.com/article/mg20527471-000-my-big-fat-geek-wedding-tears-joy-and-oxytocin/.

18. Paulina Pašková, "What Six Years at trivago Taught Me about Company Culture," *Medium*, November 10, 2019, https://medium.com/@pavlinapaskova/what-six-years-at-trivago-taught-me-about-company-culture-c80fc550b1cf.

19. Tania Singer et al., "Empathic Neural Responses Are Modulated by the Perceived Fairness of Others," *Nature* 439, no. 7075 (January 26, 2006): 466–69, https://doi.org/10.1038/nature04271.

20. Hetal Kabra, "VaynerMedia Net Worth 2022," *MD Daily Record*, May 21, 2021, https://mddailyrecord.com/vaynermedia-net-worth-2021-2022-2023.

21. Gary Vaynerchuk, "Giving without Expectation," *Gary Vaynerchuk*, blog, 2016, https://www.garyvaynerchuk.com/giving-without-expectation/.

CHAPTER 8

1. Jennifer Liu, "1 in 4 Workers Quit Their Jobs This Year," *CNBC Make It*, October 14, 2021, https://www.cnbc.com/2021/10/14/1-in-4-workers-quit-their-job -this-year-according-to-new-report.html.

2. Liu, "1 in 4 Workers Quit Their Jobs This Year."

3. Sara Silverstein and Rachel Cohn, "An Organizational Psychologist Explains Why Introverts Will Make Better Leaders in the Future," *Business Insider*, March 4, 2019, https://www.businessinsider.com/adam-grant-explains-why-introverts-will -make-better-leaders-in-the-future-2019-2.

4. Susan Cain, *Quiet: The Power of Introverts in a World That Can't Stop Talking* (New York: Crown, 2013).

5. Maureen Downey, "Teaching Introverts: Do Schools Prefer Big Talkers to Big Thinkers?," *Atlanta Journal-Constitution*, May 5, 2016, https://www.ajc.com/blog /get-schooled/teaching-introverts-schools-prefer-big-talkers-big-thinkers/idC1OLJlIP gYM21e0z01bL/.

6. Richard E. Lucas et al., "Cross-Cultural Evidence for the Fundamental Features of Extroversion," *Journal of Personality and Social Psychology* 79, no. 3 (2000): 452–68, https://doi.org/10.1037//0022-3514.79.3.452.

7. Neil G. MacLaren et al., "Testing the Babble Hypothesis: Speaking Time Predicts Leader Emergence in Small Groups," *Leadership Quarterly* 31, no. 5 (October 2020), https://doi.org/10.1016/j.leaqua.2020.101409.

8. MacLaren et al., "Testing the Babble Hypothesis."

9. Michael C. Ashton, Kibeom Lee, and Sampo V. Paunonen, "What Is the Central Feature of Extraversion? Social Attention versus Reward Sensitivity," *Journal of Personality and Social Psychology* 83, no. 1 (July 2002): 245–52, https://doi .org/10.1037/0022-3514.83.1.245.

10. Ashton, Lee, and Paunonen, "What Is the Central Feature of Extraversion?"

11. *The Ultimate Quotable Einstein*, ed. Alice Calaprice (Princeton, NJ: Princeton University Press, October 2010).

12. Colin Cooper and Richard Taylor, "Personality and Performance on a Frustrating Cognitive Task," *Perceptual and Motor Skills* 88, no. 3, pt 2. (1999): 1384, https:// doi.org/10.2466/pms.1999.88.3c.1384.

13. Sana Noor Haq, "How Do You Become a Chess Grandmaster? Magnus Carlsen Is Here to Tell You," *CNN*, October 1, 2021, https://www.cnn.com/2021/10/01/sport /magnus-carlsen-chess-grandmaster-spt-intl/index.html.

14. Vikas Kapil et al., "Dietary Nitrate Provides Sustained Blood Pressure Lowering in Hypertensive Patients," *Hypertension* 65, no. 2 (February 2015): 320–27, https:// doi.org/10.1161/HYPERTENSIONAHA.114.04675.

15. Avram J. Holmes et al., "Individual Differences in Amygdala-Medial Prefrontal Anatomy Link Negative Affect, Impaired Social Functioning, and Polygenic Depression Risk," *Journal of Neuroscience* 32, no. 50 (December 12, 2012): 18087–100, https://doi.org/10.1523/JNEUROSCI.2531-12.2012.

16. D. L. Johnson et al., "Cerebral Blood Flow and Personality: A Positron Emission Tomography Study," *American Journal of Psychiatry* 156, no. 2 (February 1, 1999): 252–57, https://doi.org/10.1176/ajp.156.2.252.

17. Karene Booker, "Extroverts Have More Sensitive Brain-Reward System," *Cornell Chronicle*, July 10, 2013, https://news.cornell.edu/stories/2013/07/brain-chemistry-plays-role-extroverts.

18. Steve Wozniak and Gina Smith, *iWoz: From Computer Geek to Cult Icon: How I Invented the Personal Computer, Co-Founded Apple, and Had Fun Doing It* (New York: Norton, 2006).

19. Lesley Sword, "The Gifted Introvert," *High Ability*, October 2021, https://highability.org/the-gifted-introvert/.

20. Chris Weller, "Scientists Studied 5,000 Gifted Children for 45 Years. This Is What They Learned about Success," *World Economic Forum/Business Insider*, September 16, 2016, https://www.businessinsider.com/what-scientists-learned-about-genius-2016-9.

21. Douglas Brinkley, *Rosa Parks: A Life* (Waterville, ME: Thorndike Press, 2000).

22. Brinkley, *Rosa Parks*.

23. Sanna Tuovinen, Xin Tang, and Katariina Salmela-Aro, "Introversion and Social Engagement: Scale Validation, Their Interaction, and Positive Association with Self-Esteem," *Frontiers in Psychology*, 11 (November 2020), https://doi.org/10.3389/fpsyg.2020.590748.

24. Jack Samuels, "Personality Dimensions and Criminal Arrest," *Comprehensive Psychiatry* 45, no. 4 (July–August 2004): 275–80, https://doi.org/10.1016/j.comppsych.2004.03.013.

25. "The Skinny Confidential: Robin McGraw and Dr. Phil," on *The Skinny Confidential Him & Her Podcast*, 439, podcast, https://tscpodcast.com/episodes/439-dr-phil-mcgraw-robin-mcgraw/.

26. Cain, *Quiet*.

27. Cain, *Quiet*.

28. John Kounios and Mark Beeman, "The Cognitive Neuroscience of Insight," *Annual Review of Psychology*, 65 (2014): 71–93, https://doi.org/10.1146/annurev-psych-010213-115154.

29. Jonathan Schooler, Stellan Ohlsson, and Kevin Brooks, "Thoughts beyond Words: When Language Overshadows Insight," *Journal of Experimental Psychology: General* 122, no. 2 (1993): 166–83, https://doi.org/10.1037/0096-3445.122.2.166.

30. Werner Stritzke, Anh Nguyen, and Kevin Durkin, "Shyness and Computer-Mediated Communication: A Self-Presentational Theory Perspective," *Media Psychology* 6, no. 1 (2004): 1–22, https://doi.org/10.1207/s1532785xmep0601_1.

31. Michael Kraus, "Voice-Only Communication Enhances Empathic Accuracy," *American Psychologist* 72, no. 7 (October 2017): 644–54, https://doi.org/10.1037 /amp0000147.

CHAPTER 9

1. Marian Schembari, "10 of the Best Companies with Paid Maternity Leave," *Penny Hoarder*, January 10, 2022, https://www.thepennyhoarder.com/make-money /career/companies-paid-maternity-leave/.

2. James Ball, "Women 40% More Likely to Develop Mental Illness Than Men," *The Guardian*, May 22, 2013, https://www.theguardian.com/society/2013/may/22 /women-men-mental-illness-study.

3. David P. Schmitt et al., "Personality and Gender Differences in Global Perspective," *International Journal of Psychology*, 52, suppl. 1 (December 2017): 45–56, https:// doi.org/10.1002/ijop.12265.

4. Julia Hartley-Brewer, "Guilt May Damage the Immune System," *The Guardian*, April 16, 2000, https://www.theguardian.com/uk/2000/apr/17/juliahartleybrewer1.

5. Louise Chang, MD, "Is Guilt Getting the Best of You?," *WebMD*, May 8, 2006, https://www.webmd.com/balance/features/is-guilt-getting-best-of-you.

6. Anne Diamond and Laura Tenison, "French Minister Rachida Dati's Return to Work Just Five Days after Giving Birth Has Sparked the Great NoTernity Debate," *Daily Mail UK*, January 13, 2009, https://www.dailymail.co.uk/femail /article-1114684/French-minister-Rachida-Datis-return-work-just-days-giving-birth -sparked-great-NO-TERNITY-debate.html.

7. "Jaimie O'Banion," *The Skinny Confidential Him & Her Podcast*, podcast, episode 353, May 3, 2021, https://tscpodcast.com/episodes/353-jamie-obanion/.

8. Miranda Bryant, "'I Was Risking My Life': Why One in Four US Women Return to Work Two Weeks after Childbirth," *The Guardian*, January 27, 2020, https://www.theguardian.com/us-news/2020/jan/27/maternity-paid-leave-women -work-childbirth-us.

9. Anna Gromada, Gwyther Rees, and Yekaterina Chzhen, "Worlds of Influence: Understanding What Shapes Child Well-Being in Rich Countries," UNICEF, 2020, https://www.unicef-irc.org/publications/1140-worlds-of-influence-understanding -what-shapes-child-well-being-in-rich-countries.html.

10. Gromada, Rees, and Chzhen, "Worlds of Influence."

11. Chang Che, "ByteDance Invents Entirely New Product Category with Dali Smart Lamp," *SupChina*, April 21, 2021, https://supchina.com/2021/04/21/edutech -bytedance-invents-entirely-new-product-category-with-dali-smart-lamp/.

12. "Landmark Report: U.S. Teens Use an Average of Nine Hours of Media Per Day, Tweens Use Six Hours," *Common Sense Media*, November 3, 2015, https://www .commonsensemedia.org/press-releases/landmark-report-us-teens-use-an-average-of -nine-hours-of-media-per-day-tweens-use-six-hours.

13. Olga Tymofiyeva et al., "Neural Correlates of Smart Phone Dependence in Adolescents," *Frontiers in Human Neuroscience*, 14 (October 7, 2020), https://doi.org/10.3389/fnhum.2020.564629.

14. Sarah Kliff, "1 in 4 American Moms Return to Work within 2 Weeks of Giving Birth—Here's What It's Like," *Vox*, August 22, 2015, https://www.vox.com/2015/8/21/9188343/maternity-leave-united-states.

15. Samuel Gibbs, "Apple's Tim Cook: 'I Don't Want My Nephew on a Social Network," *The Guardian*, January 19, 2018, https://www.theguardian.com/technology/2018/jan/19/tim-cook-i-dont-want-my-nephew-on-a-social-network.

16. Bjorn Lindstrom, Martin Bellander, et al., "A Computational Reward Learning Account of Social Media Engagement," *Nature Communications* 12, no. 1 (February 26, 2021): 1311, https://doi.org/10.1038/s41467-020-19607-x.

17. Mike Allen, "Sean Parker Unloads on Facebook: 'God Only Knows What It's Doing to Our Children's Brains,'" *Axios*, November 9, 2017, https://www.axios.com/sean-parker-unloads-on-facebook-god-only-knows-what-its-doing-to-our-childrens-brains-1513306792-f855e7b4-4e99-4d60-8d51-2775559c2671.html.

18. Olga Mecking, "American Parenting Styles Sweep Europe," *BBC Worklife*, February 26, 2020, https://www.bbc.com/worklife/article/20200225-the-parenting-style-sweeping-europe.

19. Steven Pinker, *The Language Instinct* (New York: HarperCollins, 1994).

20. Meredith F. Small, *Our Babies, Ourselves: How Biology and Culture Shape the Way We Parent* (New York: Anchor Books, 1999).

21. Richard B. Lee and Irven DeVore, eds., *Kalahari Hunter-Gatherers: Studies of the ¡Kung San and Their Neighbors* (Cambridge, MA: Harvard University Press, 1976).

22. Charmaine Patterson, "Ryan Reynolds on Taking a Break from Acting," *MSN*, December 7, 2021, https://www.msn.com/en-us/movies/celebrity/ryan-reynolds-on-taking-a-break-from-acting-i-don-t-want-to-miss-this-time-with-my-kids/ar-AARA9Sa.

23. Meghan Collie, "Men Who Take Paternity Leave Are Likely to Have Longer Relationships: Study," *Global News*, February 11, 2020, https://globalnews.ca/news/6535198/paternity-leave-relationships/.

24. Frauke Suhr, "Mehr Männer nehmen Elternzeit—zumindest kurz," *Der Statista Infografik*, November 5, 2021, https://de.statista.com/infografik/24835/anteil-der-vaeter-in-deutschland-die-elterngeld-beziehen/.

25. "A Fresh Look at Paternity Leave: Why the Benefits Extend beyond the Personal," McKinsey & Company, March 5, 2021, https://www.mckinsey.com.br/business-functions/organization/our-insights/a-fresh-look-at-paternity-leave-why-the-benefits-extend-beyond-the-personal.

26. Elseline Hoekzema et al., "Pregnancy Leads to Long-Lasting Changes in Human Brain Structure," *Nature Neuroscience*, 20 (February 2017), https://doi.org/10.1038/nn.4458.

27. "How Mother-Child Separation Causes Neuro-Biological Vulnerability into Adulthood," *Association for Psychological Science*, June 20, 2018, https://www.psy

chologicalscience.org/publications/observer/obsonline/how-mother-child-separation
-causes-neurobiological-vulnerability-into-adulthood.html.

28. Dan Barraclough, "These Were the World's Most Productive Countries in 2020," *Expert Market*, September 13, 2021.

29. Devan McGuinness, "Federal Employees of this Country Are Getting 'Summer Fridays' Forever," *Fatherly*, December 7, 2021, https://www.fatherly.com/news/federal -employees-uae-workweek/.

30. Alicia Sasser Modestino et al., "Child Care Is a Business Issue," *Harvard Business Review*, April 29, 2021, https://hbr.org/2021/04/childcare-is-a-business-issue.

31. Ben Geier, "These 32 Companies Have Concierge Services for Employees," *Yahoo! Finance*, March 28, 2016, https://finance.yahoo.com/news/32-companies -concierge-services-employees-150007644.html.

32. Kelly Gonsalves, "What Is the Mental Load? The Invisible Burden Falling on Women's Shoulders," *mindbodygreen*, June 22, 2020, https://www.mindbodygreen .com/articles/what-is-the-mental-load.

33. Nicole Hong and Matthew Haag, "Why Co-Working Spaces Are Betting on the Suburbs," *New York Times*, October 28, 2021, https://www.nytimes.com/2021/10/28 /nyregion/co-working-space-suburbs.html.

CHAPTER 10

1. Mohammed Shehata et al., "Team Flow Is a Unique Brain State Associated with Enhanced Information Integration and Interbrain Synchrony," *eNeuro* 8, no. 5 (October 12, 2021), https://doi.org/10.1523/ENEURO.0133-21.2021.

2. Helen Lee Bouygues, "Everything You Need to Know about Groupthink," Reboot Foundation blog, 2019, https://reboot-foundation.org/en/groupthink/.

3. "Attack on Pearl Harbor," *Wikipedia*, https://en.wikipedia.org/w/index .php?title=Attack_on_Pearl_Harbor&oldid=1075511929.

4. A. Gorin et al., "MEG Signatures of Long-Term Effects of Agreement and Disagreement with the Majority," *Scientific Reports*, 11 (2021): 3297, https://doi .org/10.1038/s41598-021-82670-x.

5. "Can the Brain Resist the Group Opinion?," *Neuroscience News.com*, February 8, 2021, https://neurosciencenews.com/social-influence-brain-17709/.

6. Gorin et al., "MEG Signatures."

7. Irving Janis, *Groupthink* (New York: Houghton Mifflin, 1982).

8. James C. Cobb, "Even Though He Is Revered Today, MLK Was Widely Disliked by the American Public When He Was Killed," *Smithsonian Magazine*, April 4, 2018, https://www.smithsonianmag.com/history/why-martin-luther-king-had-75-percent -disapproval-rating-year-he-died-180968664/.

9. Avi Dan, "Kodak Failed by Asking the Wrong Marketing Question," *Forbes*, January 23, 2012, https://www.forbes.com/sites/avidan/2012/01/23/kodak-failed-by -asking-the-wrong-marketing-question.

10. Shigetaka Komori, *Innovating Out of Crisis: How Fujifilm Survived (and Thrived) as Its Core Business Was Vanishing* (Berkeley, CA: Stone Bridge Press, 2015).

11. Christopher Sirk, "Fujifilm Found a Way to Innovate and Survive Digital. Why Didn't Kodak?," *CRM.org*, September 17, 2020, https://crm.org/articles/fujifilm-found-a-way-to-innovate-and-survive-digital-why-didnt-kodak.

12. Ed Catmull, "How Pixar Fosters Collective Creativity," *Harvard Business Review*, September 2008, https://hbr.org/2008/09/how-pixar-fosters-collective-creativity.

13. HBStudent11, "Pixar Animation Studios: Creative Kaizen," *Technology and Operations Management: MBA Student Perspectives*, December 6, 2014, https://digital.hbs.edu/platform-rctom/submission/pixar-animation-studios-creative-kaizen/

14. Tomas Chamorro-Premuzic, "Why Bad Guys Win at Work," *Harvard Business Review*, November 2, 2015, https://hbr.org/2015/11/why-bad-guys-win-at-work.

15. Nicola Brazil, "Assessing the Dark Triad at Work—Can Your Organization Afford Not to?" *HR Grapevine*, October 2021.

16. Chamorro-Premuzic, "Why Bad Guys Win at Work."

17. Charlan Jeanne Nemeth, *No!: The Power of Disagreement in a World That Wants to Get Along* (London, UK: Atlantic Books, 2021).

18. Nemeth, *No!: The Power of Disagreement.*

19. Charlan Nemeth, Keith Brown, and John Rogers, "Devil's Advocate versus Authentic Dissent: Stimulating Quality and Quantity," *European Journal of Social Psychology* (November 13, 2001), https://doi.org/10.1002/ejsp.58.

20. Kristin Bain et al., "Amplifying Voice in Organizations," *Academy of Management Journal* (September 13, 2021), https://doi.org/10.5465/amj.2018.0621.

21. Morton Deutsch and Harold Gerard, "A Study of Normative and Informational Social Influences upon Individual Judgement," *Journal of Abnormal and Social Psychology* (1955), https://doi.org/10.1037/h0046408.

22. Deutsch and Gerard, "Study of Normative and Informational Social Influences."

23. Alexander Stell and Tom Farsides, "Brief Loving-Kindness Meditation Reduces Racial Bias," *Motivation and Emotion* 40 (2016): 140–47, https://doi.org/10.1007/s11031-015-9514-x.

24. Yoona Kang, Jeremy Gray, and John Dovidio, "The Nondiscriminating Heart: Lovingkindess Meditation Training Decreases Implicit Intergroup Bias," *Journal of Experimental Psychology* (June 2014), https://doi.org/10.1037/a0034150.

25. Saul McLeod, "Solomon Asch Conformity Experiment," *Simply Psychology* (December 8, 2018), https://www.simplypsychology.org/asch-conformity.html.

26. Nemeth, *No!: The Power of Disagreement.*

Bibliography

Aarstol, Stephan. *The Five-Hour Workday: Live Differently, Unlock Productivity, and Find Happiness*. Carson City, NV: Lioncrest, 2016.

Branson, Richard. *Screw It, Let's Do It: Lessons in Life*. London, UK: Virgin Books, 2011.

Brinkley, Douglas. *Rosa Parks: A Life*. Waterville, ME: Thorndike Press, 2000.

Cain, Susan. *Quiet: The Power of Introverts in a World That Can't Stop Talking*. New York: Crown, 2013.

Calaprice, Alice, ed. *The Ultimate Quotable Einstein*. Princeton, NJ: Princeton University Press, 2010.

Chouinard, Yvon. *Let My People Go Surfing: The Education of a Reluctant Businessman*. New York: Penguin, 2006.

Janis, Irving L. *Groupthink*. New York: Houghton Mifflin, 1982.

Komori, Shigetaka. *Innovating Out of Crisis: How Fujifilm Survived (and Thrived) as Its Core Business Was Vanishing*. Berkeley, CA: Stone Bridge Press, 2015.

Lee, Richard B., and Irven DeVore, eds. *Kalahari Hunter-Gatherers: Studies of the ¡Kung San and Their Neighbors*. Cambridge, MA: Harvard University Press, 1976.

Lieberman, Matthew D. *Social: Why Our Brains Are Wired to Connect*. New York: Crown, January 2013.

Mullainathan, Sendhil, and Eldar Shafir. *Scarcity: Why Having Too Little Means So Much*. New York: Times Books, 2013.

Nemeth, Charlan Jeanne. *No!: The Power of Disagreement in a World That Wants to Get Along*. London, UK: Atlantic Books, 2021.

Pinker, Steven. *The Language Instinct*. New York: HarperCollins, 1994.

Schor, Juliet B. *The Overworked American: The Unexpected Decline of Leisure*. New York: Basic Books, 1993.

Small, Meredith F. *Our Babies, Ourselves: How Biology and Culture Shape the Way We Parent*. New York: Anchor Books, 1999.

Walker, Matthew. *Why We Sleep: Unlocking the Power of Sleep and Dreams*. New York: Scribner, 2017.

Wozniak, Steve, and Gina Smith. *iWoz: From Computer Geek to Cult Icon: How I Invented the Personal Computer, Co-Founded Apple, and Had Fun Doing It*. New York: Norton, 2006.

Zak, Paul J. *The Moral Molecule: How Trust Works*. New York: Plume, 2013.

Index

217

About the Author

Friederike Fabritius, MS, is a neuroscientist and trailblazer in the field of neuroleadership. Her brain-based leadership programs have transformed how Fortune 500 executives think, innovate, and navigate change. Fabritius is a thought leader and keynote speaker, known for engaging global audiences at organizations such as Google, Ernst & Young (EY), Boston Consulting Group (BCG), Adecco, Accenture, Deloitte, BMW, Bayer, SAP, Harvard Business Review, trivago, and Audi. An alumna of McKinsey & Company and the Max Planck Institute for Brain Research, she serves on the prestigious German Academy of Science and Engineering. Fabritius is author of the award-winning book *The Leading Brain: Neuroscience Hacks to Work Smarter, Better, Happier*. She is fluent in six languages and lives with her husband and five children in Heidelberg, Germany.

For more resources and guidance on your journey to be a Brain-Friendly Workplace, please visit: fabulous-brain.com